Wollstonecraft's daughters

WOLLSTONECRAFT'S DAUGHTERS

WOMANHOOD IN ENGLAND AND FRANCE 1780–1920

edited by Clarissa Campbell Orr

Manchester University Press

Manchester and New York

✠

distributed exclusively in the USA and Canada by St Martin's Press

Published by Manchester University Press
Oxford Road, Manchester M13 9NR, UK
and Room 400, 175 Fifth Avenue,
New York, NY 10010, USA

*Distributed exclusively in the USA and Canada
by* St Martin's Press, Inc.,
175 Fifth Avenue, New York, NY 10010, USA

British Library Cataloguing-in-Publication Data
A catalogue record is available from the British Library

Library of Congress Cataloging-in-Publication Data
Wollstonecraft's daughters : womanhood in England
and France, 1780-1920 / edited by Clarissa Campbell Orr.
p. cm
ISBN 0-7190-4241-0
1. Women's rights—France—History—19th century.
2. Women's rights—England—History—19th century.
I. Orr, Clarissa Cambell
HQ1236.5.F8W65 1996
305.42'0944—CC20 95-21695

ISBN 0 7190 4241 0 *hardback*

First published in 1996
99 98 97 96 95   10 9 8 7 6 5 4 3 2 1

Typeset in Monotype Columbus
by Koinonia, Manchester
Printed in Great Britain
by Bookcraft Ltd, Midsomer Norton

CONTENTS

LIST OF CONTRIBUTORS

Clarissa Campbell Orr is a Senior Lecturer in History at Anglia Polytechnic University, Cambridge. She contributed a chapter on 'Romanticism in Switzerland' to *The Romantic Movement in National Context*, eds Roy Porter and Mikulas Teich (Cambridge, Cambridge University Press, 1988), and has written on 'Albertine Necker de Saussure, the mature woman author and the Scientific Education of Women' for *Women's Writing*, June 1995, special issue on Science and Women. She is also editor of and contributor to *Women in the Victorian Art World* (Manchester University Press, 1995). Her current projects include research on women and Anglo-French liberalism and the Victorian historian, Agnes Strickland.

Máire Fedelma Cross is a Senior Lecturer in the Department of French at the University of Sheffield. Since the publication of her thesis, *The Feminism of Flora Tristan* (Oxford, Berg, 1992), she has continued to work on aspects of nineteenth-century French feminism. With Felicia Gordon she is co-editing an anthology, *1830–1930: One Hundred Years of Feminist Protest Writers in France* (Cheltenham, Edward Elgar) and is also translating Flora Tristan's *Tour de France* for Berg, Oxford. She contributes regularly to *Modern and Contemporary France*, *French Studies*, and *European History Quarterly*.

Marion Diamond is a Senior Lecturer in the Department of History, University of Queensland. She has published two books on Australian colonial history, *The Sea Horse and the Wanderer: Ben Boyd in Australia* (Melbourne, 1988) and *Creative Meddler: The Life and Fantasies of Charles St. Julian* (Melbourne, 1990). She has also written several articles on Victorian women activists including Florence Nightingale. She is currently completing a full biography of Maria Rye, and working on a study of Australian trade in Asia and the Pacific in the nineteenth century.

Felicia Gordon is a Principal Lecturer in European Philosophy and Literature at Anglia Polytechnic University, Cambridge. She is the author of *Preface to the Brontës*, London, Longman, 1989), and *The Integral Feminist: Madeleine Pelletier, 1874–1939*, (Cambridge, Polity Press, 1990). She has written on feminist auto-biography, ('Les Femmes et L'Ambition' in *Logique et infortunes d'un combat pour l'égalité*, ed. Christine Bard, (Paris, Côté Femmes, 1991)) and published articles on Sartre, eugenics, birth control, nineteenth-century anthropology and feminism. The anthology she is co-editing with Máire Cross comprises textual commentary and translations of Flora Tristan, Pauline Roland, Jeanne Deroin and Madeleine Pelletier.

Pam Hirsch is a Senior Research Associate at Homerton College, University of Cambridge and supervises student dissertations throughout the University on nineteenth-century topics. She has written on Mary Wollstonecraft, George Sand, George Eliot, and Elizabeth Barrett Browning and is currently writing a biography of Barbara Leigh Smith Bodichon.

James F. McMillan is Professor of European History at the University of Strathclyde. He is a leading authority on Modern French History and the author of *Housewife or Harlot: the Place of Women in French Society 1870–1940* (London, Harvester Press, 1981), as well as many articles on the history of women in France.

Hazel Mills was until December 1994 Fellow and Director of Studies in History at Fitzwilliam College, Cambridge. In addition to various articles on women and philanthropy in nineteenth-century France, she is preparing a full-length study on the subject for publication by Oxford University Press, *Woman and the Catholic Church in France, 1800–1850*.

Jane Rendall is a Senior Lecturer in the History Department and the Centre for Women's Studies at the University of York. She is interested in eighteenth- and nineteenth-century British and comparative women's history. Her publications include: *The Origins of Modern Feminism: Women in Britain, France, and the United States 1780–1860* (London, Macmillan, 1985), *Equal or Different: Women's Politics 1800–1914* (Oxford, Basil Blackwell, 1987), and most recently, with Karen Offen and Ruth Roach Pierson (eds), *Writing Women's History: International Perspectives* (London, Macmillan, 1991).

K. D. Reynolds is currently a Research Editor with the *New Dictionary of National Biography*. Her 1995 University of Oxford DPhil thesis on the public roles of aristocratic women in the nineteenth century will be published by Oxford University Press.

Henrietta Twycross-Martin is a Lecturer at Goldsmiths' College, London University. Until the late 1980s she specialised in Old Norse, Old English and Middle English, but after completion of an M.A. in Women's Studies at Anglia Polytechnic University in 1990, has broadened her teaching to include Victorian literature and women's writing. She is researching a full-length study of Sarah Stickney Ellis.

ACKNOWLEDGEMENTS

Some books reflect more closely than others the academic environment in which they were conceived and nurtured. I must express my appreciation for several facets of my present position which have helped to shape this collection of essays. When I first joined Anglia Polytechnic University, (then known as Cambridgeshire College of Arts and Technology), my research had already led me to a comparative framework embracing late eighteenth-century Geneva, France and England, but I then had the opportunity to teach French history much more extensively, as it formed a substantial part of the Modern Languages degree. This was immeasurably enhanced by the happy practice of regularly visiting our students in their university placements abroad. Driving across the length and breadth of France over a ten-year period enriched my sense of its historical and regional diversity as no amount of reading could have done, and I must thank my colleagues John Harris, Mike Davison and Judith Purnell-James of the French Division, whom I at various times accompanied, for their tolerance of my historical obsessions and their help in orienting me to contemporary France. As one of our regular destinations was the delightful university town of Besançon, it was all the more of a pleasure to meet Hazel Mills and discover her work on its diocese.

In 1987–88 I was able to enjoy a sabbatical year linked to York University, which facilitated my research on Albertine Necker de Saussure in her Genevan context. This year brought me into much valued and profitable contact with two of the contributors in this book, Jane Rendall and Jim McMillan.

When I returned to Anglia, an inter-disciplinary team was developing an M.A. in Women's Studies. Here I must express a special debt to Felicia Gordon, with whom I taught elements on this course which further refined my Anglo-French comparative perspective and focused it more closely on women's history. I have benefited from many conversations with her, and she also introduced me to Máire Cross and Pam Hirsch. Henrietta Twycross-Martin was one of our first graduates from this course, and interests initiated then have enabled her to contribute to this collection.

This book began as a conference with the same title held in October 1992 at Anglia Polytechnic University under the auspices of the History Division, at which earlier versions of five of these papers were given. My thanks go to John Harris, Susan O'Brien, and Mary Abbott for their enthusiastic support; I am also indebted to the latter for introducing me to Marion Diamond. Sadly, another colleague represented at the conference, Norah Crook, was prevented by other commitments from contributing to the book. As General Editor of **The Novels and** *Selected Works of Mary Shelley*, she gave a superbly witty and erudite paper on Mary Wollstonecraft's actual daughter, and readers of her edition will benefit greatly from her insights as the conference audience was able to do in a different format. I have learnt from discussions with her in the course of completing this book. I also very much enjoyed discussing elite English women with Kim Reynolds when she was a colleague here for a year.

My Head of Department, John Harris, has always been supportive of my activities in research, conference organising and writing, as have my History colleagues David Weigall and Leonardo Castillo. John Pollard and Theo Schulte have consistently been a stimulus in engaging with European history and contemporary issues.

As I have found when editing a previous collection of essays, the alleged burdens of editorship disappear when one's contributors are such an agreeable and able team. It has truly been a pleasure to work with them.

I also want to thank my mother, who has extended her interest and sympathy, especially during the closing stages of this work. My father (1913–93) will not see the completion of this project, but if I am interested in the nineteenth century 'woman question' it is certainly not because I have any experience of discouraging patriarchal fathers.

An editor is also aware that her contributors have delivered their manuscripts when their lives have often been replete with human vicissitudes, comings and goings, and manifold responsibilities. I pay tribute to their working on this collection in addition to everything else.

Katharine Reeve and Vanessa Graham at Manchester University Press have been most accommodating and supportive editors and I am indebted to the keen eye and editorial acumen of my copy-editor, Annie Eagleton and my indexer, Annette Musker.

INTRODUCTION

Cross-channel perspectives

Clarissa Campbell Orr

THE legacy of Mary Wollstonecraft was a linkage of feminism with moral and political radicalism in popular perception of the 'woman question', when it was discussed in the nineteenth century. This linkage made it harder for women wanting moderate improvement to identify themselves explicitly with women's rights. Wollstonecraft has also been the subject of selective interpretations by twentieth-century historians, sometimes because feminists have looked to the past for foremothers. While the search for precedent can open areas of neglected historical enquiry, it can also obscure others. As our understanding of Wollstonecraft's complex legacy grows, we can better refine and redefine what it has meant for her nineteenth-century 'daughters' to live after her, and explore their roles as mothers, educators, writers, historians and religious activists, which are the principal concerns of this book.

Books with comparative perspectives always raise the problem of comparing like with like. However this collection of essays is focused as much on the ways feminists and anti-feminists in the two countries thought about each other, and on how an assessment of Wollstonecraft could function as a point of reference, as on the actual similarities and differences for women in France and England. If this mutual awareness held true for contributors to the 'woman question', it was equally characteristic of nineteenth-century philosophers and critics, political and social theorists, or writers and painters, for whom either country could be used as a mirror for the other, usually in a selective and distorting way.[1]

Mutual awareness between the two countries was characterised more by anxiety than enthusiasm, largely because France had turned itself inside out by a Revolution and still seemed dangerously unstable, and England persisted in fearing Revolutionary contagion, including popular agitation for rights of any description, men's or women's. This extreme wariness lasted at least until after the 1848 Revolutionary fervour in Europe turned out to have spared Britain, with the 1848 mass Chartist demonstration passing off peacefully. From this point, British complacency toward continental styles of politics in comparison with its parliamentary tradition grew, but as G. K. Chesterton shrewdly observed, 'the most important event in English history happened in France'.[2]

A relationship of guarded ambivalence between the two countries was nothing new; political antagonism had a long history, revived in the war years of 1793–1815, and although after that peace reigned in Europe, with an alliance between Britain and France against Russia in the Crimean War (1854–56), the two remained colonial rivals further afield. British culture in the nineteenth century, with a Hanoverian Queen and a Saxon Prince Consort, was on the whole more enamoured of German than French culture; while unlike the *philosophes* of the Enlightenment, nineteenth-century French intellectuals were not especially Anglophile. While Mary Wollstonecraft bequeathed to her daughters a legacy grounded in Enlightenment rationalism, the full range of her writing, particularly her fiction and her travel book on Scandinavia, discloses elements of Romantic sensibility. Romanticism in the arts has a later appearance in France than in England, and in important senses was a dialogue with German culture, as for example in Mme de Staël's pioneering exploration of German literature, *De L'Allemagne*. Thus Romantic themes such as the revaluation of Shakespeare were mediated through the French translation of Schlegel's *Lectures on Drama* by de Staël's cousin, Albertine Necker de Saussure, (who appears in Chapter 2 of this book in her role as educationalist), rather than through a direct absorption of English Romantic preoccupations which had been so important to German developments. With the social romanticism of the first half of the nineteenth century, which provides the context for Wollstonecraft's admirer, Flora Tristan, as explained in Chapter 6, it is France which influences England.[3]

The three main themes of this collection are the impact of the French Revolution on styles of motherhood and the conduct literature addressed to women; religion and the empowerment of women; and women's engagement with the human sciences. Some preliminary comparative remarks on France and England may be useful before introducing these essays more specifically.

State, Church, law, society: comparative frameworks

At first glance, France and England seem more different than similar in the nineteenth century. France had startled Europe first by the collapse, in 1789, of an apparently absolute State in a wealthy, well-populated country which was a keen rival of Britain in colonial trade and expansion; and then by its execution of the monarch (1793) and various attempts to create an egalitarian republic of patriotic citizens, one version of which

(1792–95, the Jacobin Republic) would also briefly defy France's long religious history as the 'eldest daughter of the Christian Church', by trying to root out Christianity completely. As a consequence of its Revolution, France also disturbed the international balance of power and convulsed Europe in a series of wars lasting intermittently from 1793 to 1815, which re-drew the map of Europe, and launched the idea of the modern nation-state on its fateful career. The wars against France were crucial to the formation of a type of modern British patriotism, and for inducing a mood of conservative resistance to change, including any changes to the position of women.[4]

After the rise to power of Napoleon, France completed some of the internal restructuring initiated by the Revolution, and in 1801 made peace with the Catholic Church (without however withdrawing full rights of toleration from Protestants and Jews), inaugurating a period of internal stability. But the defeat of Napoleon at Waterloo and the Restoration of the Bourbon Monarchy (1814–15) did not solve the question of how France should be governed. The legal and administrative framework created under Napoleon remained in place, but it became plain as the century progressed that as far as hearts and minds were concerned there were now two Frances: one willing to accept the gains of the Revolution, such as civil equality and a secular state controlling the Catholic Church and other tolerated faiths, and the other, wedded to the monarchy and the religious values of a rejuvenated, but socially and intellectually conservative, Catholicism. Political allegiances were complicated by divisions within each side: monarchists were divided between Bourbon supporters, or Legitimists, and the Orleanists who had adhered to the parliamentary monarchy formed in July 1830 under Louis-Philippe, and lasting until 1848. But these liberals who accepted the Revolution and worked for the establishment of constitutional monarchy often disagreed with republicans, and later with Bonapartism in its revived form under Napoleon III (1852–70). A second attempt to create a republic in 1848 was defeated by the coup of Louis Napoleon, 1851, who transformed himself from elected President to Emperor Napoleon III in 1852, but his regime did not survive French defeat by Prussia in 1870.

The Third Republic (1870–1940), the first regime to see the formation of various kinds of organised French feminism, was the result of a negative consensus: the form of government, in Adolphe Theirs's phrase, which divided Frenchmen the least. Until the 1880s monarchists hoped that a strong presidential republic could prepare the way for the return of the throne, and the collective blow to French confidence inflicted by Prussian defeat in 1870 gave fresh impetus to Catholic piety in order to expiate what was construed as a divine judgement on French sins. It was not until 1894 that the Pope urged the French faithful to 'rally' to the republic as an established, if not legitimate, kind of government. The Third Republic saw the country as divided as ever between the two Frances, as graphically demonstrated when old wounds were re-opened and new ones created by the Dreyfus affair, (1894–99) in which a Jewish staff officer, from a family which cherished its French citizenship after their emancipation in the Revolution, was accused of spying for the Prussians. Exposure of the Army's collusion in a miscarriage of justice, and the campaign to rehabilitate Dreyfus, conducted against an atmosphere of anti-Semitism orchestrated to a significant degree by the Assumptionist Order's newspaper *La Croix*, resulted in a realignment of the French Right which became the matrix for twentieth-century versions of virulent nationalism. During the affair, republicans became convinced that the Republic itself was in danger, while socialists, initially slow to take up Dreyfus's cause, found common ground with republicans over anti-clericalism (though little else) resulting in the separation of Church and State (1905–06).[5]

It is noteworthy that Thiers's phrase implied that the formation of a political regime was a matter for French *men* to discuss and create. Women had a different history in relation to all these political regimes, for in spite of the universalist rhetoric of the Revolution, which created equality before the law for men, all of whom were also enfranchised after 1848, women were not citizens, and could not vote until 1944. The efforts during the Revolution of 1789 by some feminist leaders like Olympe de Gouges and Etta Palm d'Aelders to give women a clear political role came to an abrupt end when the Government closed the women's clubs in 1793. 'Citoyennes' were to be mothers and wives of 'citoyens', but not to participate directly in the State. As we shall see, their alleged conservatism and devotion to clerical ideals in the nineteenth century meant that the division of the two Frances was also conceptualised as a gender division between men's and women's social and political values.

In comparison with the frequent changes of political regime in France, England seemed a model of constitutional stability, and indeed prided herself as such. But this complacency was riddled with anxiety. Revolutionary France was an inspiration to English radicals in the 1790s, Mary Wollstonecraft included, though many, like her, were soon disillusioned; while to the political elite, France was a salutary reminder of the pitfalls awaiting a State that refused to adapt. Being at war with its old adversary after 1793 meant that challenges to the *status quo* were deemed unpatriotic, and even constitutional reformism was temporarily halted. However after 1815 the momentum for change gathered pace. Britain never made a formal commitment to full religious toleration and the Church of England retained its privileged position in the State, but between 1828 and 1829 Protestant Dissenters and Catholics began to have full civil rights. The reform of Parliament in 1832 to enfranchise the middle classes more adequately was speeded on by France's 1830 Revolution, which occurred in reaction to the attempts of Charles X to manipulate the constitution. Reactionaries in England took his failure and enforced abdication as a salutary warning against frustrating the process of change. In contrast with France, men took longer to gain universal suffrage, being enfranchised by stages in 1867 and 1884. However when the property qualification for male voters was extended in 1867, John Stuart Mill tried, unsuccessfully, to extend the vote to women of equivalent property by inserting the gender-free term 'person' into the Bill.[6] In the event women waited less time than their French counterparts to attain the vote, gaining it in 1919, but were (and are) subjects of the Crown rather than citizens of a State. The legacy of the Revolution remained a permanent contrast in the modern political cultures of the two countries; latterly women's rights have been better protected by European Union directives, based on a continental model of citizenship, than they have been under Britain's parliamentary tradition.

However, precisely because the Ancien Régime polity in Britain proved so adroit at making timely concessions, nineteenth-century England appeared to be the more liberal polity. Freedom of association and freedom of the press were better established in practice, and before the formation of mass political parties, Parliament was shown to be susceptible to large-scale pressure groups formed to campaign on single issues. Women's participation in movements such as the campaign against slavery, or the anti-Corn Law League, illustrate the way some women negotiated a role in the public sphere, in spite of their formal political exclusion and a rhetoric discouraging such activism. By the end of the century, the British State could tolerate mass demonstrations confidently, though policing any violence assiduously. On her visit to Britain in 1908, the socialist and feminist Madeleine Pelletier, subject of Chapter 9, was to marvel at the scale and organisational discipline of the Women's Social and Political Union rally in London, which would have been impossible in France not only because of lack of mass feminist support but also because the last thing police would allow would be large-scale rallies. Pelletier and her associates were much more aware of being under constant police surveillance than their British counterparts; but once any militant British suffragette was arrested for direct action, she could be brutally treated by the police, courts and prisons, where hunger strikes were notoriously dealt with by force-feeding.[7]

Because Britain, unlike France, was not a centrally administered State,

but relied on a subtle interplay between power at Whitehall and Westminster, and voluntary, unpaid local government, women were able to
take public office locally decades before entering Parliament, and were
sitting on School Boards, Poor Law Unions, and local councils at various
stages after 1870, often using the rhetoric of women's special sphere in
their favour.[8]

Britain also had a different religious culture from France, as Voltaire
had observed to be true even before the reforms benefiting Catholics and
Dissenters between 1828 and 1829. Alongside the Church of England's
privileged role, Britain had an array of religious denominations. Smaller
groups such as Unitarians and Quakers, introduced their female members
to public activism in behalf of their civil rights, or issues their Churches
especially adopted, such as the campaigns to end slavery and the slave
trade. These groups also tended to be more sympathetic to women's
education, often fostering an egalitarianism born of the doctrine of the
equality of souls and providing an instructive contrast to mainstream
Anglican attitudes. It is significant that organised feminism in France
included a disproportionate number of women from Protestant backgrounds, such as the pastor's daughter Sarah Monod, though as some of
these essays suggest, it is possible to over-exaggerate the contrast
between Protestant and Catholic attitudes to women's activism.

Catholic Emancipation in England did not lead to any diminution of
anti-Catholic prejudice; rather to the contrary, as the small minority of
old Catholic families in England was joined by Catholic Irish immigrants.
Once the Anglican Oxford Movement started to defend the Church as a
sacred institution which could not be subjected to secular reform by a
pro-Dissenter Whig ministry, and to talk of the Catholic element in the
Thirty-Nine articles of Anglican faith, there was anxiety that this could
only end in conversion to Rome. With the reception of Newman and
Manning by the Church of Rome these fears were realised. The re-
establishment of the Catholic hierarchy in 1850, also nourished patriotic
Protestant fears that this meant the return of such un-English practices as
the veneration of saints, the cult of the Virgin Mary, and the return of
religious Orders. But as we shall see, some feminists in England were to
be attracted to the idea of female sisterhoods and convents, which were
also revived in the High Church wing of Anglicanism.

Women in the two countries experienced different legal regimes,
although the net effect was broadly similar, particularly for married
women. In France there was a codified system of law with a clear statement of penalties for infringement. Napoleon's Civil Code defined
married women as minors, subject to the husband's authority. He con-
trolled the property she brought to the marriage, but as James McMillan

has pointed out, in practice it was a matter of family honour to safeguard a dowry, and a husband's tacit consent to a wife's expenditure was assumed, this being crucial for the running of small enterprises. A wife had no right to reside away from the marital home and needed her husband's permission to attend university or to work. The husband was sole legal guardian of children and had the final say over their education. Women had been able to divorce, albeit on less favourable terms than men, under the Code, but the right was withdrawn in 1816, only to be restored in 1884. Men however could divorce a wife for infidelity, and would be acquitted for the murder of her lover. The double standard of morality was enshrined in law: a woman had no right to institute paternity proceedings to support an illegitimate child, and prostitution was regulated by the State, creating a clear division between 'respectable' and 'fallen' women, based essentially on class. As well as being unable to vote or hold public office, women had no civil personality – that is to say they could not witness legal proceedings.[9]

The position of English women lacked the clarity of a codified legal system, and was determined by statute and legal precedent.[10] A married women's legal and economic personality was subsumed by that of the husband; since two persons were now considered to be one, her property and earnings were his, (not just under his administration), and she could not make a will or a contract. A husband was supposed to provide sufficient maintenance for his wife and was liable for her debts. It was possible to create legal trusts, making a married woman a beneficiary, in order to protect her property. These legal settlements were the English parallel of the French dowry system. Until Caroline Norton helped to changed the law in restricted cases for separated women, mothers had no custody over their children. Nor was there a secular divorce law until 1857, though up to that time courts would recognise separation from the matrimonial home, without freedom to remarry; otherwise divorce needed a private act of Parliament, limiting it in effect to the rich who felt like facing out the scandal. The law of 1857 meant that women had still to prove more against their husbands than vice versa, but in practice the category of cruelty was interpreted to include mental cruelty and thus cover extreme incompatibility.[11]

It can also be said that French and English women experienced a different biological and social history. Given the great regional diversity of French society, generalisations are even more problematic than they are for Britain, so it must be emphasised that my remarks concentrate only on a few salient features.

To increasing consternation among pundits and moralists, especially after defeat in 1870, the French birth rate declined as the century progressed; France seems to have been the first European country to practise wide-scale family limitation while English society adopted it more unevenly. This would mean that motherhood in France would during the nineteenth century increasingly be defined as a patriotic contribution. The preoccupation with demographic decline affected the character of most French feminist thought, which tended to see women in a family rather than an individual context.[12]

French women also continued the practice of wet-nursing much longer than Englishwomen, especially those running small shops or services in conjunction with their husbands, who needed to make an uninterrupted contribution to their family earnings. Married women formed 42 per cent of the work-force in the 20–24 age-group in 1901, compared with 25 per cent in England, a statistic partly explicable in terms of the later marriage age in England.[13]

Marriages in France, among the notables at the top of society down to many levels within the middle classes, were more obviously a matter of arrangement and based on property considerations, while peasant culture equally exhibited a hard-nosed attitude toward romantic love, and valued strategies based on furthering family economic interests, be it only by the acquisition of a fraction of a field.[14] In contrast, women in English society may have *felt* they chose their partners freely and much of English fiction turned on the drama of these choices. But the management of social networks at various levels meant that young people were prevented as much as possible from meeting unsuitable partners – and unsuitable meant financially deficient as well as socially or morally unacceptable. It is probable that being single was marginally easier in England than in France, but neither society was especially hospitable to the spinster.[15]

There was no real peasant sector in England, and agriculture, though modernised and capital-intensive was declining in relation to trade and manufacture from its approximately half share in the middle of the century. Young people in rural areas followed well-established patterns of leaving home in their early teens to work in domestic or agricultural service, postponing marriage until their mid-twenties, by which time choices were made with less parental or customary supervision. This freedom was even more characteristic for town-dwellers. Finally, the differential rate of social change toward factory-based work and the concomitant separation of work and household, meant that in France women were visible in manufacturing industry and white-blouse occupations at a later date than their counterparts in England, although the invention of the department store, a significant employer of female labour in Paris, happened as early as the 1850s. Factory-based work in France lagged a generation behind that in England, beginning only in the 1830s, and the textile industry continued to be based on the smaller workshop.[16]

Revolution and motherhood

Many of the women discussed in this book would have shunned the name of Mary Wollstonecraft and repudiated her as a foremother. In Chapter 1 Pam Hirsch traces this demonisation of her reputation to her association with radical English politics, and the unconventional elements of her private life. Although the direct heirs and heiresses of her political align-ment among English Unitarian culture had access to a less distorted view, she had been effectively discredited until well into the nineteenth century, when the efforts of her grand-daughter by marriage, Jane St John, to set the record straight began to bear fruit. It took a century for her to be classified as an 'Eminent Woman', worthy to be included in a biographi-cal series of two dozen such women commissioned by Macmillan, which included her daughter, Mary Shelley, and the unimpeachably respectable philanthropists Elizabeth Fry and Hannah More.

Whether or not women in the nineteenth century actively acknow-ledged or repudiated a link with Wollstonecraft, her views on women could not be completely obliterated. Wollstonecraft's assertion that women could be citizens – the most radical element in her ideal of rational womanhood – permanently changed the conceptual landscape. The notion could be repudiated or mocked but it could not be unthought, any more than the events of the French Revolution could be undone. The climate of religious and moral conservatism so evident after 1815 was ever conscious of the Revolutionary alternative and its possible repetition, and the 'woman question' was a recurrent motif of social and moral debate. It was because of women like Wollstonecraft that the 'woman question' had even been articulated.

The French Revolutionary era inaugurated the major issues of the modern world, such as civic rights and equality, the relationship of Church and State, or the conflict between religion and secularism. Wollstonecraft had explored these issues in her life and in a wide variety of writing in several genres: conduct manual, educational treatise, polemic, travelogue, novel, short story, review. Women subsequently addressing these questions can, in a metaphorical sense, all be considered her daughters. It is in this metaphorical sense that the present book groups together a wide spectrum of women from contemporaries of Wollstonecraft, such as the Scottish Whig, Elizabeth Hamilton discussed in Chapter 3, or the patrician Genevan Albertine Necker de Saussure, subject of Chapter 2, through writers and activists in the 1830s, 1840s and

1850s (Chapters 4–8) up to the Catholic conservative suffragist Marie Maugeret (Chapter 10) and the radical socialist feminist Madeleine Pelletier (Chapter 9), who both lived through the First World War. In a century of unprecedented social change for each generation, which affected even the most tradition-bound lives, the subjects of these essays emulated, contested or modified the patterns of womanhood which Wollstonecraft's life exemplified, and positioned themselves in relation to 'the woman question' and its changing articulation.

Integral to the polemical debate of the French Revolutionary era was a critique of gender as well as of aristocracy: the privileges of male *seigneurs*, but also of female aristocrats, and the political and cultural power they exercised. During the Revolution this focused on the Queen, Marie Antoinette: a disordered polity was symbolised by her undoubted extravagance and her alleged promiscuity, while the Jacobins also made allegations of child abuse at her trial. But anxieties about the power of women were by no means new. For at least the last third of the century in France there was a sense of profound disorientation, figured in art, literature, and moral discourse. In this pre-Revolutionary sensibility, 'things are changing between fathers and sons, between parents and children, probably also between men and women'.[17]

Dominating the literary expression of this unease was Jean-Jacques Rousseau's rejection of the Court-centred and fashionable world of Enlightened Paris, expressed most eloquently in his novels *Julie, ou La Nouvelle Héloïse* (1761) and *Emile* (1762). His anatomy of fashionable society sympathetically analysed its cultural competitiveness, which forced its women to live constantly in the eyes of others and to lack an autonomous sense of self. But such was his fear of the sexual power that facilitated their cultural and social importance, that his solution was to idealise a woman who would live only in the eyes of her husband, not one who would lay claim to rational equality with men, let alone autonomy. This was the virtuous Sophie, imagined as the mate for Emile, who would exercise her sexual charm only to retain her husband's attachment to her. Alternatively, Rousseau imagined Julie, who rejected passion for virtuous motherhood, bowing to the authority of her father and her husband.

Paradoxically, Rousseau's women readers found liberation in his constructions of femininity, making it hard for feminists then and now to get his measure. His sympathetic portrayal of the human heart – even, as with Julie, a guilty and transgressive heart, seems to have empowered women to take their inner lives more seriously and to see themselves as the heroines of their own dramas. The cult of sensibility freed men and women alike to believe in the authenticity and innocence of their feelings. Rousseau also became a mentor in the creation of a more 'natural' style of motherhood – natural, that is, to women sufficiently affluent to have hitherto delegated child-rearing to wet-nurses and governesses. Breast-feeding your own child became fashionable, in England as in France. The sentimentalisation of motherhood was susceptible of transformation into the sterner figure of the republican mother rearing her children to be good patriots, while the need for adequate maternal education attracted many more moderate voices, among them Elizabeth Hamilton, discussed in Chapter 3, and Albertine Necker de Saussure, subject of Chapter 2, who argued that better-educated women made better mothers.

Wollstonecraft's own starting-point in reflecting and writing about women's lives and needs was the 'woman question' of the later eighteenth century. Her book, *Vindication of the Rights of Woman*, was a dialogue with Rousseau, as well as with English mentors of women. She had come to mistrust his language of sensibility; it might promise a fuller sense of selfhood to women, but ran the risk of characterising them as even more susceptible to transgressive behaviour as a result of their allegedly excess-ive feeling. She envisaged women as citizens in a rational reformed republican Britain, which restored the rights of religious Dissenters, and had a fairly elected, accountable government. Aristocratic privilege would make way for meritocracy. Mothers would be of supreme impor-tance in moulding the future public-spirited citizens of this republic, which necessitated their receiving the same education as men and learn-ing like them to develop their rational moral judgement. Hamilton's views on maternal education overlapped with many of Wollstonecraft's, but she deliberately distanced herself from the latter once she had been stigmatised as a woman led by passion, mouthing dangerous Revolution-ary doctrines (see Chapter 3).

Rousseau had located his heroine Julie on the shores of Lake Léman, in an idealised reconstruction of his native city, Geneva, and the rural surroundings of the neighbouring Pays de Vaud. Switzerland became a locus of virtue in opposition to a corrupt Paris. Chapter 2 on Albertine Necker de Saussure considers how someone moulded by the republican culture of her native Geneva responded to Rousseau's ideals. She came from the highest circles of the essentially aristocratic oligarchy who governed Geneva, and had much in common with British Whig society. Her family were materially affected by the French Revolution while Geneva temporarily lost its independence to the Napoleonic Empire. During this time she was associated with the brilliant circle of liberals who opposed Napoleon, gathered together by Mme de Staël at Coppet. Her treatise on child-rearing, *Progressive Education*, (1828–33) was published in the climate of Restoration conservatism, when she was a grandmother. Her thinking on education was thus the product of many formative influences; here I concentrate on her implied critique of Rousseau and outline her view of the importance of women's autonomy within a Christian context. If necessary, little girls had to be forced to be free – to be self-reliant and purposeful; they should not be allowed to charm their way through life or be hopelessly dependent.

These views are consistent with the significant social, religious and cultural differences between Geneva and France which can be obscured by their common tongue. As James McMillan has observed, geography as well as gender is a crucial category of analysis for religious history. Similarly, the importance of regional specificity is exemplified by Hazel Mills's work in Chapter 7, which rests on detailed research in a region bordering Switzerland, the Franche-Comté.[18]

Mothers, citizens and aristocrats

There was much in Necker de Saussure's astringent rationalism which Wollstonecraft would have approved, but she might also have been made uneasy by her patrician poise and liberal self-confidence. The middle-class critique of aristocratic power in Britain articulated by Wollstonecraft and her circle shared the Jacobins' Rousseau-inspired mistrust of politically and culturally influential women. As Hirsch shows in Chapter 1, Wollstonecraft's first response to Burke's *Reflections on the Revolution in France*, her *Vindication of the Rights of Men*, took issue with his sentimental sympathy for the plight of Queen Marie Antoinette and with his misreading of the situation of working women, propelled into protest by the high cost of living. As Hirsch indicates, the descendants of the Dissenting middle classes, whether radicals or moderate constitutional reformists, included women and men who led the feminist campaigns of the mid nineteenth century, such as the Unitarian Barbara Leigh Smith Bodichon. In this tradition could be found a sympathetic account of Wollstonecraft's life and principles, and a continuing commitment to remodel Britain's Ancien Régime: to improve the legal status, political scope, and religious freedom, of men, women, slaves and religious minorities. As I have argued elsewhere, we should not be surprised to see women actively involved in this enlargement of the public sphere, for the concept that women were restricted to the private sphere requires some further refining by historians.[19]

But what of aristocratic women in Britain, the target, with their menfolk, of this middle-class reform movement? Is it possible to know how they felt about their continuing share of aristocratic power in England, exercised through the very mechanisms of family connection and influence which the radicals abhorred? Did considerations of their own unimpeachable status as titled ladies ever give way before a sisterly solidarity with legal disadvantages common to the whole sex? Could they look charitably on notions of women's equality, when these ideas were often associated with groups pressing to put an end to aristocratic predominance, and to make patronage and deference give way to a polity based on wider democratic accountability, meritocracy and professionalisation?

In fact we know remarkably little about these aristocratic women, although some have always attracted the attention of biographers working in a more *belles-lettrist* tradition of historical writing. In a laudable desire to rescue the middle and working classes from professional neglect and to broaden the subject matter of history, their elite sisters have been shunned to the point where arguably it is they who now need rescuing from the condescension of posterity.[20]

Neglect, however, has not been total. One important study has focused on the aristocratic experience of motherhood, and shown that changes did occur, albeit unevenly, leading some women to expect a companionate marriage rather than a convenient dynastic alliance, and to eschew social grandeur for a version of middle-class domesticity, in which they took a stronger interest in the rearing of their children and even in some cases breast-fed them. Much work remains to be done, which might address, among other topics, the role of aristocratic women in advancing their children's education. Such women were not immune to the educational experimentalism of the eighteenth century which had influenced their French counterparts, whom in any case they might know through family connections. Both wives of the first Marquis of Lansdowne, who appointed the scientist and Dissenter Joseph Priestley to tutor his sons, shared in the educational project and kept a record of their sons' progress. It is possible that the rearing of children was a subject of conversation when Albertine Necker de Saussure's father Horace-Bénédict de Saussure visited the Lansdownes at Bowood with his wife during their wedding-tour in 1768; disapproving of the education publicly on offer at Geneva's Collège, he would, as discussed in Chapter 2, personally supervise his own children's education.[21]

Aside from aristocratic approaches to motherhood, there is also the question of aristocratic women's political role and influence to consider, which has also been a neglected subject among professional historians. As K. D. Reynolds discusses in Chapter 4, women's position in nineteenth-century politics has mostly been approached as the 'prequel' to the suffragette movement, a tendency complemented by that of seeing nineteenth-century parliamentary politics as a story of the widening male franchise and the development of the party system.[22] If, however, we look at

nineteenth-century politics without the benefit of this hindsight, then
what stands out is the ability of the English aristocracy to adapt: on the
one hand, by continuing to control the monarchy, and on the other, to
head off Jacobin radicalism and begin admitting the middle classes to
Parliament on its own terms in 1832.[23]

In this Ancien Régime pattern of politics, students of Disraeli's career
are likely to be aware of his acknowledged debt to the patronage and
friendship of women, while women from slightly lower down the social
scale, have also had some case-studies devoted to them. These belonged
to the 'upper ten thousand' who filled the professions and government
and who were often linked to the titled aristocracy on the one hand and
to the 'intellectual aristocracy' on the other.[24]

Women in the nineteenth-century political elite were likely to see their
participation as a matter of family strategy, not as a pretext for breaking
gender boundaries and appropriating a Wollstonecraftian kind of citizenship. Such families were accustomed to providing courtiers as well as
public servants to the Crown; they would see themselves as subjects of a
monarch whom they often knew well enough to entertain in their own
homes, but to whom they nevertheless owed allegiance and deference.
The egalitarian rhetoric of the French Revolution terrified them.
Reynolds's essay on political hostesses, part of a larger study of elite
women in nineteenth-century politics, valuably fills in a gap in our present
knowledge. She argues that the political hostess, properly considered,
had something in her background which gave her an outsider element;
she further analyses why the social dimension to politics which they
helped to provide could be of such importance, and how it differed from
the normal social functions of 'High Society' presided over by less politically prominent women.

Those well integrated into the aristocratic elite might be less important
as political hostesses, but would still take an informed interest in political
affairs. Occasionally this reached beyond loyalty to class to loyalty to sex.
The trial of Queen Caroline in 1820 became a radical *cause célèbre* and
attracted women's support across ranks because of the way it illustrated
women's legal disadvantage, especially in the case of separated women
being barred from contact with their own children. It would be Caroline
Norton, who ran a literary and political salon frequented by the leading
Whigs, and both of whose sisters married into the peerage, who would
help to change the law on child custody 1837 and 1839, using her excellent connections in the Whig legal and political establishment to assist
her when her estranged husband took her own children from her.[25]

Mostly, aristocratic women took an interest in politics from a combination of principle and family interest. Lady Elizabeth Grosvenor,

whose diaries have been selectively published, provides one such example: her kin held public office both in the royal household and in the Houses of Parliament. Elizabeth's husband, Lord Belgrave, and his brother, were MPs for Chester and Cheshire respectively, in family-controlled seats which still required careful canvassing at election time, undertaken by the women as well as the men in the family. The personal and political were closely intertwined in her outlook, as illustrated by an entry at the end of 1830, when the Reform Bill had been first introduced in Parliament: 'The kingdom in a state of great general perplexity, burning, rioting etc. – the Yeomanry embodying, the Militia going to be set a-going – and I going to be confined next month for the 9th time!'[26]

An interest in politics was thus an extension, even a manifestation, of an interest in what her family was doing, but Lady Elizabeth could also be disinterested. Catholic Emancipation directly benefited her sister Mary's family, as her father-in-law, the Duke of Norfolk, was the premier Catholic peer in England, but it was also a Whig principle. Parliamentary reform was a Whig policy, but it disadvantaged her husband's family through loss of electoral interest and the sums of money expended on securing it. She recorded that her mother-in-law was even more reformist than her husband. It might have surprised Wollstonecraft and her ideological daughters how enthusiastically this aristocrat could acquiesce in the two reforms in Church and State which heralded the dismantling of England's Ancien Régime. But like most aristocrats she believed unchecked radicalism would lead to French-style instability: 'Talleyrand's sentiments are exactly my own. A small evil is preferable to a large.' When Peel resigned in 1835 after his brief ministry she feared radical influence in Melbourne's returning Whig ministry: 'We are getting too much like France to be comfortable'.[27]

Women writers and the redefinition of motherhood

The mark of an aristocratic lady was that she did not earn her living. By contrast Wollstonecraft was one of the first English women to live successfully as an independent professional writer. Beginning with reviews and translations, one of the first books she translated and discussed was by Albertine Necker de Saussure's famous uncle, Jacques Necker, *Of the Importance of Religious Opinions* (1788). As well as being discredited by her Jacobin associations, she faced difficulties as a woman writer. Hirsch shows in Chapter 1 how Wollstonecraft's reputation as a conduct-book writer and educational theorist was uncontroversial until she trespassed on the 'male' territory of political polemic. In addition, the very prominence and success of women writers at the turn of the eighteenth century, when they dominated the novel and poetry, and were increasingly prominent in the borderland between belles-lettres and serious intellectual enquiry, was producing a degree of male 'backlash', palpably present, together with anti-radical rhetoric, in Richard Polwhele's hysterical verse diatribe of 1798 against Wollstonecraft and other women writers, *The unsex'd females*.

By the early Victorian period, men of letters were experiencing acute anxiety as to whether writing was really a man's, let alone a gentleman's, profession.[28] Robert Southey told Charlotte Brontë 'Literature cannot be the business of a woman's life, and it ought not to be', in defiance of the fact that it was. Often the reason for this – as with Frances Trollope, Mary Russell Mitford, Caroline Norton, Anna Jameson – was that husbands or fathers who were supposed to provide for them were incapable of doing so, a factor generally overlooked by male critics. For women with any pretensions to ladylike status, writing was one of the few acceptable ways of earning money respectably if circumstances forced them to earn an income. This visibility of women in the literary profession provoked a misogynistic response from the satirical end of the early Victorian literary market, run as a male club. Few women were kindly treated, for instance, in Fraser's Gallery, a series of pen-portraits of over seventy writers which ran in *Fraser's Magazine*; one of the few, the poet Letitia Landon (L.E.L.), had her career ruined by the scandal linking her to *Fraser's* editor, William Maginn.[29]

When Thackeray moved from this magazine to *Punch*, he developed a running joke at the expense of Sarah Stickney Ellis, as Henrietta Twycross-Martin shows in Chapter 5. Ellis had come to prominence and literary profit with her series of conduct books on women's role as wives, mothers, daughters, and so on, published between 1838 and 1843, and aimed quite specifically at the middle classes. She was from a Yorkshire Quaker background and married a prominent Congregational missionary; her books clearly appealed to Evangelical Christians who prided themselves patriotically on England's moral fibre: 'how intimate is the connection which exists between the *women* of England, and the *moral* character maintained by their country in the scale of nations'. Both Ellises were active in the temperance movement and Twycross-Martin's current research underlines how important were temperance themes in Ellis's fiction.[30]

Chapter 5 also shows how women like Geraldine Jewsbury, notorious for her social forwardness, who carved a niche for themselves in the male literary world and adopted masculinist values, could be very uncharitably disposed to the women who cultivated a conventionally feminine literary persona and audience. Both Thackeray and Jewsbury were aware of the way that women exploited the ambiguities inherent in the notion of women's separate sphere so as to extend their social and moral power; both were unforgiving of what they could only interpret as a recipe for manipulativeness. Their sarcasm might have been kinder than the excoriation heaped on Wollstonecraft, but Ellis shared with her the risk that female authorial prominence was problematic. Ironically, women writers on both sides of the Channel were convinced that writing was easier for their counterparts in the other country, as discussed later. But there can be no doubt that the superior moral nature often attributed to women by moralists from Wollstonecraft to Ellis, rooted in a Christian interpretation of the world, was an important source of empowerment to women, even when there was still such marked ambivalence toward them as authors, or reluctance to grant them civic power. Chapter 2 explores Albertine Necker de Saussure's conviction that Christianity could provide women with a source of moral energy and a set of principles against which their personal obligations should be measured, and relates her ideal of self-possessed, self-reliant womanhood to codes of femininity endorsed in her native Geneva. Religious institutions both Protestant and Catholic also gave women scope to redefine their role and to exercise considerable initiative and organisational powers; it even enabled them to argue that the vote was compatible with Christian womanhood, as demonstrated in Chapters 7 and 10.

Religion and the empowerment of women

The debate on separate spheres for men and women as formulated by nineteenth-century moralists like Sarah Stickney Ellis, and taken up, sometimes uncritically, by twentieth-century historians, has its counterpart in France, summed up in the phrase *'La Femme au Foyer'*. The term *'ménagère'*, or housewife, has, it is important to note, different nuances of meaning in the two languages, with the strong connotation at this period of household administrator for the French term, while the English suggests a more direct immersion in household chores. As in England, there was a strong contribution from French and French–Swiss women writers to the literature of maternal education, as witnessed in Chapter 2. The cult of motherhood was followed by aristocratic as well as bourgeois women, the former often having had to assume direct responsibilities for the rearing of their children to a far greater degree because of the dislocations of the French Revolution.[31]

This cult of motherhood flourished in a culture which had a marked rhetorical tradition of invoking *'La Femme'* as an abstract ideal and, with reference to the salon culture of the two previous centuries, as an historical fact. As Catherine Bodard Silver has observed of France: 'Surely no other western culture has developed more elaborated and intricate ideas about women and more closely interwoven them with the "high culture" and the style of life of whole social classes'.[32] The mystification of actual women into the construct 'woman' served to mask the actual deterioration of the rights some women had enjoyed before the French Revolution and had resulted in all women being classified in the same way as non-citizens.

The treatment of women also needs to be understood in the context of French State formation after the Revolution. This had swept away all the intermediary institutions coming between individuals or families and political authority, including any regional political institutions, the higher law courts such as the *parlements*, the privileged Church and religious Orders, and guilds, town councils, or other corporate bodies. The Jacobin Republic in power between 1792 and 1795 had been particularly intrusive in its policing of the French nation, introducing military conscription, and the notorious law of suspects which had made possible the Reign of Terror. Republicans had to live down the perception associating republicanism with authoritarianism, and liberals made the minimalist state an article of faith, although royalists tended to advocate paternalist authority in the name of the public good. The net effect of the Revolutionary and Napoleonic eras was to elevate the family into the one institution that protected the individual from the glare of the French State's incandescent authority. To many of the ideologues who argued that women reigned in the home sphere, and transmitted manners and culture as well as elementary education to the coming generation, it could seem that women – or Woman – had been granted a great deal of power in a way that complemented rather than conflicted with the male sphere. But because of the legal restrictions on women, as well as their lower earning power, women operated in what many twentieth-century historians would define as an essentially masculinist culture.[33]

Whatever the nineteeth-century arguments over the nature of the French polity, endorsement that woman's place was in the home could be found right across the political spectrum, epitomised in the aphorism of the socialist and anarchist Proudhon '*ménagère ou courtisane*': woman's choice was between housewife and whore.

That the proper role of women as essentially a familial one was also widely endorsed by the church. This fact has to be addressed in connection with the point signalled earlier, that the division between the two Frances was also conceptualised as a division along gender lines. To ardent republicans such as the politician Ferry, or the historian and social philosopher Michelet, there was a split between 'enlightened, rational, progressive and anti-clerical husbands, and pious, pratiquantes, religiously ordered wives'.[34]

To republicans anxious to establish the Third Republic more securely, this was especially obnoxious: they alleged that not only did husbands rule over the family, they also predisposed women against the republic and in favour of the monarchy. Women in consequence could not be trusted with the vote, a view which helped republicans consistently to deny it to them. After all, as they already could vote, male republicans had little to gain from supporting women whom they believed to be hostile to their political ideals; however, to counteract priestly influence, Ferry embarked on a policy for state provision of a secular education to all women.

Until recently, historians have had a tendency to take this republican rhetoric at face value as an accurate historical depiction of separate spheres in the nineteenth century. That it was a substantial historical reality cannot be denied; the split between an extremely pious and royalist mother and an anti-clerical republican father coloured the upbringing and outlook of the socialist and feminist Madeleine Pelletier, for example, and she pitted herself very consciously against her mother's delineation of womanhood (See also Chapter 9).[35] But the question is how far the generalisation can be allowed to go.

Both McMillan and Mills have been engaged in reappraisals of religion and gender, the former by offering a wider perspective on the range of Catholic activities, the latter by exploring what adherence to Catholicism actually meant to women and in what ways in took them beyond a narrow female sphere. These critiques are further advanced in this volume. In Chapter 10 McMillan expands on earlier arguments that it was not necessarily less rational or progressive to be Catholic, by examining the career of the Catholic feminist Marie Maugeret, who led an influential pressure-group for women's suffrage. This is an essay which complements a previous study of how social Catholicism harnessed the philanthropic energies of women.[36]

Hazel Mills has contributed to the understanding of religion in the lives of French women by looking at their role as lay or religious sisterhoods. There was a dramatic expansion of female religious Orders between 1789 and 1880; if four in a thousand women were members of an Order on the eve of the Revolution, a century later this was seven in a thousand, and they were also three-fifths of all religious, in contrast with a third in 1789. The Enlightenment in France had been strongly critical of monasticism, and the Government had also discouraged monks and nuns from activity outside the cloister. The nineteenth-century emphasis was on religious activity that was socially useful rather than on the strictly devotional life followed by enclosed Orders.

Thus Mills argues that Mary Wollstonecraft's denigration of convent life as enclosing and stifling women into uselessness would not have been applicable to this time (though Flora Tristan's view of nineteenth-century convents in Peru echoed the former's distaste). Mills has shown elsewhere that the cultural conditioning which accorded women 'powers' of sympathy and altruism, while men were allocated civic 'power', was not an impassable boundary so much as a negotiable frontier. Women might seem at a disadvantage in the Catholic tradition – as Wollstonecraft believed – because of the idealisation of celibacy and the cult of reverence for the Virgin Mother whose role was by definition unique. (The cult itself does not appear to have attracted more women than men, and was paralleled by the increasing use of feminine imagery in the new emphasis on a loving God.)[37] The pastoral and devotional literature directed at women argued that they needed to be saved from their worst tendencies – their capacity to be, like Eve, temptresses and destroyers of men. But even if there could only be one Virgin Mary, ordinary women who became wives and mothers could express, by their piety and virtue, a kind of spiritual virginity and begin to conquer the Eve within them. In this way, the ideal of the 'femme forte' was developed.[38]

In Chapter 7 Mills shows that while such women did not overtly challenge men's civic prerogatives, they became major providers of welfare and social services of all kinds, particularly when attempts by the State to be too interventionist would have been unwelcome. Women ran hospitals, dispensaries, schools, orphanages and soup kitchens; and in organising and managing these activities displayed considerable administrative and tactical skills – one might say political skills, in the broader sense – and showed a surprising willingness to challenge male episcopal and civic authority. We see in Chapter 10 that this tradition of public-spirited activism can suggest why Maugeret found a following by the end of the century among Catholic women who were now ready to demand the vote, and to see this demand as being in line with patriotic Christian womanhood.

Philanthropy and women's nature

It has been argued that while French women – such as those Mills discusses – turned to philanthropy, they did so in a less independently-minded way than their British counterparts. Both the church and the municipality organised charity, and this has been interpreted as inhibiting female initiative, and contrasted with the organisational inventiveness of leading British philanthropists like Louisa Twining and Florence Nightingale.[39]

However, Mills's work suggests a great deal of female initiative in philanthropy even within an ecclesiastical framework, and that this particular Catholic/Protestant contrast, characteristic of Anglo-American reserve toward Catholicism, and taking an early cue from Wollstonecraft's negative judgement of convents, may be overdrawn. French priests and bishops were male, but so were the English clergy to whom women deferred when running Sunday schools or church-sponsored charities (or in the case of Anglo-Catholics, to whom they confessed as to their spiritual directors). Women also often had to rely on men as trustees for their charitable finances because of married women's lack of property rights. However it is possible that as Protestant clergy could marry, there could be a spirit of collaboration between husbands and wives, though the clergyman's wife was the classic example of a wife incorporated into her husband's profession. In Marion Diamond's essay on the philanthropist and feminist Maria Rye in Chapter 8, she dryly observes that the Revd Charles Kingsley's wife actually ran the parish where Rye lived, though doubtless without making this overtly apparent.[40]

Indeed, when some philanthropic English women assessed their situation, they did not necessarily relish having to make up things as they went along. They might envy their Catholic (and Lutheran Protestant) counterparts the role provided by lay and religious sisterhoods, and be involved in founding equivalent organisations on their side of the Channel. One of the most positive evaluations, some 'anti-popery' notwithstanding, came from Anna Jameson in her 1855 lecture, *Sisters of Charity, Catholic and Protestant, Abroad and at Home*, which had a significant influence:

> we may smile at the childish and melancholy legend of St. Ursula and her eleven thousand virgins, and at the skulls heaped up in a certain mouldy tawdry chapel at Cologne; but of the Ursulines, as a community, we may be allowed to think seriously and even reverently. Their peculiar vocation was the care and instruction of poor children. They had their infant and ragged schools long before we thought of them.[41]

Britain needed to learn from continental examples, Jameson argued, as it made no real provision for the training of men or women in public service or welfare work. She deplored the fact that Florence Nightingale had had to learn abroad from the sisterhood established by Pastor Fleidner at Kaisersworth.

Nightingale had also admired the example of nursing provided by French sisterhoods. Indeed, Cardinal Manning had hoped to win her to Catholicism, one attraction for her being its structured recognition of

women's philanthropic vocation. As she wrote to him after his conversion, 'you do know now what a home the Catholic Church is. And what
is she to you compared with what she would be to me? No one can tell,
no man can tell, what she is to women, their training, their discipline,
their hopes, their home ... For what training is there compared to that of
the Catholic nun?'[42]

Religious commitment was important to many English feminists, and
often nerved them to act against prejudice and on behalf of others by
strengthening a sense of mission. Yet denominational divisions could
often be a source of tension between them, even when they shared a
commitment to improve the legal, educational and occupational status of
women. This was the case with the Langham Place group of feminists,
with whom Maria Rye was associated, as Chapter 8 makes clear. The
group's leaders included Bessie Rayner Parkes, whose later conversion
from Unitarianism to Catholicism was partly prompted by admiration for
French Catholicism's provision for female philanthropy. She wrote
several articles on French women including Soeur Rosalie, whose work
was similar to those discussed by Hazel Mills in Chapter 7, which were
published in the feminist magazine she edited, *The English Woman's
Journal*.[43] Parkes's closest friend, Barbara Leigh Smith Bodichon, had
access through her Unitarian upbringing to a positive evaluation of Mary
Wollstonecraft, and introduced her *Vindication of the Rights of Woman* to
another Langham associate Emily Davies, from an Anglican Evangelical
background, and to her friend (but not fellow activist at Langham Place),
the Evangelical-turned agnostic George Eliot. As Hirsch shows in the first
Chapter, the gradual Victorian rehabilitation of Mary Wollstonecraft
always carefully insisted on her religiosity; hence her eligibility for
inclusion in the Macmillan series with Fry and More. Whether or not
contemporary historians would endorse nineteenth-century assessments
of her religious sympathies, feminists are only now beginning to explore
this component of her life and to counterbalance the way she was constructed as a rational, secular, egalitarian by feminists in the 1970s.[44]

The Langham Place feminists were exercised by the problem of so-
called 'surplus' women, that is to say the demographic imbalance between
men and women and the social codes surrounding acceptable marriages,
which made it hard for middle-class girls to find husbands. One reason
for the attraction to sisterhoods was that they seemed to give dignity to
the single state; other solutions were found in the informal sisterly net-
working and support offered by friendship.[45] Maria Rye's anti-popery,
product of her ardent Evangelical background, would have made her
hostile to anything that smacked of convents; for her, the answer to the
problem of 'surplus women' was to assist female emigration to the

colonies. As Diamond shows in Chapter 8, the contemporary assessment of this work at the end of her career put these efforts in the context of philanthropy rather than feminism. Rye's belief in separate spheres for men and women, and in the latter's superior capacity for altruism, led her to oppose female suffrage as unsuited to women's special nature. But there is an important sense in which work on behalf of women can be seen as an extension of the idea of 'woman's mission' to 'women's mission to other women': the boundaries between conservative Christian philanthropy and active feminism are fluid.[46]

Given the scope for action afforded French women by philanthropy in the first half of the century, it is not surprising that when organised feminism appeared in France during the 1860s, its defining characteristic, aside from the link with republicanism already mentioned, was philanthropic and ameliorative, and that it was sometimes influenced by English examples. There was a strong emphasis on ending the double standard of morality: an important feminist goal, attained in 1912, was the right to institute paternity proceedings. There were campaigns against State-regulated prostitution inspired in part by Josephine Butler's crusade against the Contagious Diseases Acts, (under which any woman in a garrison or dockyard town could be arrested on suspicion of being a diseased prostitute), and Butler came and spoke in France. Another cross-Channel inspiration was the urban settlement movement at Toynbee Hall London, a model for the work of the Social Catholic activist Mlle Gaherny.[47]

Socialism, Flora Tristan, and female messiahs

Whether Catholic, republican or socialist, most activists and male sympathisers believed in women's essential difference, which usually implied (as with Maria Rye), their supposed moral superiority and superior altruism. A notable exception to this view was the socialist feminist Madeleine Pelletier, who had no truck with this romanticisation of women. She believed firmly in equality and the same capacity for good or bad behaviour in each sex. A radical critic of the family, she thought women should be as free as men to enjoy their sexuality and to separate it from motherhood through contraceptive knowledge and the right to abortion. Children born out of wedlock should not be stigmatised, and collective arrangements in place of the family could provide adequate child-rearing. But this was an unusual perspective for French socialists, and her personal celibacy was a recognition that a nonconformist lifestyle would discredit the cause. Her cropped hair and male attire was already sufficiently notorious. Thus most feminists joined with their opponents in seeing women in a relational capacity, to use Karen Offen's phrase.[48]

Male socialist rhetoric played on the way that working-class women were sexually victimised by bourgeois men; to this they opposed an image of the proletariat as the site of domestic virtue, while the stay-at-home wife bore witness to male earning power. But women in practice frequently entered the work-force, full-time or periodically, in order to supplement the family wage. Socialists were divided from feminists over the suffrage; for most socialists, the class struggle was more important than women's emancipation, and women's issues became a bone of contention within an already fissiparous socialist movement. Pelletier was again unusual in trying to unite women's suffrage and socialism in a twin-track strategy.[49]

However, later nineteenth-century and early twentieth-century socialism contrasts with the position in the 1830s, when the differing socialisms of Saint-Simon, Fourier, and Flora Tristan all had a feminist dimension. The latter, like Mary Wollstonecraft, is difficult to pigeon-hole. She operated as an independent activist and articulated her own unique combination of feminism and socialism. Máire Cross has advanced elsewhere an interpretation which underlines her debt to Wollstonecraftian liberalism, as well as clarifying in what sense she is a socialist.[50] But as she is often discussed in connection with the Saint-Simonians, a few brief points on the movement will be useful![51]

After the death in 1825 of the social philosopher Henri de Rouvroy, Comte de Saint-Simon, the movement began among friends and admirers such as Prosper Enfantin, Olinde Rodrigues, the brothers Pereire, and Gustave d'Eichthal, who wanted to apply and develop his ideas. They were aware of the economic growth made possible by industrial processes, and also of the social costs this had inflicted on working people. They believed that society now had the historic opportunity to reorganise work and social relations on the basis of co-operation, not competition, and to use capital investment to increase productivity and diffuse prosperity for all. But there was more to their outlook than an economic critique of unproductive wealth and a desire to harness enterprise in the service of social justice and harmony. Imbued with the Romantic optimism of their epoch, there was also a visionary quality to their idealism which led to their goals being cast in an essentially religious framework, albeit a secular religion of their own making. They believed society would progress only if it respected and empowered the female principle in humankind. The new society needed to be built on love; women were especially associated with love; the 'woman principle' therefore needed to be enhanced and worshipped. God was redefined as both male and female, father and mother.

The movement constituted itself as a church in 1829, with an organisation borrowing improbably from Catholic and Freemasonic hierarchies and rituals. Enfantin was appointed to be one half of the 'couple-pope' who would lead the movement; beside his place a chair was left empty for the female messiah who would be found to complete the leadership. The year 1833 was even designated the Year of the Woman, and some Saint-Simonians set off to Constantinople and to Egypt in search of the woman messiah. The value placed on the 'woman principle' was accompanied by a reversal of traditional Christian teaching on the separation of spirit and matter, and the denigration of the flesh. Women were not to be seen as Eve-temptresses, and the flesh was to be rehabilitated. Relationships were to be based solely on love; bourgeois marriage, founded on property arrangements, was seen as another form of prostitution; divorce was again to be permitted. The isolation of the married couple was to be overcome by communal living, which would also facilitate social experimentation and ease the responsibilities of child-rearing.

The sexual radicalism of the Saint-Simonians as well as their cultish behaviour – their ceremonies, communities, and special costumes – attracted both hostility and ridicule. In 1832 the authorities prosecuted the leaders for corruption of public morals. Cartoonists like Daumier in *Le Charivari* derided the men who formed a rural retreat at Menilmontant for dabbling in 'women's work' (household tasks) or mocked women who adopted experimental dress and spoke in public. The critique of marriage and the rehabilitation of the passions made it all too easy to equate socialism and feminism with free love, and dismiss it as a terrible warning of mistaken views.

The movement was not confined to France; 'missionaries' were sent to England, among other destinations, where they made contact with Utopian socialists like Anna Wheeler, William Thompson, and the followers of Robert Owen's Co-operative movement. Their English counterparts attracted the same fear and ridicule, and the same association in the public mind that talk of improving women's status was socially subversive; in short, the demonisation of Wollstonecraft was repeated.[52]

The experience of women in the movement was that equality was more talked in theory than experienced in practice – which has parallels with English Owenite women.[53] Enfantin's rhetoric had overlooked women's economic and social dependency on men, and the difficulties of separated women in raising children. Women including Eugenie Niboyet who had been associated with Saint-Simonianism contributed to and ran the later *Gazette des Femmes*, (1836–38), which addressed issues such as the need for divorce, and borrowed from the English anti-slavery movement the idea of petitioning the Government. Flora Tristan's first publications included a pamphlet in 1837 petitioning the Government to restore women's right to request divorce, and at this point she was acquainted with the *Gazette's* editorial circle.[54]

But Tristan's was always a singular approach, one that fed directly on her cross-Channel experience, including, as Cross shows in Chapter 6, her homage to Mary Wollstonecraft's kind of Revolutionary feminism. Unlike the Saint-Simonians' secular messianism, hers was exercised in her own right, not as the 'other half' of the 'couple-pope'. She cast herself in the role of pariah and outcast, drawing on the Romantic idealisation of the artist-outsider as well as the prophetic element of social theorising in the 1830s; her womanly love of humanity would transcend the barriers her class and gender would otherwise have placed between herself and the proletariat. Denied her proper social position as an aristocrat (the marriage between her Peruvian aristocratic father and her French mother was not legally valid, rendering her illegitimate), Tristan would minister to the poor in a superior interpretation of *noblesse oblige*. Her self-identification as pariah and redeemer parallels the Christian message but is obviously a far cry from the ethos of serving the poor espoused by the *saintes soeurs* and *femmes fortes* discussed by Mills in Chapter 7. Tristan was profoundly anticlerical, and appealed to these Catholic charitable women to redirect their energies to raise funds which would help workers to help themselves.[55]

As Cross demonstrates in Chapter 6, there are definite parallels between Wollstonecraft and Tristan: the former was an important role model for the latter. In her analysis of English society, Tristan concluded that even upper-class women were in a subservient condition, unable to control their property and forced in their loveless marriages to condone a sexual double standard for male behaviour. They even lacked the powers inherent in household management, as their husbands took charge, she believed, of the household money and keys. Nevertheless, Tristan believed that women's native intelligence enabled them to survive and gave them a keen insight into human behaviour, which bore fruit in their literary achievements: 'The books of these English women are a shining phenomenon which lights up the intellectual world, especially if we consider the absurd education they had to settle for, and the stupefying influence of the milieu in which they grew up'.[56] Mary Wollstonecraft was Tristan's muse and unsung heroine, who stood out for her courageous criticism of woman's position, but she also praised women who excelled in different kinds of writing without being feminists: Lady Morgan and Lady Blessington, Rosina Bulwer (daughter of the socialist Anna Wheeler), Harriet Martineau, Mrs Gore and 'Mrs Shilly'. This can be none other than Wollstonecraft's daughter Mary Shelley, now as a widow making a name for herself as a novelist, poet and critic. Tristan must have been unaware of the misogynistic backlash which the visibility of English women writers provoked in male literary circles, from which Sarah Stickney Ellis, among others, suffered.[57]

But if Tristan was inspired by the growing numbers of English women earning a living as professional writers, the latter paradoxically looked to France as a place where clever women enjoyed greater cultural recognition and intellectual equality, and women like Mme de Staël, or her fictional alter ego, the poet Corinne, were seen as icons of female literary achievement.[58] None the less, Tristan felt her singularity as a female writer, and her choice of title for her journey to Peru, Peregrinations of a Pariah (1835), may have been influenced by the rueful assertion of none other than Mme de Staël, that a woman of intellect 'leads her peculiar existence, like all Pariahs in India, in between all the classes to which she may not belong, because she is supposed to exist all on her own, an object of curiosity, perhaps of envy, and in fact deserving only pity'.[59]

History and the science of 'Man'

As Mme de Staël's daughter, the Duchesse de Broglie, observed, 'history is the muse of our time; we are, I think, the first who have understood the past'.[60] The hugely expanding historical enterprise of the nineteenth century had its roots in the philosophical histories of the Enlightenment, as well as in the efforts of Wollstonecraft and her 'daughters' to make sense of the unprecedented events they witnessed. Wollstonecraft herself began a history of the French Revolution as well as combining social observation and personal reflection in her travel writings on Scandinavia, showing the way forward for women who wanted to appropriate 'masculine' genres to themselves.

Eighteenth-century 'philosophical history' shared with the natural sciences the ideal of scientific understanding and aimed to find the defining principles which would unify historical explanation, just as Newton's principle of gravitation had unified explanation in the physical sciences. Historical understanding was closely linked with the new science of sociology. It was also harnessed to a critique of Ancien Régime society, by showing how other societies differed, or by revealing contrasting patterns in the national or European past. The doyen of French social theory, Montesquieu, was constructing a science of society but also contributing to the contemporary debate on historical progress, religious toleration, and civic virtue. Voltaire emphasised historical achievement in terms of cultural and intellectual activity instead of military and political triumphs, and wished to show that Christian society was neither chronologically anterior nor morally superior to Chinese or Indian civilisation. History could therefore be harnessed to anti-clerical polemic against the perils of 'priestcraft'. An historical topic given fresh attention in the Enlightenment was the transition from Rome's republican origins to its

rise and decline as an empire, a subject explored most eloquently by
Gibbon, and one which had particular resonance to the ruling elites in
France and England who were competitors in imperial expansion and
concerned about the shortcomings of an imperial polity.[61]

Where did women fit into this burgeoning historical enterprise, either
as the subjects of history or the writers of it? Jane Rendall, who contributes in Chapter 3 an essay on Elizabeth Hamilton, has raised these
questions in several contexts. In her comparative survey of early feminism
in France, Britain and America, she showed that by articulating the debate
over the relative importance of nature versus culture in the development
of human society, the Enlightenment began to include questions about
gender as a part of its projected science of society. A growing grasp of the
varied historical experience of being female counteracted trends attempting to impose a particular definition of femininity as essentially and
eternally valid. The sciences of 'man' could also become an enquiry into
the sciences of woman.[62]

A common theme in Enlightenment philosophical histories was an
analysis based on the idea of progressive stages of human society,
advancing from barbarism to civilisation through the hunting, pastoral,
agricultural and commercial stages. The treatment of women was often
taken as one index of the attainment of civilisation; another was the
abolition of slavery. Women activists campaigning to abolish the slave
trade would later in the nineteenth century echo this debate by comparing women's condition, especially their legal status, to slavery and
arguing that progress had yet to be made from might to right. The
analogy is strongly made by Harriet Taylor in *The Enfranchisement of
Women* (1851), and by John Stuart Mill in *The Subjection of Women* (1869),
which was a key text of liberal feminism on both sides of the Channel.

Enlightenment histories of a Christian as distinct from an anti-clerical
tenor attributed to Christianity the abolition of slavery and the elevation
of women to a more respected status, often citing the cult of chivalry with
its elaborate romantic reverence for a woman as evidence. Suzanne
Necker, who as Mlle Churchod had been the object of Gibbon's youthful
love, was the patron of Antoine Thomas (1732–85) author of *Essai sur le
caractère, les moeurs et l'esprit des femmes dans les différents siècles* (1772), one of
several French and Scottish conjectural historians who argued precisely
this theme.[63] His historical sociology was followed by Albertine Necker
de Saussure, Mme Necker's niece by marriage, in her brief survey of the
treatment of women through history in *Education Progressive*. Chapter 2
gives an account of this. Other themes pursued by these historians included women's role in the growth of 'politeness', that is the civilised
social interaction characteristic of modern commercial society. Women

were seen as key agents in the transmission of manners, namely, social behaviour and moral culture, through their role as maternal educators. Recognition of this historically important role could open the way for comment on the need to improve women's education, for while there was agreement that women were better off overall than they had been in the earliest, 'savage' state, it was recognised that this did not justify complacency about their present position.

There was ambivalence about the nature of feminine influence, however. History could be viewed as a feminising process, replacing brute force with peaceful kinds of co-existence regulated by social etiquette; but at what point did the feminisation of society mean women's subjection of men and their effeminacy? Rousseau had been quite clear that this dreaded emasculation would be the outcome of women's sexual, social and cultural power, and accordingly envisaged his ideal woman as a submissive helpmeet, as discussed in the first section of this introduction. Another anxiety was women's attraction to the 'luxury', or as we would say, the consumer culture, of the new commercial society. Women could become the agents of corruption through this hedonism.[64]

Women were not only the subjects of history but writers of it. Jane Rendall's essay on Elizabeth Hamilton in Chapter 3 is part of a wider investigation she is making into how British women were beginning to write a national history incorporating their standpoint and experiences.[65] History was not yet a fully professionalised academic discipline, but it was nevertheless regarded as a masculine preserve because women were thought to be intellectually incapable of the powers of generalisation and analysis it required, besides being excluded from crucial sources because they usually lacked classical scholarship. Nevertheless, the boundaries between history, antiquarianism and literature were fluid, and this fluidity, combined with the expanding literary market, enabled some women to push against the restrictions of gender and genre, which otherwise confined them to children's primers or anecdotal and biographical sketches, and to devise their own kinds of history incorporating their perspectives and preoccupations. Moreover there was an illustrious foremother in the eighteenth century, Catherine Macaulay, pictured in Richard Samuel's famous picture of the *Nine Living Muses* (1779) as Clio, the Muse of History. Macaulay had written history with a clear political agenda, that of eighteenth-century republicanism, but had not directly addressed the question of women's status in her history of Britain.[66] However Macaulay's last book, *Letters on Education*, published in 1790, discussed education as part of a wider review of government, society, and the proper upbringing of children, and argued for boys and girls to receive the same schooling. Wollstonecraft reviewed this book and it may have been an important catalyst in showing how a woman writing on educational theory could at the same time be offering comprehensive cultural and social criticism.[67]

Wollstonecraft offered this searching criticism in her philosophical history of the French Revolution. Titled significantly *An Historical and Moral View of the Origin and Progress of the French Revolution and the Effect it has produced in Europe*, it combined personal interpretation (a 'view') with analysis ('historical and moral') based on the idea that the progress of reason, including its attack on 'priestcraft', had prepared the ground for a renewal of the French State, which had lapsed into degeneracy. Mary's contemporaries Mary Hays and Helen Maria Williams as well as Elizabeth Hamilton were also to experiment with historical genre.[68]

Elizabeth Hamilton, if known at all today, is usually cited as the novelist whose *Memoirs of Modern Philosophers* (1800) parodied Wollstonecraft as Bridgetina Botherim. Yet before the politicisation and stigmatisation of Wollstonecraft's life and works described in Chapter 1, she and Hamilton had shared common ground in their conviction that women must be given an essentially rational education. But Hamilton's introduction to literary life had been much easier than Wollstonecraft's, being facilitated by the moral and financial support of a brother who encouraged her scholarly leanings and opened the door of the 'masculine' classics to her.

Jane Rendall's exploration in Chapter 2 of Hamilton's debt to the Scottish Enlightenment again underlines the importance of cultural specificity. Edinburgh was not London, just as Geneva was not Paris. Between Whig Edinburgh and liberal Geneva there were some significant similarities, too, both being cultures shaped by Calvinism, with many links between Edinburgh University and Geneva's Academy. Rendall shows how Hamilton's work is shaped by Scottish psychological theory on the development of the intellect, as well as Scottish conjectural history on the development of society. Hamilton's choice of Agrippina as an historical subject, a member of the Roman Imperial family in the early years of its transition from republic to empire, puts Hamilton squarely in the historical debate on the contrasts between the 'barbaric' yet noble simplicity of the northern German tribes, and the decadence already apparent in the Roman imperium. This was also a debate on gender relations, since German tribal society was viewed as notable for its monogamy and respect for women. Agrippina and her husband, while enjoying a rational companionship based on mutual esteem, can learn from the German women's self-reliance and patriotic resistance to Roman domination.

Hamilton's history, unlike some Enlightened histories, was also a Christian history; as Rendall shows, it is a morality tale for the British

Imperial conscience. Thirty years later, Sarah Stickney Ellis would put her conduct books into the context of a British Christian mission, linking domestic virtues at home to wholesome influence abroad, speaking of the dangers of self-indulgent materialism and spurious refinement:

> as far as the noble daring of Britain has sent forth her adventurous sons, and that is to every point of danger on the habitable globe, they have borne along with them a generosity, a disinterestedness, and a moral courage, derived in no small measure from the female influence of their native country.[69]

Sarah Stickney's husband, the Revd William Ellis, was a noted missionary who wrote accounts of the flora, fauna and ethnography of Polynesia and Madagascar. After their marriage Sarah assisted him in writing accounts of his travels. William Ellis was in no doubt that Christian influence could ensure the the advancement of civilisation abroad, especially in abolishing infanticide, enhancing the status of women, replacing alcohol abuse with temperance, and creating a fair as distinct from an exploitative commercial relationship. His ethnographic studies were sympathetic to the peoples they depicted without assuming western superiority in every respect.[70]

International travel and national histories

The travel accounts which contributed to the comparative history of human civilisation from the Enlightenment into the twentieth century were no more the exclusive preserve of male writers than were the historical analyses which resulted from them. Women wrote actual and fictional travel books which often regarded family and marriage customs and the condition of women with a critical eye and as a device for introducing comparative perspectives on the condition of women. As a reviewer of travel books for the *Analytical Review*, Wollstonecraft was familiar with the spectrum of travel writing in her time, and approved those books which eschewed mere anecdote for a unifying point of view: 'the art of travel is only a branch of the art of thinking'.[71]

When she wrote her own travel book, Wollstonecraft helped create a change of direction for her future 'daughters'. Her *Letters written during a Short Residence in Sweden, Norway and Denmark* (1796) showed how sociological enquiry could be united to intense personal reflection and susceptibility to nature; the book has been seen as a seminal document in the shaping of English Romanticism. The format she used, that of letters to her (unnamed) lover, Imlay, on behalf of whose business ventures the trip was made, did not disguise from readers that the author was unhappily in love. Yet the keen eye for detail and constant curiosity about a country

that embodied the contrasts beloved of Enlightenment historiography
between northern 'barbarism' and southern 'luxury' provoked from one
of her hosts the comment that she asked 'men's questions'.[72]

In France, travel literature, whether factual or fictional, served a parallel function of providing comparative insights to show the variability of
women's status, and linking discourses on colonialism and feminism.
Mme de Graffigny's best-selling novel *Lettres d'une Péruvienne* (1747) had
used the device of a Peruvian princess captured and brought to Paris
where she observed the contrasts between her native culture and 'civi-
lized' Paris. Modern critics see the colonial motif as a metaphor for how
women's experience is appropriated by a masculinist culture.[73] Editions of
the book continued to appear until 1835, the same year that Flora Tristan
published her account of her journey to Peru to try to secure some of her
inheritance, *Pérégrinations d'une Paria, 1833–4*. It too dramatised the plight
of different women in Peruvian society, while her experiences confirmed
her view of herself as an pariah whose destiny she now made her own.
Tristan's first piece of writing, *Nécessité de faire bon acceuil aux femmes
étrangères*, was on behalf of the special needs of women travellers, whose
plight was a test-case of the vulnerability of women in an inegalitarian
world. Her sociological study of England anticipated Engels's critique of
industrial conditions, while she spent her remaining strength touring and
lecturing in France, as shown in Chapter 6.

Travel accounts from a variety of writers: the leisured amateur,
missionaries, colonial administrators, settlers, and entrepreneurs, therefore provided comparative and historical material which could be utilised
in an historicised, scientific account of the development of civilisation.
This continued to be true a century after Wollstonecraft's death, when
feminists continued to appropriate and re-interpret the human sciences
and contest their domination by male intellectuals.

The prestige accruing to scientific forms of knowledge meant that
there was a continuing attempt to give history a scientific base, and relate
it to the new historical sciences of the nineteenth century: geology,
paleontology, and anthropology. These were transforming the older
accounts of the stages of civilisation, but given that scientific discourse is
not impermeable to the values of the people and institutions who shape it,
the new anthropology interpreted its ethnographic raw material to tell a
story of progress, culminating in nineteenth-century styles of western
civilisation and endorsing the subordination of women, children, and
'primitive' races.[74]

In Chapter 9, Felicia Gordon shows how two women, one French, one
English, both socialists and both therefore imbued with a materialist emphasis
on human history, developed a feminist interpretation of anthropology.

Madeleine Pelletier, who specialised in psychiatric medicine, experimented with craniometry (the measurement of the brain) in order to refute assumptions about the relationship of brain size to women's alleged intellectual inferiority. Edith Simcox offered an ambitious interpretation of Egyptian, Mesopotamian and Chinese civilisation which undermined late-Victorian assumptions about the 'natural' social order of gender hierarchy, showing that the pattern of earlier civilisations was one of gender reciprocity. Neither sex was privileged over the other in its possession of wealth; and the dominant social values were not the male, public-oriented, civic virtues of Graeco-Roman culture, but domestic virtues of interdependence. She also relativises nineteenth-century sexual codes by her discussion of Egyptian sibling marriage, a relativisation which Gordon relates to Simcox's hidden homosexual identity and her ability to free herself from a Eurocentric, imperial imagination.

The historical imagination was also more narrowly harnessed into a nationalist context in the nineteenth century. Cultural and political nationalism relied heavily on constructing an account of national origins, and this was the case even for well-established nation-states like Britain and France. Women's historical writing was (as we have already seen in the case of Hamilton's moral, patriotic aims) included in this creation of a national past. It could have a feminist dimension, by offering a gallery of past 'women worthies' who could inspire women to new levels of achievement and reassure them that there were precedents for their endeavours, or a conservative one, holding up models of traditional female roles for patriotic emulation. Maria Rye, whom Diamond discusses in Chapter 8, used her magazine articles to highlight the history and prospects of British women. The internationalist sympathies of nineteenth-century feminism meant that their re-telling of women's past often transcended a merely national context. A third of the Eminent Women biographies published by Macmillan were devoted to French women, reflecting the English preoccupation with a French construct of 'woman' noted above.

Historical writing in France clearly reflected and indeed helped to articulate the division between the two Frances. The great caesura of the Revolution had to be explained and its violence confronted. Liberals, for example, could rehabilitate the Revolution by relating it to a tradition of French constitutionalism with roots in the medieval town commune, and explain Revolutionary excess as a perversion of this tradition by the Jacobins. The eloquent and influential Romantic historians, such as Quinet or Michelet, projected a vision of national destiny which apotheosised the development of the nation and people of France, and demonised the monarchy and the Catholic church for hindering this destiny. Such historical visions were invariably deeply gendered. For Michelet, history witnessed the struggle of society to emancipate itself from nature; women were more closely assimilated to nature than to society. Nature was thus 'the mother to be denied, the lover to be escaped'. Later he was to emphasise a more complementary view of the masculine and feminine principle in human development. But women could never transcend their femininity; biology rendered them vulnerable, even pathological, and dependent on male protection. Michelet's was one of the most powerful voices contributing to the republican, anti-clerical belief that women's childlikeness predisposed them to religious deference and made them unfit to be citizens, views which were now given historical authority in his sweeping account of national destiny.[75]

Furthermore, once evolutionary theory had begun to imply that the human race itself might have developed through natural selection, implying no moral or qualitative difference between animals and humankind, the tensions deepened between science and religion. Auguste Comte's positivism was ranged against ultramontane Catholic conservatism, and the Vatican's Syllabus of Errors seemed to close the door on the modern historical and biological sciences.

The struggle over competing accounts of the French past was also a struggle for the possession of national symbols. One such struggle centred on the figure of Joan of Arc. Originally associated with the monarchy and patriotic struggle against England, in the nineteenth century she became a symbol of the people. But which people? Anti-clerical patriots who saw her as a representative of the peasantry and the victim of priesthood (for the Church had condemned her as a witch)? Or the radical Right for whom she was a sainted representative of France, 'the oldest daughter' of the Catholic church? As McMillan shows in Chapter 10, Marie Maugeret used the symbol of Joan of Arc to appeal to Catholic women, so as to link patriotism with piety, and counteract the republican symbol of Marianne, who figured increasingly in the public imagery of the Third Republic. Looking further back into European history, Maugeret contrasted Luther the heretic with Loyala the founder of the Jesuit Order, directly obedient to Rome. Aligning herself with the anti-Dreyfusards, she interpreted recent times in virulently anti-Semitic terms. Elements of an older Christian anti-Semitism were blended the economic conspiracy theories of the Belle Epoque which demonised Jews as the exploitative beneficiaries of the new financial capitalism.[76]

Women in France in England during the nineteenth century were unable to fulfil Wollstonecraft's dream of full citizenship. But they pushed hard at boundaries defining their proper sphere, redefining motherhood and insisting on better education to prepare themselves for it; they found in religious activism an extended field of labour, often premised on a view of essential womanhood granting them considerable moral power and energy; and they contested the masculine world of scholarship and science, beginning to enter it and challenge its definitions of women's nature and capacities with their own interpretations. Wollstonecraft helped to articulate the great modern debates about citizenship and womanhood, religion and secularism, history and progress. As these essays illustrate, women are integral to these debates; not only are they the subject of discussion, they also speak for themselves; they are Wollstonecraft's daughters. Two centuries after Wollstonecraft's death, the historical profession strives to hear what they had to say and understand their lived experience. This book is a contribution toward a continuing historical endeavour that will, this editor hopes, make it unthinkable to separate historical enquiry of men – and ideologies of masculinity – from the history of women, and ideologies of femininity.

Notes

1 Comparative perspectives on women include Jane Rendall, *The Origins of Modern Feminism: Women in Britain, France and the United States, 1780–1860* (London, Macmillan, 1985); Erna A. Hellerstein, Lesley P. Hume, and Karen M. Offen (eds), *Victorian Women: A Documentary Account of Women's Lives in Nineteenth-Century England, France, and the United States* (Stanford, Stanford University Press, 1981), and the stimulating cultural study by Doris Y. Kadish, *Politicizing Gender: Narrative Strategies in the Aftermath of the French Revolution* (New Brunswick), Rutgers University Press, 1991). Rosemary O'Day, *The Family and Family Relationships, 1500–1900: England, France and the United States of America* (London, Macmillan, 1995) appeared while this was in the press. Two attempts to trace the picture of France held by English writers are Christophe Campos, *The View of France: From Arnold to Bloomsbury* (Oxford, Oxford University Press, 1965), which however quite explicitly takes as a guide the imaginary figure of a young man of letters and does not consider whether women writers may have had a view of France; and Ceri Crossley and Ian Small (eds), *Studies in Anglo-French Cultural Behaviour: Imagining France* (London, Macmillan, 1988).

2 Cited from G. K. Chesterton, *The Victorian Age in Literature*, p. 17, by David Newsome, *The Convert Cardinals: John Henry Newman and Henry Edward Manning* (London, John Murray, 1993), p. x.

3 For Britain and German culture, see Rosemary Ashton, *The German Idea: Four Writers and the Reception of German Thought 1800–1860* (Cambridge, Cambridge University Press, 1980); and Noel Annan, *Leslie Stephen: The Godless Victorian*, revised and expanded edition (London, Weidenfeld and Nicolson, 1984). My remarks on Romanticism simplify and summarise some very complex issues, and my comments should not be taken to underestimate the importance of French pre-Romanticism including its assimilation within Germany, to the full development of the movement, e.g. in the contribution of the Francophone but Genevan Jean-Jacques Rousseau. For some comparative perspectives on Romanticism, see Roy Porter and Mikuláš Teich (eds), *Romanticism in National Context* (Cambridge, Cambridge University Press, 1988), and

Lillian R. Furst, *Romanticism in Perspective*, 2nd ed. (Macmillan, London, 1979). For French adoption of the English dandy style, which became an important element in the pose of French aestheticism, see Ellen Moers, *The Dandy, Brummell to Beerbohm* (London, Secker and Warburg, 1960) and, for women and Romanticism, the pioneering study by Anne Mellor, *Romanticism and Gender* (London, Routledge, 1993). Some aspects of women, national romanticism and the visual arts are addressed in Clarissa Campbell Orr, 'The Corinne Complex: Gender, Genius and National Character', in Campbell Orr (ed.), *Women in the Victorian Art World* (Manchester, Manchester University Press, 1995).

4   See Linda Colley, *Britons: Forging the Nation, 1701–1837* (New Haven, Yale University Press, 1990).

5   Roger Magraw, *France 1814–1915: The Bourgeois Century* (London, Fontana Press, 1983) and James F. McMillan, *Twentieth Century France: Politics and Society in France 1898–1991* (London, Edward Arnold, 1992) provide accessible introductions; from the enormous literature on Dreyfus and the French Right, Michael Burns, *Dreyfus: A Family Affair 1789–1945* (London, Chatto and Windus, 1992) and Eugen Weber, *My France* (Cambridge, Mass., Harvard University Press, 1991) provide penetrating insights.

6   An overview of English political and religious change is provided by Eric J. Evans, *The Forging of the Modern State, 1783–1870* (Harlow, Longman, 1983), and E. J. Feuchtwanger, *Democracy and Empire: Britain 1865–1914* (London, Edward Arnold, 1985).

7   The seminal article on women's part in public activism is Alex Tyrrell, ' "Women's Mission" and Pressure Group Politics in Britain, 1825–1860', *Bulletin of the John Rylands University Library*, 63 (1980), 194–229. I have discussed recent debates among historians about the concept of separate spheres (demarcating men to the public and women to the private), and its usefulness for understanding women's historical experience, in the introduction to Campbell Orr, *Women*. Pelletier's visit to England and experience of French police surveillance is discussed by Felicia Gordon in *The Integral Feminist: Madeleine Pelletier, 1974–1939* (Cambridge, Polity Press, 1990).

8   See Patricia Hollis, 'Women in council: separate spheres, public space', in Jane Rendall (ed.), *Equal or Different? Women's Politics 1800–1914*, (Oxford, Basil Blackwell, 1987).

9   McMillan, *Housewife or Harlot: The Place of Women in French Society 1870–1940* (Brighton, Harvester Press, 1981) summarises the legal position in theory and practice. Margaret Darrow, *Revolution in the House: Family, Class and Inheritance in Southern France, 1775–1825* (Princeton, Princeton University Press, 1989), is a case-study for the Montauban area of how the Napoleonic Code supplanted law and custom in marriage and family matters.

10 Lee Holcombe, *Wives and Property: Reform of the Married Women's Property Law in Nineteenth Century England* (Toronto, University of Toronto Press, 1983).

11 A. James Hammerton, *Cruelty and Companionship: Conflict in Nineteenth Century Married Life* (London, Routledge, 1992).

12 Karen Offen, 'Feminism, Anti-feminism, and National Family Politics in Early Third Republic France', in Marilyn J. Boxer and Jean H. Quataert (eds), *Connecting Spheres: Women in the Western World, 1500 to the Present* (Oxford, Oxford University Press, 1987). Historical arguments on the extent of contraceptive practices in England are reviewed in F. M. L. Thompson, *The Rise of Respectable Society: A Social History of Victorian Britain, 1830–1900* (London, Fontana Press, 1988).

13 McMillan, *Housewife or Harlot*; George Sussman, *Selling Mother's Milk: The Wet-Nursing Business in France 1715–1914* (Urbana, University of Illinois Press, 1982).

14 See McMillan, *Housewife or Harlot*; Eugen Weber, *Peasants into Frenchmen* (London, Chatto and Windus, 1976); M. Segalen, *Love and Power in the Peasant Family* (Oxford, Blackwell, 1983).

15 Jenny Uglow, *Elizabeth Gaskell: A Habit of Stories* (London, Faber and Faber, 1993), depicts these networks well for Unitarian provincial culture; Leonore Davidoff, *The Best Circles: Society, Etiquette, and The Season* (London, Croom Helm, 1973), describes the workings of London Society's marriage market; Joan Perkin, *Women and Marriage in Victorian England* (London, Routledge, 1989), offers a wider discussion. Barbara Corrado Pope, 'Angels in the Devil's Workshop: Leisured and Charitable Women in Nineteenth-Century England and France', in Renate Bridenthal and Claudia Koontz (eds), *Becoming Visible: Women in European History* (Boston, Houghton Mifflin, 1977), makes some acute observations on the different marriage markets.

16 McMillan, *Housewife or Harlot*; Elizabeth Roberts, *Women's Work 1840–1949* (London, Macmillan, 1988); Jane Rendall, *Women in an Industrializing Society: England 1750–1880* (Oxford, Basil Blackwell, 1990).

17 Michel Vovelle, 'The pre-Revolutionary Sensibility', in *Ideologies and Mentalities* (Cambridge, Polity Press, 1990). See also Lynn Hunt, *The Family Romance of the French Revolution* (London, Routledge, 1992), and Madelyn Gutwirth, *The Twilight of the Goddesses* (New Brunswick, Rutgers University Press, 1992); Sara Maza, *Private Lives and Public Affairs: The Causes Célèbres of Pre-Revolutionary France*, (Berkeley, University of California Press, 1993). Similar analyses based on cultural and literary studies for the post-Revolutionary era can be found in Sara E. Melzer and Leslie W. Rabine, *Rebel Daughters: Women and the French Revolution* (Oxford, Oxford University Press, 1992).

18 James F. McMillan, 'Religion and Gender in Modern France: Some Reflections', in Frank Tallett and Nicholas Atkin, *Religion, Politics and Society in France since 1789* (London, The Hambledon Press, 1991).

19 See Campbell Orr, *Women*, Introduction; also Patricia Levine, *Feminist Lives in Victorian England: Private Lives, Public Commitment* (Oxford, Basil Blackwell, 1990).

20 David Cannadine's *The Decline and Fall of the British Aristocracy* (New Haven, Yale University Press, 1990), mentions little about women. Dominic Lieven, *The Aristocracy in Europe 1815–1914* (London, Macmillan, 1992) includes some discussion of women but admits his treatment could be more extensive. J. V. Beckett's *Aristocracy in England, 1660–1914* (Oxford, Basil Blackwell, 1986), contains so little on women one wonders whether the aristocracy reproduced itself by parthogenesis. Even a chapter on the aristocracy at home, supposedly the women's domain, mentions virtually nothing about women's cultural role in building or altering house or gardens and parks, or their estate management in the absence of their husbands. An exception is some mention of Elizabeth Montagu, the bluestocking hostess, but the point is omitted that most of her architectural patronage was exercised when she was a widow and thus fully in control of an extensive fortune. See also Trevor Loomis and Jan Marsh, *The Woman's Domain: Women and the English Country House* (London, Viking, 1990), for example of women from *chatelaines* to housekeepers. The scholarly study of elite women currently being prepared by Linda Colley will be of immense value. For a preliminary view, see her article 'The Power behind the Patronage: The Female Elite of Eighteenth and Nineteenth Century England', in *Past and Present*, forthcoming.

21 Schneid Lewis, *In the Family Way: Childrearing in the British Aristocracy 1760–1860* (New Brunswick, Rutgers University Press, 1986); Randolph Trumbach, *The Rise of the Egalitarian Family: Aristocratic Kinship and Domestic Relations in Eighteenth-Century England* (New York, Academic Press, 1978). See also Stella Tillyard, *Aristocrats* (London, Chatto and Windus, 1994), for an especially illuminating contrast between the first and second marriages of Emily and Sarah Lennox, both of whose second marriages followed a more middle-class model. Indeed Emily's second marriage was to her children's tutor, appointed to educate her children on Rosseauesque principles. An exhibition at Bowood House in 1994 focused on the education of the sons of the first

first Marquis of Lansdowne (1737–1803) and displayed his journal entries by his first wife, Lady Sophia, recording her sons' health and educational progress.

22 See however Michael Bentley, *Politics without Democracy 1815–1914* (London, Fontana Press, 1984).

23 M. Bush, *The English Aristocracy: A Comparative Synthesis* (Manchester, Manchester University Press, 1984).

24 Pat Jalland, *Women, Marriage and Politics 1860–1914* (Oxford, Oxford University Press, 1988); Barbara Caine, *Destined to be Wives: The Sisters of Beatrice Webb* (Oxford, Oxford University Press, 1988); M. Jeanne Petersen, *Family, Love and Work in the Lives of Victorian Gentlewomen* (Bloomington and Indianapolis, Indiana University Press, 1989); Noel Annan, 'The Intellectual Aristocracy', in J. H. Plumb (ed.), *Studies in Social History* (London, Longman, 1955).

25 Thomas Laquer, 'The Queen Caroline Affair', *Journal of Modern History*, 54 (September 1982), 417–66, and E. A. Smith, *A Queen on Trial: The Affair of Queen Caroline* (Stroud, Alan Sutton Publishing, 1994), esp. ch. 6. The languages of support for Caroline included a rhetoric based on chivalrous sympathy for a wronged woman as well as an equal rights kind of discourse, in which 'Caroline's cause became self-consciously the cause of 'out-door' politics, of public opinion against the coterie politics of court and parliament'. (Laquer, 'Queen Caroline'). I address the relationship of this language of chivalry to women's rights in a forthcoming article: 'Women's History, Women's Rights: Agnes Strickland, Caroline Norton, and the Victorian cult of Chivalry'.

26 Gervase Huxley (ed.), *Lady Elizabeth and the Grosvenors: Life in a Whig Family, 1922–1839* (London, Oxford University Press, 1965), p. 96.

27 *Ibid.*, pp. 98, 109. Some British aristocrats had become acquainted with French émigré aristocrats who had fallen out with the republican regime and taken refuge in England; the 4th Marquis of Landsdowne married the daughter of one such exile, Charles de Flahault.

28 See for example, Norma Clarke, 'Strenuous idleness: Thomas Carlyle and the Man of Letters as Hero', in Michael Roper and John Tosh (eds), *Manful Assertions* (London, Routledge, 1991); Stuart Curran, 'Romantic Poetry: the I altered' in Anne K. Mellor (ed.), *Romanticism and Feminism* (Bloomington and Indiana, Indiana University Press, 1988), and Gary Kelly, 'Revolutionary and Romantic Feminism: Women, Writing, and Cultural Revolution', in Keith Hanley and Raman Selden (eds), *Revolution and English Romanticism: Politics and Rhetoric* (London, Harvester Wheatsheaf, 1990).

29 Miriam M. H. Traill, *Rebellious Fraser's* (New York, Columbia University Press, 1934).

30 Sarah Stickney Ellis, *The Women of England: Their Social Duties and Domestic Habits* (London, 1838), p. 37; see Linda Colley, *Britons*, for the moral and religious base to British patriotism during and after the Napoleonic wars. Thackeray's 'A Shabby Genteel Story' portraying a downwardly mobile family fraying at the edges through drink and narrow means but buoyed up by snobbery doubtlessly parodies the genre of temperance fiction written by Ellis and others. D. J. Taylor, (ed.), *William Makepeace Thackeray: A Shabby Genteel Story and Other Writings* (London, Everyman, 1994).

31 Rendall, *Origins*; Margaret F. Darrow, 'French Noblewomen and the new Domesticity, 1750–1850', *Feminist Studies*, 5 (Spring, 1979), 41–65.

32 Catherine Bodard Silver, 'Salon, Foyer, Bureau: Woman and the Professions in France', in Mary S. Hartman and Lois Banner (eds), *Clio's Consciousness Raised: New Perspectives on the History of Women* (New York and London, Harper and Row, 1974).

33 See Silver, 'Salon, Foyer, Bureau', and the analysis of masculinism offered by Patrick Kay Bidelman, in *Pariahs Stand Up! The Founding of the Liberal Feminist Movement in France, 1858–1889* (Westport, Connecticut and London, The Greenwood Press, 1982), ch. 1.

34 McMillan, 'Religion and Gender'.

35 Gordon, *Integral Feminist*; see also Bonnie C. Smith, *Ladies of the Leisure Class: The Bourgeoises of Northern France in the Nineteenth Century* (Princeton, Princeton University Press, 1981), ch. 6 for some documented examples of wives opposing their husbands' anti-clericalism in local politics.

36 On Social Catholicism, see McMillan, 'Women in Social Catholicism in late Nineteenth and early Twentieth Century France', in *Women in the Church*, eds, W. J. Sheils and Diana Woods, *Studies in Church History*, 27 (1990) where he concludes: 'Social Catholic Christian women may have been constrained by a certain Christian discourse, but they were not crushed by it'. Further perspectives on religion, anti-clericalism and gender are offered by Ralph Gibson, 'Why Catholics and Republicans couldn't stand each other in the nineteenth century', in Tallett and Atkin, *Religion, Politics and Society*. In my view Bonnie C. Smith's *Ladies of the Leisure Class*, richly researched study though it is, is flawed by its lack of historical perspective on religious history, and a conceptual approach to religion that resembles nineteenth-century positivism. It also betrays logical inconsistency by demonstrating a clear disjunction between the leisured later nineteenth-century women and their unsentimental and not very observant Catholic foremothers, who worked full-time in family enterprises, yet at the same time speaking of women *maintaining* an uninterrupted religious world-view while their menfolk acquired progressive modern views: e.g. 'While men abandoned their mythical or religious deities, women not only maintained their relationship with the Christian God, but invented a new cult of the virtuous heroine who ruled a domestically constructed universe'; 'science, rationality, and the values of liberal society passed her by as she maintained a reactionary posture', pp. 12, 25. She regards her boureoises as if they were a virtually alien culture, deploring the 'unpleasant' way women's history reveals 'primitivism and antirationalism', p. 216.

37 Gibson, *A Social History of French Catholicism* (London, Routledge, 1989); see also Marina Warner, *Alone of All Her Sex: The Myth and Cult of the Virgin Mary* (London, Weidenfeld and Nicolson, 1976).

38 Hazel Mills, 'Negotiating the Divide: Women, Philanthropy, and "The Public Sphere" in Nineteenth Century France', in Tallett and Atkin, *Religion, Politics and Society*.

39 Pope, 'Angels'.

40 A clearer example of gender dynamics in a companionate clerical marriage is discussed by Seth Koven, 'Henrietta Barnett, 1857–1936: The (Auto)biography of a late Victorian Marriage', in Susan Pedersen and Peter Mandler (eds), *After the Victorians* (London, Routledge, 1994).

41 The lecture was printed in London in 1855; I quote from pp. 31–2. See also Martha Vicinus, *Independent Women: Work and Community for Single Women, 1850–1920* (London, Virago, 1985).

42 Cited by Susan O'Brien in '*Terra Incognita*: The Nun in Nineteenth-century England', *Past and Present*, (November 1988), 110–40 (p. 115).

43 These were published in book from as *Vignettes* (London, 1966). Other books included travel sketches celebrating religion and localism: *La Belle France* (1868), and *Historic Nuns* (1898).

44 Barbara Taylor's forthcoming study will reassess her religion. See also Taylor's 'Mary Wollstonencraft and the Wild Wish of Early Feminism', *History Workshop Journal*, 33 (1992), 197–219.

45 See Campbell Orr, *Women*, especially the essay by Jan Marsh, 'Art, Ambition and Sisterhood in the 1850s' and Martha Vicinus, *Independent Women*.

46 See Anne Digby, 'Victorian Values and Women in Public and Private, in T. C. Smout (ed.), *Victorian Values* (Oxford, Oxford University Press, 1992). Digby discusses how

philanthropy was a significant border zone for women negotiable between strictly
public and strictly private spheres; her terminology reviewing the English debate
echoes Mills' description of 'negotiating a divide'.

47 See McMillan, *Housewife or Harlot* and 'Women and Social Catholicism'.
48 McMillan, *Housewife or Harlot* Bidelman, *Pariahs Stand Up!*; Charles Sowerwine, *Sisters or Citizens? Women and Socialism in France since 1876* (Cambridge, Cambridge University Press, 1981); Offen, 'Feminism, Anti-feminism, and National Family Politics'.
49 Gordon, *Integral Feminist.*
50 Máire Cross and Tim Gray, *The Feminism of Flora Tristan* (Oxford, Berg, 1992).
51 I have based my account chiefly on Claire Goldberg Moses and Leslie Wall Rabine, *Feminism, Socialism and French Romanticism* (Bloomington and Indianapolis, Indiana University Press, 1993).
52 A particularly vituperative attack was made by J. M. Kemble, editor of the *British and Foreign Review*. He linked together current grievances over women's education and legal status, with Saint-Simonianism and English women writers, such as Martineau, Wollstonecraft, Frances Wright and Caroline Norton, who were described as 'Britomarts' (i.e. warrior women). This debate is explored by the pre-feminist but extremely valuable study by John Killham, *Tennyson and The Princess: Reflections of an Age* (London, The Athlone Press, 1958). Killham argues that the image of France as a place of social experimentation concerning women's role is reflected in the lines toward the end of Tennyson's poem: 'and far beyond, imagined more than seen, the skirts of France'.
53 Barbara Taylor, *Eve and the New Jerusalem: Feminism and Socialism in the Nineteenth Century* (London, Virago Press, 1983).
54 Moses and Rabine, *Feminism*, which wants to characterise Tristan as more closely associated with organised feminism than Cross and Gray would allow.
55 Cross and Gray, *Feminism*, pp. 81–2; see also their discussion of Tristan's novel, *Méphis*.
56 *Flora Tristan's London Journal* (translation of *Promenades dans Londres*), trans. Dennis Palmer and Giselle Pincetl (London, George Prior, 1980) p. 191.
57 The translator's suggestion of this identification of Mrs Shilly has been confirmed by my colleague Norah Crook, who suggests the misspelling may be because Tristan had been told the identity of Shelley's anonymous poetic contributions to the Annuals by editors like Morgan or Norton, who knew Shelley personally. I am grateful to Crook for her illuminating discussion of this issue. Thackeray's satirical pen was directed against fashionable novelists such as Mrs Gore, Lady Blessington and Lady Morgan, as well as pious moralists like Ellis; see his 'Fashionable Authoresses' reprinted in D. J. Taylor (ed.), *A Shabby Genteel Story.*
58 A full account of De Staël's function as an icon of woman's literary power remains to be given. My discussion in 'The Corinne Complex: Gender, Genius and National Culture', in Campbell Orr (ed.) *Women* is by no means exhaustive. See also Angela Leighton, *Writing Against the Heart: Victorian Women Poets* (London, Harvester Wheatsheaf, 1992). A fuller discussion of English women writers' view of France will be essayed in my forthcoming article, '"Those wonderful women of France": Womanism, Liberal Feminism, and the Victorian woman writer'.
59 This is the suggestion of Sandra Dijkstra, *Feminism in the Age of George Sand* (London, Pluto Press, 1992), who cites Mme de Staël on p. 12.
60 Cited by Stanley Mellon, *The Political Uses of History* (Stanford, Stanford University Press, 1958), p. 1.
61 J. Brumfitt, *Voltaire, Historian* (Oxford, Oxford University Press, 1970); short studies by Judith N. Shklar, *Montesquieu* (Oxford, Oxford University Press, 1987), and J. W.

Burrow, *Gibbon* (Oxford, Oxford University Press, 1985), are useful guides to the scholarship on these *philosophes*.

62 Jane Rendall, *Origins*, ch. 1, 'The Enlightenment and the Nature of Women'; Sylvana Tomaselli. 'The Enlightenment Debate on Women', *History Workshop*, 20, (1985), 201–4, and 'Reflections on the History of the Science of Woman', *History of Science*, 29 (1991), 185–205. Norah Crook has also discussed with me her view that Wollstonecraft's biological daughter, Mary Shelley, may have been consciously exploiting the linguistic ambiguity in early nineteenth-century usage of 'man' meaning either 'humankind' or 'male person', in her novel *The Last Man*.

63 Published in Paris, 1772; two English translations followed in 1773 and 1781, the latter by a Mrs Kindersley.

64 Tomaselli, 'The Enlightenment Debate'; G. Barker-Benfield, *The Culture of Sensibility* (Chicago, University of Chicago Press, 1993); John Brewer and Roy Porter (eds), *Consumption and the World of Goods* (London, Routledge, 1993).

65 Jane Rendall, Introduction, William Alexander, *History of Women* (Bristol, Thoemmes Press, 1995); '"Does History Speak?" Writing a National History for British Women (c. 1780–1810)', unpublished paper delivered at Women's History Network Conference, Nottingham, October 1994.

66 Bridget Hill, *Republican Virago* (Oxford, Oxford University Press, 1992).

67 Kelly, *Revolutionary Feminism: The Mind and Career of Mary Wollstonecraft* (London, Macmillan, 1989), p. 83. Her translation and discussion of Jacques Necker may also have helped her discuss 'masculine' social issues, Kelly argues.

68 Gary Kelly, *Revolutionary Feminism*, and also *Women, Writing and Revolution, 1790–1827* (Oxford, Clarendon Press, 1993).

69 Ellis, *Women of England*, pp. 52–3.

70 For William Ellis's career see *Dictionary of National Biography*; William Ellis (ed.), *Christianity: The Means of Civilization* (London, 1837).

71 Cited by Mitzi Myers, 'Mary Wollstonecraft's *Letters written in Sweden*: Towards Romantic Autobiography' *Studies in Eighteenth Century Culture*, 8 (1979), 167.

72 Richard Holmes (ed.) Mary Wollstonecraft, *A Short Residence in Sweden, Norway and Denmark* and William Godwin, *Memoirs of the Author of the Rights of Woman* (Harmondsworth, Penguin, 1985), Introduction. Quotation from p. 68.

73 Judith Curtis, 'Françoise d'Issembourg d'Happencourt de Graffigny', in Eve Martin Sartori and Dorothy Wynne Zimmermann (eds), *French Women Writers* (Westport, Connecticut, Greenwood Press, 1991).

74 Even were they were not hostile to women, liberal anthropologists tended to interpret human historical experience in terms of progress that could be extended to weaker persons (women) or races: Henrika Kuklick, *The Savage Within: The Social History of British Anthropology 1885–1945* (Cambridge, Cambridge University Press, 1992).

75 The foregoing simplifies some immensely complex issues. Mellon, *The Political Uses of History*, is the classic account of liberal and conservative efforts to explain and appropriate the Revolution; for Romantic French historians, see Ceri Crossley, *French Historians and Romanticism* (London, Routledge, 1993), from whom the quote on Michelet is taken, p. 211; and for Michelet's gendered vision, see also Ludmilla Jordanova, *Sexual Visions: Images of Gender in Science and Medicine* (Madison, University of Wisconsin Press, 1989).

76 Marina Warner observes that English suffragettes borrowed the symbolism of Joan; Christabel Pankhurst's admirers called her the Maiden warrior and sported badges depicting her like Joan. *Joan of Arc: The Image of Female Heroism* (London, Weidenfeld and Nicolson, 1981). For the symbol of Marianne see Maurice Agulhon, *Marianne into*

Battle: Republican Imagery and Symbolism in France, 1789–1920, trans. Janet Lloyd (Cambridge, Cambridge University Press, 1981). David Englander (ed., *The Jewish Enigma* (Milton Keynes, Open University Press, 1992) is a useful introduction to the huge literature on European anti-Semitism.

Mary Wollstonecraft: a problematic legacy

Pam Hirsch

How long will it be before we shall have read to better purpose the eloquent lessons and the yet more eloquent history, of that gifted and glorious being, Mary Wollstonecraft? (William J. Fox in the *Westminster Review* for January 1831, p. 221)

IN 1855, Marian Evans, writing a review of Margaret Fuller's *Woman in the Nineteenth Century* (1843), felt moved to compare it with Mary Wollstonecraft's most celebrated work the *Vindication of the Rights of Woman* (1792). She commented that there existed 'in some quarters a vague prejudice against the *Rights of Woman* as in some way a reprehensible book', yet she had found it 'eminently serious, severely moral, and withal rather heavy'.[1] This immediately raises the question of why this book should have acquired a bad reputation, or rather, how Mary Wollstonecraft herself acquired a bad reputation, and it is these intertwined issues which the first part of this essay addresses. The second part of the essay charts the efforts made to excavate Wollstonecraft and her work out from under the layers of disinformation. It seems to me that, sadly, both how this vilification process operated and how the recuperative operation was organised, are not of merely historical interest, but instructive in the face of 'backlash' polemic today.

Much of Wollstonecraft's work, including the *Vindication of the Rights of Woman* belongs in the category of educational theory. It was when she dared to enter the realm of political philosophical discourse, thereby crossing acceptable gender and genre boundaries, that she fell prey to 'prejudice'. Press attacks after her death were more to do with her first vindication, *Vindication of the Rights of Men* (1790) than with her second vindication, *Rights of Woman* (1792), or rather were more to do with the political and intellectual alignment that they signified. It was Wollstonecraft's positioning of herself as intellectual daughter of the Newington

Green Unitarians which gave rise to her problematic reputation.

As the first published response to Edmund Burke's *Reflections on the Revolution in France* (1790) Wollstonecraft's *Rights of Men* established her as a 'Revolutionary Feminist'; her name was inextricably linked in the public mind with the French Revolution.[2] After her death, the name of Mary Wollstonecraft was ridiculed by an Anti-Jacobin press to the extent that her intellectual daughters were at worst filled with fear, or at best regarded her as something of an embarrassment to the women's movement.[3]

The Wollstonecraft family's wandering life, as outlined by her many biographers, was thoroughly unsettled and disorientating. However, it also, as Kelly observes, provided Mary Wollstonecraft with an almost unique opportunity to observe the 'regional, class, gender and cultural divisions of late-eighteenth-century Britain'.[4] For the purposes of this essay I will take as a starting point her arrival in Newington Green in 1784, where she set up a school in order to provide a living for herself, her sisters Eliza and Everina, and her friend, Fanny Blood. Although the head of her all-female family, she adopted a daughterly position in relation to her Newington Green mentors, Richard Price and Hannah Burgh (widow of the educational writer, James Burgh). The Unitarians' views about the relations between the sexes, their belief in the right of women to a liberal education and their refusal to accept that women's duties in the domestic sphere should render them unfit for general intellectual and cultural activity, together made a distinctive contribution to the development of feminist thinking in Britain. The legal and political disabilities that they suffered under the Test and Corporation Acts – Unitarians were not to become full citizens in law until 1813 and were excluded from taking Oxford and Cambridge degrees – meant that, not surprisingly, they formed a significant pressure group for political reform.[5]

In the late eighteenth century, two remarkable men brought the Unitarians into a special prominence, the Reverend Richard Price (1723–91) and Joseph Priestley (1733–1804). As Dissenters, university careers were not open to them although the Dissenting academies in which they trained arguably provided a more up-to-date academic training. In any case, they were recognised as major intellectual figures. At Newington Green, Mary Wollstonecraft, although brought up an Anglican, attended Richard Price's Unitarian chapel as often as her own church, and, in effect, adopted him as her intellectual father. Price's sermons were not only moral assaults on the legitimacy of the established social and political order, but also, on occasion, articulated explicit political philosophy. In this environment Mary had available to her the free intellectual exchange she enjoyed, embued with typical Unitarian optimism grounded in the potential of individual human reason to change the world for the better.

Mary Wollstonecraft's allegiance to the Unitarian way of thinking is evident in her early work. Above all Unitarians stressed the role of reason in the quest for truth, the concomitant of which was a keen interest in all aspects of education. They were prominent among the provincial leaders who set up the Literary and Philosophical Societies of the 1780s and 1790s and promoted many non-denominational educational experiments. In the late eighteenth century one of the most influential educational treatises was Rousseau's *Emile* (1762) in which education was acknowledged as the key to transforming society. However, unlike the Unitarians' theories, Rousseau's prescription was gendered. For Emile, Rousseau designed an education that would turn the boy into a virtuous citizen; for Sophie, however, he had designed an education which constructed her as representative of only domestic virtues. Mary Wollstonecraft's first book written in 1786, *Thoughts on the Education of Daughters*, outlined, by contrast, a more rational education than was usually afforded middle-class girls.[6] Close reading suggests a debt (perhaps even in its title) to the Unitarian James Burgh's *Thoughts on Education* (1747).[7] Although Burgh had devoted only five pages of his *Thoughts on Education* to female education, there are several aspects of it that make it seem likely that Mary Wollstonecraft had read it. Burgh was convinced that women were as rational as men, and that they should concentrate on developing the beauty of their minds rather than external beauty, as the former, unlike the latter, would not fade with time. Burgh thought that plays and novels were dangerous for young women as they made them susceptible to male rakishness. Lastly, he laid great stress on rational marital partnership; all these ideas recur in Mary Wollstonecraft's writing, albeit nuanced by her various personal experiences as a daughter, a paid companion and a schoolteacher.[8] Central to her educational theories, was her conviction that intellectual and moral development were inextricably linked, and therefore girls and boys should have essentially the same access to knowledge and culture.

Apart from, and even including, a brief interlude as a governess in Ireland,[9] Mary Wollstonecraft stayed closely in touch with the Newington Green community via her publisher, and another father-figure, Joseph Johnson.[10] From 1787 she found her livelihood as a reviewer for the *Analytical Review*, founded, by Johnson and a fellow Unitarian from Scotland, Thomas Christie, in order to bring continental ideas into better circulation in England. Her second educational book, *Original Stories from Real Life; with Conversations Calculated to Regulate the Affections and Form the Mind to Truth and Goodness* (1788) established her reputation as a pedagogical writer, and it seems likely that if she had continued to write in this genre, she would have made a steady if unremarkable income, and enjoyed posthumously a steady and unremarkable reputation.[11] The heroine of *Original Stories* is a governess – Mrs Mason – who takes in hand the moral education of two young girls whom she leads, through a series of chastening tales and situations, to understand that reason and compassion are the grounds of virtue. Mrs Mason inculcated such human virtues as initiative, independence and courage, attributes Rousseau would have considered appropriate to boys rather than girls. It was her most popular book, reprinted for generations. The second edition was illustrated by the poet and artist William Blake, one of Johnson's 'Academy' of intellectuals. His representation of Mrs Mason, as a surprisingly young and lovely woman is possibly the first extant representation of Mary Wollstonecraft. The visual vocabulary Blake employs – the simple, unfussy dress, Mrs Mason's protective attitude towards the two young girls, the positioning of the girls to look up at their governess as moral exemplar – is an interesting example of late eighteenth-century iconography. It is ironic, given our hindsight of the trials of Mary Wollstonecraft to come, that her figure is in the shape of a cross (Plate 1).

This likely reputation, however, was to be thwarted by events. In July 1789 the Revolution began in France, followed with keen interest and excitement by Mary Wollstonecraft's Newington Green friends. On 4 November, the anniversary of the 1688 Revolution in England, Richard Price delivered a sermon in which he claimed the Revolution in France as following the model of 1688 and that in turn it would serve as a model for the further emancipation of Dissenters in England. The text of his message was published with the sermon as *A Discourse on the Love of our Country*. To the surprise of Johnson's circle this provoked an attack by Edmund Burke, the veteran Whig luminary, who had previously promoted political reforms to reduce the influence of the Court, a cause supported by Dissenters in their attempts to obtain full civil rights. Burke's *Reflections on the Revolution in France, and the Proceedings of Certain Societies in London Relative to that Event* (1 November 1790) made him the leading spokesman of what was to crystallise into aristocratic conservatism. A telling cartoon by Gillray dated 3 December 1790 depicts Burke holding the emblems of Church and King; on the wall of Price's study Gillray includes a picture of Charles I being executed (Plate 2). Mary Wollstonecraft, assuming the role of female knight, rushed to the defence of Richard Price. Her pamphlet was the first of half a dozen attacking Burke. The second edition of *Vindication of the Rights of Men* was published with her name. Her female signature marked her entry into the world of political discourse.[12]

Wollstonecraft's central admonition to Burke sprang from the feminist insight that 'your politics and morals, when simplified, would undermine

1
Engraving by William Blake of 'Mrs Mason' for *Original Stories from Real Life: With Conversations calculated to regulate the Affections and form the Mind to Truth and Goodness* (London, Joseph Johnson, 1788, by permission of the Syndics of Cambridge University Library)

2
Gillray: 'Smelling out a rat, or, the atheistical revolutionist disturbed in his midnight calculations' (by permission of the Trustees of the British Museum)

religion and virtue to set up a spurious sensual beauty, that has long debauched your imagination'.[13] Although the *occasion* of her anger was Burke's attack on her friend, it seems clear that what had most provoked her was Burke's protectiveness towards Marie Antoinette, depicted by Burke as the beautiful, helpless aristocratic woman. Burke had described the procession which led Marie Antoinette to Paris as a mêlée of 'horrid yells, the shrilling screams, and frantic dances, and infamous contumelies, and all the unutterable abominations of the furies of hell, in the abused shape of the vilest of women'.[14] Burke described the Revolutionary women as monsters; Mary quoted these lines of Burke's against him with the retort that: 'Probably you mean women who gained a livelihood by selling vegetables or fish, who never had any advantages of education'.[15] In attacking Burke's moral aesthetic, in her view the product of a debauched imagination, she was typically attempting to uphold the dignity of women. In Burke's *Philosophical Enquiry into the Sublime and the Beautiful* he had written 'The beauty of women is considerably owing to their weakness or delicacy, and is even enhanced by their timidity, a quality of mind analogous to it'.[16] In *Vindication of the Rights of Men*, Mary Wollstonecraft roundly denounced this strategy:

> You may have convinced them that *littleness* and *weakness* are the very essence of beauty; and that the Supreme Being, in giving women beauty in the most supereminent degree, seemed to command them, by the powerful voice of Nature, not to cultivate the moral values that might chance to excite respect, and interfere with the pleasing sensations they were created to inspire. Thus confining truth, fortitude, and humanity, within the rigid pale of manly morals, they might justly argue, that to be loved, woman's high end and great distinction! they should 'learn to lisp, to totter in their walk, and nick-name God's creatures'.[17]

Mary Wollstonecraft had exposed the fact that women like the French Revolutionary women, who are active and assertive are defined as 'not beautiful', even 'not-women' but monsters. In so doing, she had identified in advance precisely the process of demonisation which would be applied to herself.

The revelation that an almost unknown woman had dared to produce such a bold challenge to the great Burke. added to its éclat. After years of obscurity and struggle Mary Wollstonecraft enjoyed the widespread acclaim of the radical intellectuals with whom she had aligned herself. Her entry into the public domain was marked by a portrait, commissioned by the Unitarian philanthropist and anti-slavery campaigner William Roscoe (1753–1831) (Plate 3).[18] Both the representation of Mary Wollstonecraft in the 'Roscoe' portrait and her own self-presentation in the introduction to her next book *Vindication of the Rights of Woman* is that of a stern moral

3
The 'Roscoe' portrait, by an
unknown artist (The Walker
Art Gallery, Liverpool, by
permission of the Board of
Trustees of the National
Museums and Galleries on
Merseyside)

4
Engraving of 'Mrs Godwin' in
The Monthly Visitor, February
1798 (by permission of the
Corporation of London, Great
London Record Office,
History Library)

philosopher, as unadorned in her style of clothing as she claimed to be in her prose.[19] She began the *Vindication of the Rights of Woman* by refusing to 'cull her phrases or polish her style', an indirect attack on Burke, whom she had accused in her advertisement for the *Rights of Men* of levelling 'many ingenious arguments in a very specious garb'.[20] Her attack indicates that she believed Burke to be a 'philosophical wanton', confused by externals, whilst she herself could get to the heart of the matter.[21] That heart, as we have already seen, was her concern for the dignity of women, which in turn must begin with a rational education. In her second vindication she extended the discoveries she had made about Burke's debauched imagination to the works of Milton and Rousseau.[22] When the *Vindication of the Rights of Woman* first appeared, it was reviewed widely and favourably; by the end of 1792 Johnson had published a second edition and the book appeared in Boston and Philadelphia, in two French translations, and one German translation. Although it is now her most celebrated work (the one most likely to be studied on Women's Studies courses, for example), nevertheless, it was the publication, and more particularly, the timing of her first vindication, that of the *Rights of Men*, that had such a powerful impact on her later reputation.

It was the first vindication's association with the French Revolution which led to her posthumous demonisation as one of 'the furies of hell, in the abused shape of the vilest of women'.[23] Like many radical intellectuals of the time, she went to Paris and there wrote *An Historical and Moral View of the Origin and Progress of the French Revolution* between late 1793 and April 1794. Again, like many of her Unitarian friends, while condemning the Terror, she would not condemn the ideals of the Revolution. By the time she returned to London in April 1796, counter-revolutionary panic had set in; all progressives were viewed as dangerous Jacobins, and any manifestations of social discontent as the beginning of a general Revolution. Richard Price was dead and the new centre of the radical intellectual group in London was William Godwin, the author of *Political Justice* (1793). It seemed inevitable that these two would form an alliance of some kind. In *Political Justice* Godwin had condemned marriage as an affair of property and had argued for its abolition. Similarly Mary Wollstonecraft had commented that marriage was often no more than legal prostitution as it existed under contemporary laws. However, she had already had one child out of wedlock and when she became pregnant by Godwin the two agreed to marry, rather to the scorn of their immediate circle, who felt that they were betraying an important principle.[24] Tragically, following complications which set in after giving birth to a second daughter, Mary Wollstonecraft died, aged thirty-eight on 10 September 1797.

After Mary's death the obituaries were initially respectful, even those written by the enemies of her liberal political views. The *Vindication of the Rights of Woman* was not considered objectionable in 1792. However, the intensifying climate of counter-revolutionary anxiety meant that when Godwin chose to publish four volumes of his wife's *Posthumous Works* and his *Memoirs of the Author of the Vindication of the Rights of Woman* early in 1798, his timing was particularly unfortunate, and doomed her reputation.[25] His honest, but extraordinarily naive account of his wife's love affairs had reinforced a connection in the minds of the public between 'Liberty' and sexual licence.[26] He unwittingly provoked a kind of feeding frenzy in the Anti-Jacobin press. The Reverend Richard Polwhele drew the connection between Wollstonecraft and the French Revolutionary women whom Burke had described as 'harpies ... sprung from night and hell' in his poem *The Unsex'd Females* (1798).[27] The conservative periodical, *The Anti-Jacobin Review* reviewed Godwin's *Memoirs* in 1798, seizing on them as 'proof' that the inevitable results of liberalism and free thinking would be moral collapse; it added insult to injury by placing in the index, under the heading 'Prostitution', an entry which simply says 'See Mary Wollstonecraft'. Cartoons and scurrilous poems attacked the English 'Jacobins' in general and Mary Wollstonecraft and Godwin in particular. In 1801, the *Anti-Jacobin Review* published an anonymous poem called 'The Vision of Liberty' in which the author sneered at Godwin's extraordinary frankness:

> William hath penn'd a waggon-load of stuff,
> And Mary's life at last he needs must write,
> Thinking her whoredoms were not known enough,
> Till fairly printed off in black and white.
> With wondrous glee and pride, this simple wight
> Her brothel feats of wantonness sets down,
> Being her spouse, he tells, with huge delight,
> How oft she cuckolded the silly clown
> And lent, O lovely piece! herself to half the town.[28]

However, the *Anti-Jacobin Review* was a periodical founded to express conservative political views and its calumnies would be unlikely to mislead a more liberal readership. From this point of view, a more moderate review of Godwin's *Memoirs* in a women's magazine, *The Monthly Visitor* of 1798, was ultimately perhaps more subtly damaging. Although the reviewer is fair to the work – a great point this – nevertheless, the summing up of Mary's character implied that intellectual arrogance was the ground of her feminism, not the desire for justice:

> She was a woman of high genius; and, as she felt the whole strength of her powers, she thought herself lifted, in a degree, above the ordinary trammels of civil communities. She inveighed bitterly against a code of regulations

which she deemed derogatory to her sex; nor did she for an instant reflect that unless women were equally qualified with herself to act on the grand principles of all morality, independent of tuition and restraint, the doctrine she inculcated, if received, must overturn the basis of every civilised state.[29]

The engraving that accompanied this article looks like no other extant representation of Mary Wollstonecraft. Her fine, even sharp, features are not represented; this face looks rather coarse (Plate 4). Claire Tomalin in her biography of Mary Wollstonecraft suggests that the hat 'resembles hats worn by French revolutionary women'. However, it seems more likely that the representation is a caricature in the style of an Irish Revolutionary woman; indicating, perhaps, the dangerous spread of Jacobin ideas.[30] In the same year of 1798 a liberal-minded women's journal was 'relieved to report' that:

> the champions of female equality, who were as inimical to the happiness and interest of the sex, as those who preached up the doctrine of liberty and equality to the men, are no longer regarded as sincere and politic friends.[31]

Plotting the changing climate towards Mary Wollstonecraft's ideas in the immediate aftermath of her death makes it clearer why Marian Evans took so long to 'discover' the *Vindication of the Rights of Woman*. Mary Wollstonecraft's association with Jacobinism had separated her off in the public mind from her place amongst a wide spectrum of women writers, all of whom, in their different ways, sought to endow women's role with more dignity. Some, like Maria Hays, Helen Maria Williams and Elizabeth Hamilton clearly tempered their earlier liberalism to this new climate, as Jane Rendall's essay on the latter, and Gary Kelly's recent survey show.[32] For a generation at least Mary Wollstonecraft's ideas went underground, in the sense that her name was more likely to be invoked by working-class radicals than in middle-class drawing-rooms. The collapse of the Owenite communities in a welter of financial mismanagement and free-love scandals did nothing to help.[33] The discrediting of Mary Wollstonecraft's character and the association of feminism with free love caused a generation of middle-class women to draw back from her, even some of the Unitarian women one might have expected to applaud her ideas. We find Harriet Martineau, for example, in her *Autobiography* (1855) commenting:

> It seemed to me, from the earliest time when I could think on the subject of Woman's Rights and condition, that the first requisite to advancement is the self-reliance which results from self-discipline. Women who would improve the condition and chances of their sex must, I am certain, be not only affectionate and devoted, but rational and dispassionate, with the devotedness of benevolence, and not merely personal love. But Mary Wollstonecraft was,

with all her powers, a poor victim of passion... The Wollstonecraft order ....
do infinite mischief; and, for my part, I do not wish to have anything to do
with them.[34]

The trashing of Mary Wollstonecraft's work by reference to the supposed
immorality of her life had been accomplished. So far, so bad.

However, as Mitzi Myers has convincingly demonstrated, Wollstonecraft, although radical in her demand for equal political rights for women,
was typical of 1790s female educators in 'downgrading the ornamental
and pleasing to magnify the useful and moral'.[35] Even cautious 'feminine'
writers such as Katherine Elwood felt able to include Wollstonecraft in
her *Memoirs of The Literary Ladies of England* (1843) which she said was
'intended only for such of her own sex, who, not feeling themselves equal
to profound and abstract subjects, can derive amusement and information
from what is professedly too light for the learned, and too simple for the
studious'. She blamed inadequate parental guidance for Mary's 'errors'
and her relationship with Fuseli for Mary's 'wild and visionary ideas' and,
in her defence, stressed Mary's role as the 'good genius' of her family (by
which she means financial provider).[36] However, some of the liberal
feminists who were active from the 1850s onwards, the Langham Place
group, had direct access to Wollstonecraft's work in their own family
libraries. Furthermore, many Unitarian chapels ran lending libraries from
their vestries and they faithfully kept copies of the works of their adopted
daughter, even though no new editions of her work were being published.

The women of the Langham Place group who came from Unitarian
families – Barbara Leigh Smith, Bessie Rayner Parkes, Octavia Hill,
Elizabeth Whitehead Malleson, Clementia Taylor – were likely to have
heard sympathetic accounts of Wollstonecraft's work within their family
circles. Nor were they likely to have been misled by lurid accounts of her
as a dangerous revolutionary. Bessie Rayner Parkes's grandfather Joseph
Priestley, along with other Dissenters in Birmingham, had his house
burnt down by a 'Church and King' mob in July 1791 and subsequently
had to take his family to safety in America. Barbara Leigh Smith's
grandfather, William Smith, M.P. first for Sudbury and then Norwich,
had been the chief parliamentary advocate for the Unitarians at precisely
the time when Burke had been calling them traitors. When Burke had
accused Dissenters in Parliament of intending to subvert and overturn
every establishment, whether political or religious, William Smith had
asserted that the Unitarians 'were as firm and steady friends of the
constitution as the right honourable gentleman'. French intelligence
agents in England in late 1792 quite erroneously considered that a French
declaration of war on Britain would be a signal for rebellion in Ireland,
separation in Scotland and civil war in England. In November 1793,

William Smith was prevailed upon by a contact of his friend, Helen Maria Williams (also a friend of Mary Wollstonecraft), to write a letter indicating that the French were entirely mistaken in this assumption. This letter was discovered by British intelligence agents in the hands of the French spy, William Jackson, and William Smith was questioned by the Privy Council. Joseph Priestley urged him to escape to America but Smith courageously remained in England, reiterating his own loyalty and the loyalty of all Unitarians to England.[37] Both Barbara Leigh Smith and Bessie Parkes therefore, had forebears whose own reputations had been attacked, during the highly charged atmosphere of conspiracy in 1793 and 1794.

In 1858, when these two young women founded the *English Woman's Journal*, they pushed the Unitarian/Wollstonecraftian line, in that they campaigned for better education for women and for the possibilities of useful work for middle-class women. Like Mary Wollstonecraft, they did not decry the virtues of the domestic sphere, but pleaded for enlightened educated mothers and challenged the assumption that a role as daughter, sister, wife or mother somehow mysteriously disqualified women as citizens.[38] Furthermore, these radical young women from Unitarian backgrounds encouraged their friends from orthodox Anglican backgrounds to study Mary Wollstonecraft's work. Emily Davies reported that when she met Barbara Leigh Smith in Algiers in 1858, Barbara told her to read the *Vindication of the Rights of Woman*. The two women went on to campaign for better education for middle-class girls and to found, with encouragement from their friends, the first university college for women, Girton College, Cambridge.[39]

Barbara Leigh Smith may well have introduced Wollstonecraft's work to Marian Evans, as it was unlikely to have been recommended reading in her father's home, where Robert Evans, as the estate manager of the Newdigate family at Arbury Hall in Warwickshire, followed the Tory and Anglican politics of his employers. Marian was more likely to have been familiar with Chalmers *The General Biographical Dictionary* (1814), where the entry for 'Godwin, Mary' argued that she 'unfolded many a wild theory on the duties and character of her sex' that she was 'a voluptuary and a sensualist' and had 'rioted in sentiments alike repugnant to religion, sense and decency'.[40] After the death of her father, Marian Evans came to London to make her living as a journalist, where she was influenced, although not persuaded on every issue, in her thinking about the 'woman question' by Barbara Leigh Smith. Her article which implicitly identified Margaret Fuller as one of Wollstonecraft's daughters, proved a neat and effective rescue job. She wrote: 'In both writers we discern, under the brave bearing of a strong and truthful nature, the beating of a loving woman's heart, which teaches them not to undervalue the smallest offices of domestic care or kindliness'.[41] First, as I demonstrated at the beginning of the essay, there is an invitation to the intelligent reader to read the book and not fall prey to 'vague prejudice'. Second, there is a quiet insistence that intellectual prowess is in no way incompatible with a (nineteenth-century) construction of femininity.

Mary Wollstonecraft's daughter by Godwin, Mary Wollstonecraft Shelley, had, as her mother had died shortly after her birth, only known her mother by her writings and by her father's memoirs. Godwin, by making Mary Wollstonecraft's life an open book, had, no doubt unintentionally, offered her up for all men to gaze upon.[42] Mary Wollstonecraft Shelley grew up revering her parents but, not surprisingly, she was hypersensitive to the dangers of memoirs. Her own elopement with Shelley, she felt, had become linked in the public mind with her mother's sexual liaisons – she herself had become the doubly disgraced daughter of a disgraced mother. Widowed early, Mary Shelley made her living as a writer, but also expended a great deal of energy into defending her dead husband's reputation. However, it was to be her daughter-in-law, Jane St John (later Lady Shelley), who began a determined project of recuperating the reputations of Godwin and Mary Wollstonecraft. Jane St John was one of nine illegitimate children of the banker, Thomas Gibson of Newcastle-upon-Tyne, a fact that may have influenced her decision to be the champion of her husband's illustrious, but supposedly morally dubious, forebears. After the death of Mary Shelley in 1851, Jane had discovered a cache of manuscripts in a nailed-down box. In early 1857, Thomas Jefferson Hogg was entrusted with some of these papers, in order to write a biography of the poet Percy Bysshe Shelley. The first two volumes, which came out in 1858, pained Jane and her husband so much that they refused to allow Hogg access to their papers for a sequel. At this time Lady Shelley was friendly with Bessie Rayner Parkes and Barbara Leigh Smith, being a subscriber to the *English Woman's Journal*, which they ran. She consulted Bessie about the possibilities of an introduction to a more suitable biographer. In the event, Lady Shelley waited nearly twenty years before entrusting the papers to Charles Kegan Paul for him to study before writing *William Godwin: His Friends and Contemporaries* (1876). Paul (1828–1902), author and publisher, was the son of an Anglican cleric. He had been destined for a career in the church but changed allegiance in 1874, identifying himself as a Unitarian, where his radical politics seemed less out of place. The Godwin biography was followed by a reprint of Mary Wollstonecraft's *Letters to Imlay* (1879) in which Paul's prefatory memoir attempts to recuperate Mary Wollstonecraft from 'obloquy and scorn' by assuring the reader that she was a Christian to the end, notwithstanding Godwin's atheism.[43] Paul's work seems to have

achieved the family's desired aim in that it marked a turning-point for
Wollstonecraft's (and Godwin's) reputation.

In 1885 W. H. Allen & Co. commissioned a biography of *Mary Wollstonecraft Godwin* for their 'Eminent Women Series'; in this series Mary
Wollstonecraft appears in the respectable company of Elizabeth Fry and
Hannah More. Elizabeth Robins Pennell, the author they chose, began by
acknowledging Paul's recuperative work and then commenced her own
endeavour with a flourish. 'Few women', she wrote, 'have worked so
faithfully for the cause of humanity as Mary Wollstonecraft Godwin, and
few have been the objects of such censure.'[44] After these recuperative
enterprises Emma Rauschenbusch-Clough, in her biography of 1898,
seemed to feel free to concentrate on demonstrating that what was at
stake in Mary Wollstonecraft's critiques of Burke and Rousseau was her
attempt to establish a parity between the abstract rights of man and the
abstract rights of woman. However, even at this late date, she felt it
necessary to insist that Mary Wollstonecraft had neither betrayed women
nor tampered with men's affections.[45]

It appears, on this evidence, to have taken at least a century to rescue
Mary Wollstonecraft's work from the calumny against her character. In
the 1970s a cluster of new Wollstonecraft biographies emerged, emblem-
atic perhaps of the women's movement's need for heroines, but even these
did not necessarily fully engage with the 'intellectual trends in the formation of [Mary Wollstonecraft's] ideas'.[46] Emily Sunstein, in her biography
of Mary Shelley commented that 'both idealizers and defamers of controversial figures select qualities relevant to larger arguments of their own
times.'[47] This is precisely the point of my essay: Wollstonecraft has been
praised and damned, re-praised and co-opted by a succession of commentators all of whom (and I cannot be excluded from this) will be impli-
cated in an agenda which may or may not be made explicit. The reputation of Mary Wollstonecraft's work acts as a 'test case' of the fragility of
political visions. We should not be surprised, perhaps. Feminists doing
the kind of work today which might seriously challenge the *status quo* are
still savaged by the conservative press using disconcertingly similar terms
of abuse to the ones used against Mary Wollstonecraft. The 'problematic'
element in the legacy of Mary Wollstonecraft turns out to be the sour
knowledge that women's work can be dismissed or distorted by a hostile
press, and that one of the easiest ways to do this is by attaching sexual
scandal to the name of the woman in question.[48] Like the feminists of the
1850s we need always to remind ourselves to give serious critical attention
to women's work, not take reviews and biographies on trust, even (perhaps
especially) if they are by friends or lovers. Mary Wollstonecraft herself
wrote: 'Those who are bold enough to advance before the age they live

in, and to throw off, by the force of their own minds, the prejudices which the maturing reason of the world will in time disavow, must learn to brave censure.'[49] An alert sense of Mary Wollstonecraft's originality and courage may well be the best prophylactic against acts of bad faith in our own critical work.

Notes

1 Marian Evans (later to become famous as the writer 'George Eliot') in 'Margaret Fuller and Mary Wollstonecraft' in the *Leader* 6 (13 October 1855) reprinted in *Essays of George Eliot*, ed. Thomas Pinney (London: Routledge and Kegan Paul, 1963), pp. 199–206 (p. 201).

2 *Vindication of the Rights of Men, in a Letter to the Right Honourable Edmund Burke* (London, Joseph Johnson, 1790); *Vindication of the Rights of Woman with Strictures on Political and Moral Subjects* (London, Joseph Johnson, 1792). Gary Kelly in *Revolutionary Feminism: The Mind and Career of Mary Wollstonecraft* (Basingstoke, Macmillan, 1992) defines a Revolutionary feminist as 'an advocate of the rights or claims of women in a specific revolutionary situation' (p. 1).

3 Jane Rendall, *The Origins of Modern Feminism* (Basingstoke, Macmillan, 1985), p. 33.

4 Kelly, p. 23.

5 See Raymond V. Holt, *Unitarian Contribution to Social Progress* (London, Lindsey Press, 1952) and John Seed, 'The role of Unitarianism in the formation of liberal culture 1775–1851', Ph.D. thesis (Hull 1981).

6 See Mitzi Myers, 'Impeccable Governesses, Rational Dames, and Moral Mothers: Mary Wollstonecraft and the Female Tradition in Georgian Children's Books', *Children's Literature*, 14 (1986) 31–59. She points out that Wollstonecraft was one of a generation of professional women who at the turn of the century found an outlet for their talents in writing didactic children's books. In an era of educational reform they were addressed to the mothers as much as the children. *Vindication of the Rights of Woman* was identified by its initial reviewers as an educational treatise.

7 When Mary arrived in Newington Green, she was 'mothered' by Burgh's widow Hannah, who had run a successful academy for the Dissenting community at Newington Green with her husband until his death in 1775. Hannah Burgh (1710–88) gave Mary a great deal of practical support including money to start her school.

8 See G. J. Barker-Benfield, 'Mary Wollstonecraft: Eighteenth Century Commonwealth woman', *Journal of the History of Ideas* (1989).

9 She worked as a governess for Viscount and Lady Kingsborough. One of the daughters, Margaret King, later Lady Mount Cashell, was deeply influenced by her unusual governess. She was active in the Irish rebellion of 1798 and had left her husband and eight children to live with her lover in Italy. On many occasions she helped Mary Shelley, Wollstonecraft's daughter by Godwin. Lady Mount Cashell lived in Italy under the pseudonym 'Mrs Mason'. Such scandals helped to pin the label on Mary Wollstonecraft of revolutionary virago.

10 'Mr. Johnson ... assures me that if I exert my talents in writing I may support myself in a comfortable way ... you know I am not born to tread in the beaten track, the peculiar bent of my nature pushes me on'. Letter to her sister Everina, dated 7 November 1787, *The Collected Letters of Mary Wollstonecraft*, ed. Ralph M. Wardle (Ithaca, N.Y. and London, Cornell University Press, 1979), p. 60.

11 The *Monthly Review* said that the *Stories* had 'excellent principles and morals'. See 'Impeccable Governesses', p. 40.

12   The *Gentleman's Magazine* of 1791 found it ridiculous that the rights of men should be
     asserted by a woman. See *A Wollstonecraft Anthology*, ed. Janet Todd, (Bloomington
     and London, Indiana University Press, 1977), p. 65. As a Tory and High Church
     journal, this may not be surprising.

13   Quoted by Mitzi Myers, 'Politics from the Outside: Mary Wollstonecraft's First Vin-
     dication', *Studies in Eighteenth Century Culture* 6 (1977), p. 121.

14   Quoted by Ronald Paulson, *Representations of Revolution 1789–1820* (New Haven and
     London, Yale University Press, 1983), p. 80.

15   *Ibid.*

16   Quoted in *A Wollstonecraft Anthology*, p. 76.

17   *Rights of Men*; *ibid.*

18   On 6 October 1791, Mary Wollstonecraft sent a letter to Roscoe to tell him how the
     painting was progressing: Liverpool City Library: Roscoe Papers [920 ROS 5328].

19   See Mary Jacobus' essay, 'The Difference of View', in *Reading Woman* (London,
     Methuen, 1986), pp. 27–40.

20   *Revolutionary Feminism*, p. 89.

21   Mary Wollstonecraft was accused of being a 'philosophical wanton' in *The London
     Review and Literary Journal* (April 1798), 246.

22   Rousseau had described Sophie as writing 'nothing but O's … always drawn back-
     wards' because she was always distracted by looking in the mirror. I note that Mary
     Wollstonecraft's entries in the *Female Reader* (1789) were insistently signed with an
     'O'.

23   Neil Hertz, *The End of the Line: Essays on Psychoanalysis and the Sublime* (New York,
     Columbia University Press) quoting from Burke's *Reflections*. Hertz in an essay about
     'Male Hysteria under Political Pressure' asks the question 'why should revolutionary
     violence be emblematized … as a hideous but not exactly sexless woman?' (p. 162).
     Why indeed?

24   In France, Mary had had a daughter, Fanny, by an American adventurer called Gilbert
     Imlay. Imlay's desertion of Mary and her child, provoked first an attempt to kill
     herself by drowning, but later it fuelled the drive to write what turned out to be her
     last piece of fiction and, as it were, the second volume of *Vindication of the Rights of
     Woman, Maria, or the Wrongs of Woman* which was published by Godwin posthu-
     mously (1798).

25   Janet Todd in *Gender, Art and Death* (Oxford, Blackwell, 1993) states that Godwin was
     guilty of giving 'his wife's story the sentimental and romantic cast she had spent most
     of her intellectual life combating' (p. 116). He inadvertently pushed Wollstonecraft
     'back into a romantic or sentimental frame' (p. 117).

26   Marilyn Butler, *Jane Austen and The War of Ideas* (Oxford, Clarendon Press, 1987)
     writes: 'It is no accident that Godwin … had begun his career as a Unitarian minister
     … In sexual matters … their advocacy of reason and restraint often makes them read
     like their opponents, the conservative moralists' (p. 451).

27   See Barbara Taylor, *Eve and the New Jerusalem* (London, Virago, 1984), p. 11, and G. J.
     Barker-Benfield, *The Culture of Sensibility: Sex and Society in Eighteenth Century Britain*
     (Chicago, University of Chicago, 1992), p. 376.

28   Quoted in full in *A Wollstonecraft Anthology* p. 17.

29   'Memoirs of Mrs. Godwin', *The Monthly Visitor and Pocket Companion* by a Society of
     Gentlemen, III (1798), 242.

30   Tomalin in a footnote to illustration 6, between pages 116 and 117.

31   'The Old Woman – No. III', *The Ladies Monthly Museum*, 1 (September 1798), 86.

32   See Gary Kelly, *Women, Writing and Revolution 1790–1827* (Oxford, Clarendon Press,
     1993).

33 Barbara Taylor in *Eve* charts the shifts in political location of feminist ideas during the nineteenth century.

34 Quoted by Tomalin, p. 235.

35 Mitzi Myers, 'Reform or ruin: "a revolution in female manners"', *Studies in Eighteenth Century Culture*, 11 (1982), 199–216, (201–2).

36 Mrs Elwood, *Memoirs of the Literary Ladies of England* (London, Henry Colburn, 1843), 2 vols, vol. I. Preface and p. 127 and p. 141.

37 When feelings against Dissenters were being whipped up by Burke in Parliament, William Smith defended Richard Price in particular and Unitarians in general as 'a meritorious and respectable body of men, who had by no part of their conduct deserved to be treated with so much scurrility' quoted by Barbara Stephen in an unfinished typescript 'History of William Smith and his Family' *c.* 1940 (Add. 7621/71 Cambridge University Library). See also Albert Goodwin, *The Friends of Liberty: The English Democratic Movement in the Age of the French Revolution* (London, Hutchinson, 1979), pp. 322–5, and my forthcoming biography of Barbara Leigh Smith Bodichon.

38 See Jane Rendall, '"A Moral Engine?" Feminism, Liberalism and the *English Woman's Journal*', in *Equal or Different: Women's Politics 1800–1914*, ed. Jane Rendall (Oxford, Blackwell, 1987), pp. 112–38.

39 Marian Evans wrote to Emily Davies: 'The answer to those alarms of men about education is, to admit fully that the mutual delight of the sexes in each other must enter into the perfection of life, but to point out that complete union and sympathy can only come by women having opened to them the same store of acquired truth or beliefs that men have, so that their grounds of judgement may be as far as possible the same'. 8 August 1868. Quoted by Barbara Stephen, *Emily Davies and Girton College* (London, Constable, 1927), p. 182.

40 Alexander Chalmer, *The General Biographical Dictionary* (London, 1914), pp. 53–5. A full account of the mutual influence of these two women and its importance for the history of feminism is given in my Ph.D. thesis 'Barbara Leigh Smith and George Eliot: an examination of their work and friendship' (Anglia Polytechnic University in collaboration with the University of Essex, 1992).

41 *Essays of George Eliot*, ed. Thomas Pinney (London, Routledge and Kegan Paul, 1963) pp. 199–206 (p. 201).

42 Elizabeth Robins Pennell, in *Mary Wollstonecraft Godwin* (London, W. H. Allen and Co., 1885), p. 2, quoted Roscoe:
    > Hard was thy fate in all the scenes of life,
    > As daughter, sister, mother, friend, and wife;
    > But harder still thy fate in death we own,
    > Thus mourned by Godwin with a heart of stone

43 Letters from Jane, Lady Shelley in Parkes Papers VI, Girton College, Cambridge. *Letters to Imlay* (London, C. Kegan Paul and Co., 1879), prefatory 'Memoir', p. v. Paul was personally fascinated with religious questions, but it is unlikely that his readings of Wollstonecraft's religious views would be accepted by current scholars.

44 Elizabeth R. Pennell, *Mary Wollstonecraft Godwin* (London, W. H. Allen and Co., 1885). Pennell (1855–1936) was an author and art critic. Her *Life of Mary Wollstonecraft* was published in America (1884) in the Roberts Brothers' Famous Women Series.

45 Emma Rauschenbusch-Clough, *Mary Wollstonecraft and the Rights of Woman* (London, Longmans, Green and Co., 1898). Emma Rauschenbusch-Clough Ph.D. was the daughter of Professor A. Rauschenbusch D.D. and second wife of Revd J. E. Clough D.D., an American Baptist missionary. Another of her books, *While Sewing Sandals: Tales of a Telegu Pariah Tribe* (London, Hodder and Stoughton, 1899) seeks to vindicate 'the humblest and most despised of the Pariahs of Southern India' (p. vii).

Perhaps the same missionary impulse inspired her defence of that other pariah, Mary Wollstonecraft.

46 *Gender, Art and Death*, p. 3.

47 Emily W. Sunstein, *Mary Shelley: Romance and Reality* (Baltimore, The Johns Hopkins University Press, 1989), p. 387.

48 Joanna Russ, *How to Suppress Women's Writing* (London, The Woman's Press, 1983) surveys the forces that work against the equitable reception of women's writing.

49 Letter from Mary Wollstonecraft quoted by her friend Mary Hays in a biographical sketch in *Annual Necrology* for 1797–98. Mitzi Myers in 'Reform or Ruin' points out that only Wollstonecraft's demands for equal *political* rights were premature, her demands 'for forceful female social leverage and for freedom from sexual exploitation were not' (p. 212).

▓▓

A republican answers back: Jean-Jacques Rousseau, Albertine Necker de Saussure, and forcing little girls to be free

Clarissa Campbell Orr

HISTORIANS who have examined in recent years the relationship of the French Revolution to questions of gender have agreed that the republican culture which emerged after the failure of a liberal, constitutionalist project to create a parliamentary monarchy (1789–92) was in many respects inimical to women. The direct political activism of the women's clubs was brought to an end by their closure in 1793. Jacobin republican culture was essentially masculinist, even misogynist. Central to its critique of the Ancien Régime was its belief that women had exercised undue influence in salon and boudoir over the cliques and secret factions inherent in Court-centred politics. Political power must instead be accountable to the sovereign people; words and deeds must be intelligible, transparent, incorruptible. Men must be citizens, acting heroically in the public sphere, reviving the civic virtue of the classical republic and if necessary dying for it. Women must acknowledge masculine authority both by exclusion from the public sphere and in deference to the male head of household in the private sphere. Yet the celebration of Roman models of patriotism which endorsed the sacrifice of family – of sons, husbands and fathers – to the needs of the *patrie* meant that Revolutionary republicanism was destructive of the very sphere, the family, assigned to women. This may have been one reason why French women in the Restoration continued to find republicanism unattractive; if it refused them citizenship, it also conceded them little real power in the private sphere.[1]

A central strand of this republican ideology was of course derived from Rousseau, and it must be recognised how ambivalent was his message to and about women. It is evident that men and women felt liberated through their identification with his fictional characters and their emotional dilemmas, and that the cult of sensibility enabled women to see themselves as the heroines of their own life-dramas. By the end of his

novel *Julie, ou La Nouvelle Héloïse* (1761) his tragic heroine had so trans-
gressed moral norms that her only 'solution' was to take her own life; but
Julie's truthfulness to her feelings portrayed a kind of emotional integrity,
none the less, while her maternal devotion helped to create the new ideal
of motherhood. However, it was also clear that Rousseau's revolt against
Parisian courtly and intellectual circles was also a revolt against the cultivated *salonière*, against her cultural power and her sexual independence.
The overt exercise of such power was to be feared.

In considering solutions to the alienation and artifice of French society,
Rousseau believed it was essential to remodel motherhood, and the cult of
natural motherhood and closer family affection indeed became fashionable even among the French Court whose values he had rejected. In the
salon of Jacques Necker, the Paris-based Genevan banker who became
finance minister to the Crown, and his wife Suzanne Churchod, a daughter
of a Swiss pastor, this familial ideal was paraded by the inclusion of their
daughter Germaine among the salon guests, who literally sat at her
mother's feet during the evening receptions. Later when the Revolution
began, Marie Antoinette was to be tried, among other charges, as a bad,
indeed a perverse, mother.[2]

Feminist historians have been divided over whether this cult of motherhood was ultimately to women's disadvantage or advantage. An emphasis
on the importance of motherhood could and did lead to arguments for the
better education of women precisely so that they could be better mothers;
but this still tended to their exclusion from the civic sphere. The social
contract was essentially between men.[3] Wollstonecraft's own personal
response to Rousseau led her to a rejection of Rousseauesque sensibility
in favour of egalitarian rationalism. She was to conclude that motherhood
necessitated participation in the public sphere for women as citizens: this,
rather than her emphasis on the rationality of women was the measure of
her radicalism.[4]

In imagining a solution to the social deformities of Ancien Régime
French society, Rousseau oscillated between the possibilities for a private
life in which individuals chose to reject the public, Court-centred world
of power, fame, social prestige, and sexual dalliance, 'opting out' to live
by their own standards, and the possibility of designing a blueprint for a
purer society, in which social mores reinforced civic culture and the
pursuit of private interests was subsumed in patriotism. In the *Social
Contract*, he had suggested that individuals might have to be forced to be
free. He may well have meant that they would need moral instruction to
recognise their civic responsibilities and check self-interest, but under the
Jacobin Republic the creation of civic virtue used the sterner mechanisms
of denunciation and the guillotine.[5]

Both solutions were imagined in the context of the Suisse Romande. The setting for *Julie* was the countryside around Lake Geneva, in the Pays de Vaud. This was politically subordinate to the canton of Berne, and its titled gentry were socially prestigious but politically powerless, as they were ineligible to serve on Berne's city councils. A virtuous private life was thus the only choice available to men and women.[6] Rousseau's theoretical political writings often had reference to his native city, Geneva, which like Berne was an oligarchic republic. But having run away from his apprenticeship, Rousseau had never lived in Geneva as a adult citizen and he idealised its virtues when he dedicated his *Discourse on the Origins and Foundations of Inequality Among Men* to its sovereign magistrates in 1754.[7]

This dedicatory letter also apostrophised the women of Geneva in the following terms:

> Could I forget that precious half of the Commonwealth which assures the happiness of the other, and whose sweetness and prudence maintain its peace and good morals? Lovable and virtuous women of Geneva – the destiny of your sex will always be to govern ours. Happy are we so long as your chaste power, exerted solely within the marriage bed, makes itself felt only for the glory of the state and the well-being of the public![8]

This was a fulsome eulogy: but was it true? And did Genevan women wish to conform to this code of femininity? How much of Rousseau's prescriptions did they accept? One way to answer this question is to look at the response of one particular Genevan woman to the debate over women's education. Such a response exists in the work of Albertine Necker de Saussure (1766–1841), whose study of education, *L'Education Progressive*, was published between 1828 and 1838. Though appearing roughly sixty years after Rousseau's *Emile* (1762) and *Social Contract* (1761), her book has deep roots in her childhood experience of being taught by her father, himself an educational reformer, in the years immediately following the publication of Rousseau's books and the controversy they engendered in Geneva. Educational reform was a preoccupation of her family and culture; she taught all four of her children herself, preparing her two sons for admission to the Collège or grammar school, and teaching her two daughters for their entire education.[9]

Before looking in some detail at her recommendations for girls' upbringing, I will outline some features of Geneva's republican culture, which had its roots in early modern forms of republicanism. Her response to Rousseau must be contextualised in terms of the ideology of femininity and the opportunities for women provided by her native city. Her response to Rousseau is a response from the heart of Geneva's own distinctive republican ethos, for her family was at the centre of the oligarchy controlling Genevan political and intellectual life. She was linked to liberal reform circles in Paris, too, through her husband, Jacques Necker, nephew of the French finance minister, and her cousin by marriage, Germaine de Staël. These contacts continued in her close friendship with de Staël's daughter Albertine and the latter's husband Victor, Duc de Broglie, who were both associated with the liberal opposition to the Bourbon Restoration. Together with Guizot and other Doctrinaires, de Broglie took office during the July Monarchy. Geneva's aristocratic republican liberalism was a political model to de Broglie as important as England's example of a parliamentary monarchy.

Necker de Saussure's republican outlook therefore represents a different republican tradition from that of the Jacobins; it was one which was liberal, religious in an ecumenical not a dogmatic way, and one which believed that girls needed to be taught self-reliance and a certain degree of autonomy even within the structure of marriage and family. Albertine Necker de Saussure's book may be read in part as an answer to Rousseau's Sophie, the imaginary helpmeet provided for the eponymous character of his novel *Emile*, who lived to serve and please first her parents and then him, thus lacking any other moral and emotional anchorage.

Geneva's most important characteristic, from the point of view of women's status and opportunities, was that the State was not extensively interventionist, and left its male citizens and their families scope to associate and pursue their own interests in civil society. Ancien Régime Genevan society rested on privilege: not all residents had civic rights, which were confined to the categories of *citoyen* and *bourgeois*. The principle of equality before the law was established only when Geneva was absorbed as a *département* of France during the Napoleonic era, and retained when it was reconstituted as a canton and then affiliated to the restored Swiss constitution in 1814–5. Civic rights then rested on a property qualification which was progressively changed in the direction of adult male suffrage.

Freedom from Napoleonic supervision allowed for fuller development in a classically liberal manner of a wide variety of voluntary organisations based variously on Christian philanthropy and utilitarianism: savings banks, Lancastrian schools, reformed prisons, though similar initiatives had been possible before this. As in England, women found in philanthropic work a convenient border zone between the public state and the private home where they could work and organise. Despite the different religious affiliation, the range of interests was similar to the activities of Catholic female philanthropy in the neighbouring Franche-Comté. However, philanthropic organisation was perhaps less gender-specific in Protestant Geneva, where there were also important examples of secular male leadership – for instance, the work of J.-A.-P. de Candolle in setting up friendly societies. His wife Sophie-Dorothée Boissier was a second cousin of Albertine Necker de Saussure and the money the couple had at their disposal came largely from the immense Boissier banking fortune. The Government also developed its cultural institutions. It restructured the Académie, founded a Music Conservatory, and instituted a botanic garden. But the State had no monopoly of cultural initiative and one of the most significant private gestures was the founding of an art museum, the Musée Rath, by the two Mesdemoiselles Rath, using their brother's fortune.[10]

Because of Calvin's association with Geneva at the Reformation, it is often mistakenly supposed that the republic was a theocracy enforcing his austere ideal for a disciplined, Christian society. Were this true, it might have truly been a blueprint for a Jacobin polity controlling religion and morals as well as politics. But Geneva was not a theocracy. Church and State were separate institutions; the former had no independent juris-dictional power, and its governing body had lay representatives. In the earlier stages of the Reformation, it was expected that Christian magis-trates would enact laws to encourage a godly society and repress ungodly tendencies; by Necker de Saussure's lifetime, such laws, covering sumptu-ary regulations or Sunday observance, were seldom rigorously enforced, and moral offences like adultery had been de-criminalised.[11]

Until Napoleon's annexation of Geneva in 1797, the only Christian worship permitted was that of the Reformed Church. But after that, Catholicism and other denominations were given equal legal rights, retained at the Restoration. This period also saw an Evangelical revival with strong links to Scotland, and a strong social agenda. In a different key were the small groups of adherents following the teachings of the mystics Mme de Krudener and the Chevalier de Langalerie. Religious diversity within a society actively observant of Christianity was the hall-mark of Geneva when Necker de Saussure began to write, and she was personally of an ecumenical disposition.[12]

There were therefore spaces for women to be active socially, culturally, and to some extent intellectually, in Geneva's liberal republican society in a way that a Rousseauesque/Jacobin republican culture would not have tolerated.[13] True, there was no Court to act as a magnet for ambition and faction, no decadent monarchy, no Parc aux Cerfs supplying nubile girls for Louis XV, or Petit Trianon to amuse Marie Antoinette. But Genevan women were not domestic ciphers.

Albertine Necker de Saussure had always been a beneficiary of this Genevan liberalism. She was a member of an interlocking and interrelated set of families who dominated the political structure of Geneva in the Ancien Régime, where real power lay with the Council of 50 and the Council of 200. Her immediate forebears included members of the

Boissier, De la Rive and Lullin families, and her aunts married into the Tronchins and Turrettinis; these were the equivalents of the Whig cousinhood of English parliamentary politics. The same families resumed positions of influence in 1815; Necker de Saussure's daughters married Turrettinis and de la Rives, and the former son-in-law served as secretary to Geneva's negotiator at the Congress of Vienna, François D'Ivernois. Albertine's husband, Jacques Necker, followed a political career, interrupted only by French annexation, serving several times as one of the four leading magistrates or *syndics*.[14]

Unusually for a family which enjoyed their wealth and connections, her father Horace-Bénédict de Saussure was not so consistently active in politics, but he made a very distinctive contribution periodically. He was a distinguished naturalist, the conqueror of Mont Blanc, and preferred to concentrate on his scientific interests and the education of his daughter and two sons, which he personally attended. His various attempts to make educational reforms in Geneva's Collège or grammar school were part of his strategy to heal the divisions in this liberal republican polity, which tempted him into the political arena.[15]

Although Rousseau idealised the republic as one which avoided extreme social divisions, there were in reality significant social and political cleavages even within the enfranchised minority who possessed civic rights. The middling sort, who were still actively engaged in business and the skilled trades, looked to Rousseau to champion their concerns, such as hostility to the idea of a public theatre. Their outlook contrasted with the sophistication of the patrician elite who lived largely on private incomes, had Francophone tastes, and enjoyed attending Voltaire's private theatricals at nearby Ferney; Necker de Saussure was later to translate A. W. Schlegel's *Lectures on Dramatic Poetry*.[16]

There was a political dimension to these cleavages too, concerning the powers of the governing Councils of 50 and 200 relative to the Great Council. Horace-Bénédict de Saussure was in office during this time and tried to act as a moderating liberal influence. After 1768 he turned away from political mechanisms to concentrate more wholeheartedly on educational reform. It was clear to him that an essentially aristocratic regime should take care to mitigate inequalities of influence and wealth by providing a modern, relevant education through the city's Collège, but the Government was in a reactionary mood and shelved the proposals.

In 1782, there were further constitutional tensions. Fearing trouble, de Saussure sent his three children in disguise into the country; a prescient decision, for the family town house was besieged and de Saussure, assisted by his wife and her two sisters, had to defend themselves. From 1788 there were fresh disturbances, influenced by rising bread prices and the French unrest. By 1792 a Jacobin style of republican government had been formed replacing the traditional magistrates. De Saussure again tried to act as a moderating influence, and made further educational reform proposals, which would have resulted in free primary education for boys and girls up to ten years of age. However, the coup of 1794 which executed seven people in a modest re-enactment of the French Reign of Terror finally put an end to de Saussure's willingness to help the cause of moderation through educational or other liberal reform strategies. None the less, his example must have shown his daughter that education was of central importance in shaping the ethos of a state, and that change might come about as much through cultural and social mechanisms as direct political participation.[17]

Women in Geneva were not able to participate directly in the political process, but in such an oligarchic system, politics was essentially about family concerns and strategies. Being au fait with public issues was tantamount to being familiar with the interests and deeds of one's father, husband, brother son and so on; there was less of a disjunction between public and private spheres. It is evident from family correspondence that Albertine's mother felt it appropriate to be well-informed on public affairs; later it was known that Albertine and her more conservative husband agreed to differ on political matters.[18]

Like her father, she also found opportunities to express her political alignments through cultural issues. During Geneva's annexation by France (1797–1814), some of its leading scholars and intellectuals expressed their pro-British, anti-Napoleonic sympathies through the *Bibliothèque Britannique*, a journal reviewing English literature and social debate. Albertine Necker de Saussure contributed several book reviews to this, including one of Robert Owen's *New View of Society*. As an intimate friend of her cousin by marriage, Germaine de Staël, who spent some of her time at Coppet, her father's chateau near Geneva, when exiled from Paris by Napoleon, Necker de Saussure also participated in the intellectual life of the brilliant Coppet circle, the heart of liberal nationalism under Napoleonic tyranny. She was believed to be even more intelligent than her more famous cousin, and enjoyed the esteem of men such as Benjamin Constant, Victor Bonstetten, Sismond de Sismondi, and A. W. Schlegel, who also encouraged her to write down her own views and not act merely as a translator.

It is incontestable that Necker de Saussure's opportunities for cultural, social and quasi-political engagement came about because of her fortunate social position. But it would I suggest be mistaken to regard her relative emancipation as characteristic of any but the elite few; rather, it represented a difference of degree, not kind, of freedom enjoyed by most Genevan women. The work of social historians suggests a pattern of intellectually developed, essentially sensible, and practically competent women similar to that associated in England with the Unitarian circles who were such an inspiration to Mary Wollstonecraft.

Whatever the economic and political contrasts between Genevan women, all were the beneficiaries of a certain kind of moral egalitarianism fostered by Calvinism. The equality of souls before God, which was a feature of Necker de Saussure's discussion of gender roles, was one element of this egalitarianism. The Calvinist ethos imposed a similar standard of sexual morality on both sexes; a double standard tolerating greater laxity in men, which was so institutionalised in French law and society, was not condoned in Geneva. Marriage was to be encouraged as an honourable state, and it was not particularly approved for either sex to remain single. Young people were left reasonably free to choose a marriage partner, and parents were not supposed to withhold financial support if this choice did not accord with worldly ambition, or to blame their offspring for rejecting candidates they particularly favoured.[19] The absence of arranged marriages based on property considerations may well have removed the practice, characteristic in French society, whereby a man maintained a mistress commanding his personal affections alongside a wife chosen for social and dynastic reasons. The small scale of Genevan society (the walled town could be traversed within twenty minutes on foot) meant that girls could walk unchaperoned, but were likely to be spotted by some friend or relative wherever they went. Similarly, the close-knit quality of Genevan society would make it hard for anyone to conduct extra-marital liaisons. The sensational scandals of pre-Revolutionary France would have been impossible in Geneva.

Women as well as men were able to initiate divorce, on the same grounds: adultery, desertion, and frigidity or impotence; and because a man leaving Geneva would lose his civic rights, it may have been that women felt they had less to lose in regularising their position. Between 1770 and 1780, sixty deserted wives petitioned successfully for divorce, higher than the the the number of male petitions. Population statistics suggest that birth control was practised, so women experienced some freedom from reproductive imperatives. Women also enjoyed high rates of literacy in an exceptionally well-schooled European city: 87 per cent of women, alongside 95 per cent of men, could sign marriage contracts by the end of the century. This can also be traced to Calvinism, where reading the Scriptures was a part of preparation for confirmation. One third of teachers employed at this primary level by 1789 were women.[20]

These trends in Genevan society seem to have been little altered by the French occupation. In the Restoration epoch women were characterised by their intellectual interests, their role as social and moral educators, and their philanthropic activity. They were valued for their relational capacity, certainly – for being wives, mothers and daughters; but Genevan society preferred to see men also acting in a family context.[21]

Albertine Necker de Saussure's recipe for the upbringing of girls is consistent with the social and cultural context sketched here of Genevan society. Her women would fulfil their religious, familial and social obligations, but they would do so in a self-possessed manner scarcely imagined by Rousseau. The advice she gives suggests that she wished to strike a balance between teaching them to be unselfish, and fostering their ability to make independent judgements. This advice was rendered in the context of a theory of historical progress characteristic of the Enlightenment.[22]

Her most immediate source for a theory of the historical conditioning of women was the work of Antoine Thomas, *Essai sur le caractère, les moeurs, et l'esprit des femmes, dans les différents siècles*.[23] Thomas, a protégé of Suzanne Necker, Mme de Staël's mother, adhered to the philosophical history of the Enlightenment which envisaged humanity experiencing different stages of progress. The advent of Christianity had been in his view beneficial to women, ameliorating their position by freeing them from chattel status and in general replacing the rule of force with the rule of law. Albertine Necker de Saussure certainly believed that in the past, social attitudes were detrimental to women's dignity, and that traces of this remained in women's sense of themselves:

> Whence then arises that lamentable alloy by which beings, evidently intended for better things, are so frequently debased? It seems to us that it is attributable in great measure to a cause of very remote date: to that degrading yoke of servitude so long imposed on them by men … its effects still remain – the trace of them is deeply impressed on the manners, the opinions, and even the thoughts of women. They have blindly adopted those humiliating maxims which it should have been their object to subvert.[24]

Against Rousseau's indictment of modern times and his belief that the earliest stages of human society were the least deforming to human nature, Necker de Saussure is an unequivocal modernist.

But modern society, Necker de Saussure argues, is still flawed in its treatment of women: men still tend to regard women as their property, not persons in their own right who may have other talents to fulfil, in addition to their roles as wives and mothers.[25] For Necker de Saussure, women cannot be exclusively defined by their relational capacities. Although in her view men and women have distinct natures, they also have gifts that are similar, including intellectual attributes. Difference of attainment is due solely to different education, not differential capacity.

Necker de Saussure's strongly criticised an education for women designed solely to meet masculine requirements: 'his object has been to

render woman an instrument either for the gratification of his passions, or
the advancement of his interests.' The result is that his aims are defeated:
'in vain will he be continually changing his system, and require from
education by turns a mistress, an artist, or a housekeeper; he will never
gain a wife, a companion, a being truly formed to be the charm and
comfort of his life.'[26]

Marriage is a likely and natural state for all women, but it is by no
means the be-all and end-all of their lives. Their upbringing should be
designed to develop their own individual potential as persons and moral
beings, as well as equip them to enter into relations with others, and be
trained to educate their own children. This sense of identity is also necessary because some women may not marry, and even the majority who do
will in the end need to find resources to meet widowhood and old age.
The outer limit of Necker de Saussure's vision therefore includes the
single woman who may have to earn her own living and will need a sense
of her worth.

Like many liberals, she did not envisage a fundamental revision of
structures and institutions. She wanted to change attitudes, so that while
society has the same forms, it was animated by a different spirit. This may
make her sound essentially conservative, but it may be argued that
because she wants to alter the way women *see themselves*, her prescriptions
are far more radical and comprehensive than if she had called for an
enlargement of women's social and economic opportunity, without first
reaching to the core of their internalised habits of deference and self-
deprecation.

In sum, she wanted to foster in a young woman 'a happy mixture of
humility and dignity'. Admittedly her sphere will be that of private life;
her special influence will be the family; but, consistent with Geneva's
view of the significance of family life, 'to perfect, to animate, to embellish
and sanctify private life' is no mean task, but 'a great and exalted object'.[27]

Women can exercise influence outside the home in philanthropic
projects, which should be undertaken individually rather that through a
public role. This seems to be a matter of tactics: even a single woman, she
believed, needed to be tactful about her initiatives, in case she sparked
some misogynist reaction which polarised the sexes: 'as they might advance
towards independence, men would advance toward indifference'.[28] A
similar pragmatism is offered as a strategy for dealing with the male's
inherent sense of superiority. As she comments wryly, indeed, unspar-
ingly, it is hard to pin down the actual grounds for this sense of superiority:

> Should we be asked in what this superiority consists, we might not, perhaps,
> find it very easy to point out any one particular quality as its cause. More
> addicted to sensual indulgences, and not either more religious, more disinter-

ested, more virtuous, or perhaps, more spiritual than we are; we yet feel that they are intended to be our masters, and that they are so in virtue of a moral, as well as physical superiority.[29]

This is scarcely complimentary, but Necker de Saussure seems to think it wisest to recognise masculine self-regard as a psychological given, and then, bearing this in mind, try to achieve social co-operation. Her advice on authority within the family is similarly pragmatic. Because children will otherwise play off one parent against another, a family needs a single source of authority. Further more, as men acquire significant responsibilities on marriage, the authority of paterfamilias provides them with psychological compensation.

Necker de Saussure accepts a traditional framework, then, but insists that women must possess a code of conduct, a set of impersonal principles beyond and above the desire to please. Like Mary Wollstonecraft, she may be seen as substituting a form of rule-based constitutional government in place of divine right monarchy as a metaphor for married life (though this analogy is not one she made herself).

A product of Geneva's rational Christianity, as well as a participant in its religious awakening or *Réveil*, she believed that Christianity was what offered women a resource for the development of a strong, internalised set of principles, without challenging the norms of society. However, although she thought women had a natural affinity to Christianity, this by no means absolved men from their obligations: 'Christianity is a religion so perfectly adapted to the whole human race, that we might perhaps appear to depreciate it if we spoke of it as peculiarly suited to women'. And if women have often been considered only in relation to men, there is no necessity for women to react against this and live only for themselves:

> Nor do we wish that her main object in life should be herself. We desire that she should devote herself to others; but we desire that man should do this also. By no other means does it seem to us that human beings can attain any great degree either of happiness or perfection.[30]

Indeed, the best form of married partnership is one where both partners are conscious of their shortcomings in relation to the spiritual demands made on humankind, and encourage each other in a spirit of mutual forbearance.

In common with English patterns of Evangelical Christianity which acted as a social discipline for men, encouraging them to play their part in the establishment of true marital partnerships and contribute to parenting, Mme Necker de Saussure's views of gender were deeply conditioned by the idea of the equality of souls before God.[31] This counterbalances the social and economic asymmetries between men and women and is the foundation of female self-esteem. A woman's right to develop her talents is based on the fact, self-evident to Mme de Saussure, that women are equally with men 'a piece of divine workmanship' and that the deity requires *both* sexes 'to do good according to their ability'.[32]

To the modern mind, it might seem that living with the goal of Christian perfection before you would be a way of deepening diffidence, a recipe for inadequacy and guilt. But Mme Necker de Saussure's religious views were eclectic and owed a particular debt to the philosophic optimism of her great-uncle, Charles Bonnet, Geneva's leading mid-century moralist and scientist. Bonnet's views encouraged her to believe that humanity was naturally progressing toward perfection, which seems to have acted as a positive and empowering belief, analogous to the role of necessitarianism in the outlook of Harriet Martineau and other English Unitarians.[33]

In addition, Necker de Saussure's religious beliefs were not so much anti-clerical as non-clerical. She deplored sectarianism and what she called methodistical bigotry, and found consolation from a variety of religious sources. Her advice on religious education for children was that it should be conducted within the home, both parents having a contribution to make. A minister's assistance would simply augment this instruction in the prelude to confirmation. So in her republicanism there was no scope for the French polarity between male anti-clericalism and female, allegedly priest-ridden religiosity. A woman conducts her own religious quest with respect for but without undue deference to the clergy.

To her, Christianity contributed to both the humility and dignity of women because it gave them a sense of perspective. Christianity therefore inoculated women from indulging in their own romantic fancy, and enabled them to respond to male infatuation with a kind of amused scepticism. Necker de Saussure's target here may be not the generalised manifestations of literary romanticism, but a more specific critique of social romanticism, whether Saint-Simonian or positivist, with its exaggerated cult of a female messiah.[34]

A rational reappraisal of romantic hyperbole will protect women from seduction, and give them a healthy perspective regarding marriage. A Genevan woman would not, following this advice, use her sexual power as an opportunity for manipulation of a partner while her influence lasted. Friendship, as in Wollstonecraft's mature conclusions, should be the basis and cement of marital partnerships. A cool and temperate mode of conducting relationships seems to have been characteristic of the Genevan style. Benjamin Constant's cousin Charles de Constant observed, 'Nos femmes, quand elles sont marieées, aiment leur maris par-dessus tout, mais c'est sans passion, sagement et prudemment' (Our women, when they marry, love their husbands first and foremost, but they love wisely and prudently, not passionately.) The tenor of Necker de Saussure's own marriage may be gauged from the term she always used in writing to her husband: 'mon ami'.[35]

It might appear that the advice given by *L'Education Progressive* errs on the side of reinforcing propriety and social hierarchy. In fact, there is an equally important element to reinforce a certain kind of responsible independence of spirit in women from an early age. This is where we come to what Necker de Saussure means by forcing little girls to be free. She had observed that girls were early aware of their charms, (just as Rousseau had pictured the imaginary Sophie as shrinking from practising the alphabet because her mirrored face, glimpsed as she concentrated, was unflattering). But unlike Rousseau, she is adamant that this coquettish tendency must be checked, because once girls learn to be insincere, they have no moral character. 'Is it not ... transparency and candour which forms the peculiar and fascinating attributes of youth and innocence?' So when little girls lose the bloom of childhood prettiness and go through a stage of looking 'plain' from around seven to ten, this could be an advantage, because it meant that a child could not get by on charm, but had to earn approbation by her actual conduct.[36]

A girls' greater willingness to please her parents in contrast to the rebelliousness of little boys (a contrast she believed was rooted in nature, not nurture), could also be a disadvantage because although it produced an outwardly biddable child, it was one whose grasp of moral responsibility was still feeble. Obedience instilled by mothers in daughters should be directed toward their acquiring a sense of impersonal duties that require fulfilment, irrespective of whether this will also please. The child's awareness that she is performing a duty, not just yielding her will to another's, will foster a sense of self-esteem; it will also teach resignation, since 'frustrated attempts and disappointed hopes must always make a part of her destiny'.[37]

What Necker de Saussure wishes to produce is a

self-command [that] constitutes the happy medium between that passive will which submits quietly to necessity, and that active will which executes its own designs in spite of natural indifference or inconstancy. This active will should be cultivated in girls; for however pliable and docile we may wish them to be, we also wish them to possess decision of character.[38]

Rousseau had talked in *Emile* about Sophie learning to love virtue, but had imagined that the chief motive for her to acquire it was to please her parents. Necker de Saussure's women were made of sterner stuff. Their characters had been deliberately moulded to make them able to make moral decisions. To nurture this decisiveness, a practical step for mothers to take was to insist that a child be given an hour each day to spend as she had decided, and afterwards to take stock as to how well she had fulfilled her intentions. 'Nothing should be absolutely required, except that she should have the consciousness of having employed her hour of liberty judiciously, and that she should render an account to herself of the manner in which it has been spent'.[39]

Since a girl lacking strength of character is at a serious moral disadvantage, a more concerted policy of fostering self-command may in some instances be required.

> If ... you observe that your daughter has not energy enough to form a will of her own, that she is governed by indolence even in her amusements, and ready to follow any guide who may be presented to her, endeavour to place her in situations which will oblige her to decide for herself. Force her to be free in spite of herself; follow her at a distance with your eye, but withdraw your guiding hand from her.[40]

Although Necker de Saussure nowhere makes explicit reference to Rousseau's theories, comments like the above suggest an implicit dialogue with the Genevan who had made such controversial claims for the inherent virtues of mankind and the careful education of young men to enable them to make moral judgements. Girls too, for Necker de Saussure, need to be given a sense of self-reliance, an inner reference point. If the family is the microcosm of society, then the nurture of girls as well as boys must provide them with a sense of individual judgement as well as social co-operation. Both sexes can then make a contribution to a sound society whose fundamental principles apply equally to both sexes, even if they do not have the same role in civic politics.

The Christian faith (and not Rousseau's civic religion recommended in The *Social Contract*, nor the deism of *Emile*) will be not so much a code of conduct *controlling* women as a set of principles *empowering* them. She was critical of presenting moral precepts simply as a means of indicating what was socially acceptable. This is to reduce religion to propriety, making it a means, not an end. Conversely, a woman imbued with a Christian sense of obligation will not hesitate to lead her household in setting standards for 'all that is pure and elevated in human life'. Her sense of spiritual imperatives will contribute to 'an internal energy – the same spirit acting in a thousand different ways, according to the exigency of the moment'.[41]

A full appraisal of Mme Necker de Saussure's prescriptions for bringing up little girls to become resourceful and characterful women would need to take into consideration her ideas on their intellectual, cultural and physical education. Like Wollstonecraft, for instance, she had no patience with girls who lay on their sofas looking pale and interesting, and she advocated periods of regular exercise. Moreover women brought up under Mme Necker de Saussure's prescriptions would have been intellectually much more self-confident than Rousseau's matrons, or the ideal Sophie who has 'the sort of mind which calls for no remark, as she never seems cleverer or stupider than oneself'.[42] A further and valuable dimension to appraising her contribution to maternal education is to explore the similarities and differences between her and mentors in Restoration French society such as Claire de Rémusat and Pauline Guizot. More broadly still there are under-explored parallels between the Scottish Enlightenment, English Dissent, and Dutch Enlightened republicanism which could be pursued both in respect of women's social formation and the wider political and religious culture.[43]

Here I have simply suggested Necker de Saussure's accord with the liberal republicanism of her native Geneva, and her implicit critique of Rousseau. His tribute to the women of Geneva rightly emphasised a culture valuing marital fidelity and family loyalty, where women did not flaunt their sexuality as they could do in Paris or Versailles, nor use it to obtain political influence. But above all if they followed Necker de Saussure's advice, they would have been women who acted according to a set of internalised principles that made them self-possessed rather than possessed by their husbands or families; they would see themselves as belonging to God, not persons – not even close family, devoted though they were to them. While respectful of the institutions of marriage and family they would behave within these structures with an inner poise and self-respect stemming from their free consent to fundamental moral rules imposed on men as well as women. It is doubtful whether Rousseau would really have admired such women with minds, consciences or wills of their own behind the conventional exterior.

Notes

1   There is a large and expanding literature on these issues; see *inter alia* Joan B. Landes, *Women and the Public Sphere in the Age of the French Revolution* (Ithaca, N.Y., Cornell University Press, 1988); Lynn Hunt, *The Family Romance of the French Revolution* (London, Routledge, 1992); Hunt, *Politics, Culture and Class in the French Revolution* (Berkeley, University of California Press, 1984); Dorinda Outram, *The French Revolution and the Body: Sex, Class and Political Culture,* (New Haven, Yale University Press, 1989); Outram, 'Le langage male de la vertu; in Peter Burke and Roy Porter (eds), *The Social History of Language* (Cambridge, Cambridge University Press, 1987); Outram, 'Revolution domesticity and feminisim', *Historical Journal,* 32:4 (1989), 971–80; Sian Reynolds (ed.), *Women, State and Revolution* (Brighton, Wheatsheaf Books, 1986); Thomas E. Crow, *Painters and Public Life in Eighteenth Century France* (New Haven, Yale University Press, 1985); Sara Maza, *Private Lives and Public Affairs: The Causes Célèbres of Pre-Revolutionary France* (Berkeley, University of Calfornia Press, 1993).

2 Selecting again from an extensive literature, the following may be consulted: Landes, *Women and the Public Sphere*; Madelyn Gutwirth, *Twilight of the Goddesses* (New Brunswick, Rutgers University Press, 1992); Simon Schama, *Citizens: A Chronicle of the French Revolution* (London, Viking 1989); Maza, *Private Lives*; P. D. Jimack, 'The Paradox of Sophie and Julie: Contemporary Response to Rousseau's Ideal Wife and Ideal Mother', in Eva Jacobs *et al.* (eds), *Women and Society in Eighteenth Century France* (London, The Athlone Press, 1979); Robert Darnton, 'Readers respond to Rousseau: The Fabrication of Romantic Sensitivity' in Darnton, *The Great Cat Massacre and Other Episodes in French Cultural History* (London, Allen Lane, 1984).

3 Joel Scwartz, *The Sexual Politics of Jean-Jacques Rousseau* (Chicago and London, University of Chicago Press, 1984); Carole Pateman, *The Sexual Contract* (Cambridge, Polity Press, 1988); Pateman, *The Disorder of Women* (Cambridge, Polity Press, 1989); Lydia Lange, 'Rousseau and Modern Feminism' in Mary Lyndon Shanley and Carole Pateman (eds), *Feminist Interpretations and Political Theory* (Cambridge, Polity Press, 1991); Susan Moller Okin, *Women in Western Political Thought* (Princeton, Princeton University Press, 1979); Victor G. Wexler, '"Made for Man's Delight": Rousseau as Anti-Feminist', *American Historical Review*, 81 (1976), 266–81; Ruth Graham, 'Rousseau's Sexism Revolutionized' in Paul Fritz and Richard Morton (eds), *Woman in The 18th Century and Other Essays* (Toronto, Hakkert, 1976). Gita May, 'Rousseau's Anti-Feminism Reconsidered' in Samia J. Spencer, (ed.), *French Women in the Age of Enlightenment* (Indianapolis, Indiana University Press, 1984).

4 Wollstonecraft's rejection of the cult of sensibility can be seen in both Chapter 3 of her *Vindication of the Rights of Woman* (modern editions include Miriam Kramnick (ed.), (Harmondsworth, Penguin Books, 1975), and in the difference between her first and last novels; see *Mary and The Wrongs of Woman*, edited with an introduction by Gary Kelly, (Oxford, Oxford University Press, 1976). For the cult of sensibility, see G. Barker-Benfield, *The Culture of Sensibility* (Chicago, University of Chicago Press, 1992).

5 Kennedy F. Roche, *Rousseau: Stoic and Romantic* (London, Methuen, 1974); J. L. Talmon, *The Origins of Totalitarian Democracy* (London, Secker and Warburg, 1952).

6 A point well explored by Tony Tanner in an illuminating essay, 'Julie and "La Maison Paternelle": Another Look at Rousseau's *La Nouvelle Héloïse*', in Jean Bethke Elshtain, *The Family in Political Thought* (Brighton, Harvester Press, 1982).

7 For the Gevevan context of his *Social Contract*, see John Stephenson Spink, *Jean-Jacques Rousseau et Genève* (Paris, Boiven et Cie, 1934), and Maurice Cranston, *The Noble Savage: Jean-Jacques Rousseau 1754–1762* (London, Allen Lane, 1991).

8 Cited from Maurice Cranston (ed.), *Jean-Jacques Rousseau, A Discourse on Inequality* (Harmondsworth, Penguin Books, 1984), p. 65.

9 *L'Education Progressive, ou Etude du cours de la vie*, 3 vols (Brussels, A. Sautelet & Cie, 1840). A fuller discussion of Albertine Necker de Saussure as educational theorist can be found in Clarissa Campbell Orr, 'Albertine Necker de Saussure (1766–1841): themes and contexts for the interpretation of *L'Education Progressive*' (M.A. thesis, Department of History, University of York, 1988); and Etienne Causse, *Madame Necker de Saussure et L'Education Progressive*, 2 vols (Geneva, Editions Je Sers, 1930).

10 For culture and society in Restoration Geneva, see Philippe Monnier, *La Genève de Toeppfer* (Geneva, A. Tallien, 1914), and Campbell Orr, 'Albertine Necker de Saussure'.

11 Harro Hopfl, *The Christian Polity of John Calvin* (Cambridge, Cambridge University Press, 1982); Linda Kirk, 'Genevan Republicanism' in David Wootton (ed.), *Republicanism, Liberty, and Commercial Society* (Stanford, Stanford University Press, 1994).

12 For the *Réveil* in Geneva, see E. Guers, *Le Premier Réveil et La Première Eglise Indépendente de Genève* (Geneva, 1871), and further discussion in Campbell Orr, 'Albertine Necker de Saussure'.

13 I offer some comparison with women writing in England on scientific education in 'Albertine Necker de Saussure, the Mature Woman Author, and the Scientific Education of women', *Women's Writing, The Early Modern Period* (June 1995).

14 The best account of Geneva's political culture before 1797 is now Kirk, 'Genevan Republicanism'. See also Spink, *Jean-Jacques Rousseau*; and R. R. Palmer, *The Age of Democratic Revolution*, 2 vols (Princeton, Princeton University Press, 1959, 1964).

15 Douglas Freshfield, *The Life of Horace-Bénédict de Saussure* (London, Edward Arnold, 1920).

16 Albertine Necker de Saussure, *Cours de Littérature Dramatique* (Paris 1914); Maza, *Private Lives*, esp. ch. 4.

17 In addtion to Freshfield's *Life* and Kirk, 'Gevenan Republicanism', Geneva's eventful history can be followed in Société d'histoire et d'archéologie de Genève, *Histoire dès origines à 1798*, and *Histoire de Genève de 1798 à 1931* (Geneva, Alexandre Jullien, 1951–6).

18 Freshfield, *Life* and Causse, *Madame Necker de Saussure*; c.f., Gervase Huxley (ed.), *Lady Elizabeth and the Grosvenors: Life in a Whig Family, 1822–1839* (London, Oxford University Press, 1965); see also the Introduction, and Chapter 4 in this volume.

19 Freshfield, *Life*; E. William Monter, 'Women in Calvinist Geneva 1500–1800' in *Signs*, 6, (1980–81), 189–209' Linda Kirk, 'Godliness in a golden age, the church and wealth in eighteenth century Geneva', in W. J. Sheils and Diana Wood (eds), *The Church and Wealth, Studies in Church History*, 24 (Oxford, Basil Blackwell, 1987).

20 Monter, 'Women'.

21 The historian Monnier wrote of Restoration women: 'Elles sont versées dans les sciences et accoutumées aux sérieux réflexions. Elles sont educatrices dans les moeurs. Elles sont essentiellement bienfaisantes et promtes à secourir les misères'. *La Genève*, p. 168.

22 Jane Rendall, *The Origins of Modern Feminism: Women in Britain, France and The United States, 1780–1860* (London, Macmillan, 1985), ch. 1; Sylvana Tomaselli, 'The Enlightenment Debate on Women', *History Workshop*, 20 (1985), 210–24, and 'Reflections on the history of the science of Woman', *History of Science*, 29 (1991), 185–205.

23 Paris, 1772; two English translations: 1773 by W. Russell as *Essays on the Character, Manners and Genius of Women in Different Ages*; 1781, by Mrs Kindersley under the title *An Essay on the Character, the Manners, and the Understanding of Women in Different Ages*, with two original essays.

24 All quotations are taken from the English edition of *L'Education Progressive, Progressive Education, or Considerations on the Course of Life*, 3 vols (London, Longman, 1839–43), vol. 3, 8–9.

25 *Ibid.*, p. 9.

26 *Ibid.*, pp. 9, 11–12.

27 p. 15.

28 *Ibid.*, p. 17.

29 *Ibid.*, pp. 32–3.

30 *Ibid.*, p. 19, p. 10.

31 Catherine Hall and Leonore Davidoff, *Family Fortunes, Men and Women of the English Middle Classes 1780–1850* (London, Hutchinson, 1987); Walter E. Houghton, *The Victorian Frame of Mind 1830–1870* (New Haven, Yale University Press, 1957).

32 Necker de Saussure, *Progressive Education*, vol. 3, pp. 10, 13.

33 Cf. R. K. Webb, *Harriet Martineau, A Radical Victorian* (London, Heinenann, 1960).

34 Necker de Saussure, *Progressive Education*, vol. 3, p. 46.

35 *Ibid.*, p. 47. Charles de Constant is cited by Monnier, *La Genève*, p. 167. I am grateful to M. A. Perrot who generously gave me access to Albertine Necker de Saussure's papers in his family's possession in 1988.

36 Necker de Saussure, *Progressive Education*, vol. 3, pp. 67, 69.

37 *Ibid.*, p. 72.
38 *Ibid.*, pp. 72–3.
39 Jean-Jacques Rousseau, *Emile*, trans. Barbara Foxley, Everyman edition (Dent, London, 1974), p. 359; Necker de Saussure, *Progressive Education*, vol. 3, p. 159.
40 *Ibid.*, p. 74.
41 *Ibid.*, p. 75.
42 Rousseau, *Emile*, p. 358.
43 I suggest some comparisons between Mme Necker de Saussure, Pauline Guizot and Claire de Rémusat in 'Albertine Necker de Saussure'. See also Jane Rendall, *Origins*, and Barbara Corrado Pope, 'Maternal Education in France, 1815–1848', *Proceedings of the Third Annual Meeting of the Western Society for French History*, 4–6 December 1975, Texas, 1976; Corrado Pope 'Revolution and Retreat: Upper Class French Women after 1789', in Carol R. Berkin and Clara M. Lovett (eds), *Women, War and Revolution* (New York, Holmes and Meier, 1980); Margaret Darrow, 'French Noblewomen and the New Domesticity, 1750–1850', *Feminist Studies*, 5 (spring 1979), 41–65. Comparative perspectives are also facilitated by G. A. Kelly's magisterial essay *The Humane Comedy: Constant, Tocqueville and French Liberalism* (Cambridge, Cambridge University Press, 1992); Roy Porter and Mikuláš Teich, *The Enlightenment in National Context* (Cambridge, Cambridge University Press, 1980), and Teich, *The Romantic Movement in National Context* (Cambridge, Cambridge University Press, 1988).

3

Writing History for British Women:
Elizabeth Hamilton and the
Memoirs of Agrippina

Jane Rendall

'The inconsistency and folly of [Rousseau's] system', said Henry, 'was perhaps, never better exposed than in the very ingenious publication which takes
the Rights of Women for its title. Pity that the very sensible authoress has
sometimes permitted her zeal to hurry her into expressions which have raised
a prejudice against the whole. To superficial readers it appears to be her
intention to unsex women entirely. (Elizabeth Hamilton, *Memoirs of Modern
Philosophers* (1800), vol. 1, p. 196)

ELIZABETH HAMILTON's novel
was intended to satirise the politics of such 'modern philosophers' as
William Godwin and Mary Wollstonecraft. In Bridgetina Botherim she
created a portrait of a feminist with 'long craggy neck' and 'shrivelled
parchment-like skin', deluded and absurd.[1] Yet such satire has obscured
Hamilton's lifelong commitment to the cause of improving the education
of women, on which subject she found much to agree with in Wollstonecraft's *Vindication of the Rights of Woman*. Hamilton's distinctive approach
owed much to the outlook of the Enlightenment in Scotland.[2] In her one
work of history – *The Memoirs of Agrippina, the Wife of Germanicus* (1804) –
she was to explore the political dilemmas which faced those who sought to
shape new roles for British women. In doing so, she also illustrated the difficulties which faced women writers, who like Wollstonecraft herself, were
ambitious to transcend the limits of genres judged appropriate for women.

Elizabeth Hamilton was largely brought up by her paternal aunt, Mrs
Marshall, near Stirling. She wrote of her paternal family, the Hamiltons of
Woodhall as 'one of the first of the *Saxon* family established in Scotland'.[3]
From the age of eight she attended a boarding school in Stirling, where
she remembered receiving good, regular tuition, though regretting her
inability to study the classics there. She remained a committed and

evangelical Christian throughout her life, though she was hostile to denominational and sectarian narrowness, and the imposition of religious dogma on young children.[4] Her first publication, in 1785, was an article in *The Lounger*, edited by Henry Mackenzie, whose periodicals marked an attempt to create a civic morality appropriate to a refined and commercial society, in which private life and the domestic circle were the chief sources of sympathy and sensibility.[5] Her brother, Charles, in India since 1772, encouraged through correspondence her intellectual ambitions. After his return in 1786, she enjoyed the access to London literary circles which he could give her. Her project to found a periodical, *The Breakfast Table*, in England on similar lines to *The Lounger* was soon abandoned. Where the hero of Mackenzie's *Lounger* had been 'Benevolus', a country gentleman attached to his community and native land, Hamilton's was to be one 'Alfred Freeman'. Her first novel, the *Translation of the Letters of a Hindoo Rajah* (1796), was published after her brother's death and very much influenced by his career. In it, she viewed her own society – and especially the situation of women and their education – through the constructed lens of a benevolent and credulous Rajah.

But Hamilton's viewpoint was as much that of an educationalist as a novelist. The educational philosophy of her next publication was based on an ambitious reading of the works of the Scottish moral philosopher Dugald Stewart.[6] In the preface to her *Letters on the Elementary Principles of Education* (1801), she noted how effectively national character, even in the early stages of society – whether among the American Indians, inured to hardship and torture, or among the Hindus, observing the dietary rules of caste from their earliest years – was shaped by the responsibility of mothers for early education, which determined a child's patterns of desire and aversion. Women's intellectual powers were capable of acquiring the knowledge of the human mind and its psychology needed for these duties, 'throughout all the stages of society'. Those duties included above all the control of the selfish passions. Hamilton here closely followed Stewart's *Elements of the Philosophy of the Human Mind* (1792), and his explanation of how the association of ideas acquired in early childhood, which regulated the succession of thoughts and actions, shaped both the intellectual powers and the moral character of the individual.[7] To watch over the associations formed in the infant mind was the task of mothers. Hamilton expected her female readers to follow her discussions of the philosophy of mind, and added a fuller explanation of the term 'association of ideas' in the second edition of the *Letters*.

Nevertheless her next project was one which sought to illustrate rather than to expound her principles. After the *Letters*, Elizabeth Hamilton saw her next task, not as writing another 'narrative of fictitious events' but using, for the first time, for her own purposes, 'the records of authentic history', in her *Memoirs of Agrippina, the Wife of Germanicus* (1804).[8]

Why history? And why Agrippina? To Hamilton, history could offer an illustration of philosophical principles, in demonstrating the workings of the passions, the affections, and the appetites, and how they had been inculcated in early life. Hamilton's writing can be located within the 'philosophical' approach to history, shared by such Enlightenment historians as Hume, Gibbon, Voltaire and Robertson.[9] Such writers assumed the uniformity of human nature across the world, attempted to construct the laws of development that governed the progressive history of societies, and were as interested in economic progress, manners and mentalities as in political and military narratives. Scottish and French historians drew upon European descriptions of the different cultures encountered in the eighteenth and earlier centuries, many of which included discussion of gender relations, forms of marriage, and the status of women, and on the European historical and classical past. They constructed a hierarchy of the stages of development, a ladder of human societies, at the top of which was the apex, European 'civilisation'. Hamilton's reference to the 'stages of society' in the Preface to her *Letters* locates her within this tradition.

Yet, for such writers as William Robertson and John Millar, these stages were imprecisely drawn. Sometimes the evidence was missing, Dugald Stewart had coined the term 'conjectural history' for the practice, already clear in the 1770s and 1780s of speculating from evidence based on similar societies on the likely course of events.[10] Sometimes admiration for the classical past, and especially for the Greek and Roman Republics, could displace a more rigid application of a hierarchical model. Even if the language of republicanism no longer seemed entirely appropriate to the modern commercial nation at the end of the eighteenth century, it might still provide a source of inspiration and imagery, as it did for Revolutionary France. The conflict of ideals between the simplicity of republican manners and the potentially corrupting wealth and luxury of modern civilisation was not entirely resolved in the work of such historians.

Few women, on the face of it, wrote history at all in the eighteenth century. Thomas Peardon's list of 157 English historians writing between 1760 and 1830 includes only three women.[11] A survey of Janet Todd's *Dictionary of British and American Women Writers, 1660–1800* produced only nine historians from 450 women writers.[12] Even among these, it is hard to find women with ambitions to write 'philosophical history', though Mary Wollstonecraft's *Historical and Moral View of the Origin and Progress of the French Revolution* (1794) was an exception. Yet as Isobel Grundy has suggested elsewhere, perhaps 'the presumed absence is merely an absence of what we have mistakenly expected to find'.[13] The

Memoirs of Agrippina have not previously been recognised as a work of history.

The absence of ambitious historical writing, in the spirit of a Gibbon or a Robertson, is unsurprising. Hamilton wrote modestly of her own incapacity for the task she had set herself. She had no Latin, read her extensive sources in translation, and called on male friends for translations of essential material.[14] She sought approval at every stage of her work from Dugald Stewart, to whom she submitted her half-finished manuscript. He gave his full support, suggesting a series of comparative biographies, with ancient characters balanced by modern, and beginning with John Locke.[15] With this encouragement she gained sufficient confidence to ask her publisher for £200 a volume, and £100 more if it went to a second edition.[16]

Why Agrippina? One part of the answer is clear. Hamilton writes of the absence of women from the historical record, a record devoted mainly to men as 'the conquerors and disturbers of the earth'. Agrippina had escaped the invisibility of women in history – largely, she says, through 'the masterly hand of Tacitus', in his *Annals of the Roman Empire*.[17] Her plan was to begin her biographical project with subjects of her own sex, the two Agrippinas, mother and daughter. Yet the biographer of a woman faced problems, for 'the springs which operate in private life' were rarely displayed by the historian. Hamilton defended the choice of an individual who was not a private citizen, but a member of an imperial family, because of the insight offered into the workings of the passions 'in the rank soil of unlimited power'. But she also claimed the right, in the spirit of conjectural history, 'in the manner that appeared most consonant to probability' for 'circumstances which it suited not the dignity of history to record' to reconstruct the domestic detail of everyday life.[18] Yet the question of why she selected the setting of the early years of the Roman Empire remains.

'It was the perusal of Tacitus, in Murphy's translation, which first excited the idea in my mind', she wrote.[19] Arthur Murphy's translation of the complete works of the Roman historian Tacitus, with fully accompanying notes, was published in 1793. Tacitus' works had for long been a political and literary weapon in the hands of translators and political commentators.[20] Murphy's translation was dedicated to Edmund Burke, in the spirit of the war against Revolutionary France in 1793: 'The regicides of France had the vanity to offer their new lights and wild metaphysics to a people who have understood and cherished Civil Liberty from the Invasion of Julius Caesar to the present hour'.

He noted that in the *Germania*, Burke would find 'the origins of that Constitution which you have so ably defended' and in the *Agricola*, 'that

holy flame of liberty' so long the envy of other nations.[21] As Howard
Weinbrot has suggested, Murphy's translation should be taken as a contribution to the emerging identity of a northern and commercial nation
with its roots in an ancient Britain and an ancient Germany.

However, Murphy's translation of the *Germania* may also be set into a
different debate, on the nature of gender relations in tribal societies. For
the *Germania* does not only describe the political and military structures of
early German tribes, but the relationships between women and men in
those tribes. It remains a point of departure for historians of early
medieval European women today.[22] Tacitus noted the participation of
women who followed men to battle, there treating their wounds, supplying food, and even helping to rally the armies (chs 7–8). He described
how the responsibility for the care of house and fields was left to women
and to men unable to fight, and gave much detail of everyday life, including dress, food and the layout of housing (chs 16, 17, 22, 23). And in three
short sections (chs 18–20), he analysed the structures and expectations of
marriage among the early German tribes, largely monogamous, in which
the husband brought a dowry to his wife, rather than the wife to husband.
The marriage ceremony was marked by an exchange of gifts, symbolising
'the most sacred bond of union, sanctified by mystic rites under the favour
of the presiding deities of wedlock'. Chastity was preserved by harsh
punishments for adulterous women.[23]

Both English and Scottish historians of the late eighteenth century had
recognised in the *Germania* a statement about the situation of women and
their high status among the early tribes, including the ancestors of Anglo-
Saxon England. That statement could be both emphasised and contested
in attempts to trace a gendered national identity within the past, and to
mark out that identity from the cultural variety of the present. Thomas
Percy's translation of Paul-Henri Mallet's *Introduction à l'histoire de
Dannemarc* (1755), as *Northern Antiquities* (1770), popularised the view of
the common heritage of northern nations, and made full use of Tacitus'
portrait of women's role in ancient Germany. Gilbert Stuart's *A View of
Society in Europe* (1778) followed Mallet, adding to the discussion a weight
of historical and antiquarian scholarship. To William Robertson, the
historian of America, and to others writing the history of progressive
stages of development in human history, women were drudges and
'slaves' in the early stages of society, in Germany as in north America. Yet
for Mallet, Percy and Stuart, the high status of women among the German
tribes described by Tacitus indicated the distinctive destiny of northern
European nations.[24]

Murphy's commentary made it clear that while drawing on an range of
scholarship on other 'savage' peoples, as well as on much classical and

historical scholarship, to illuminate Tacitus' testimony, he was contributing to the formation of a national identity, to be contrasted both with
that of Greece and Rome, and with other early peoples. He commented
for instance on Chapter 18 of the *Germania*, on marriage among the early
Germans:

> In this passage Tacitus seizes the opportunity to commend the noble simpli-
> city of the German marriages, in order to pass a pointed censure on the nuptial
> ceremonies established at Rome, and the facility with which both sexes
> violated the marriage bar. ... The simplicity and virtue of the marriage
> contract among the tribes of Germany are given by Tacitus as a striking
> contrast to the depravity of Roman manners. ... Among the wild Canadians
> it appears that women were not in the same estimation as in Germany [sic].[25]

He wrote of the superiority of 'the natural reason, the instinct, it may be
said, of the German tribes, to the boasted philosophy of Greece and
Rome!', seen in the strength of their domestic affections.

In *Agrippina* Hamilton believed that she was writing not only a historical biography, but a 'philosophical' and 'conjectural' history of women,
which also looked to the origins of the nation. Clearly hostile to Wollstonecraft's hopes for 'a revolution in female manners' on republican principles, she was committed to the war against France. Like other Scottish
Whig historians, she had come to associate ideas of liberty with the
experience of Anglicisation, and the emergence, as Colin Kidd has argued, of
an 'Anglo-British' identity which marginalised the Scottish past.[26] We
have already seen her reference to her 'Saxon' ancestry, and her use of
'Alfred Freeman'. Linda Colley has written of women's deployment of
their own language of patriotism, the language of British womanhood, as
a new and justifiable route into public affairs in the years of the Napoleonic wars.[27] Elizabeth Hamilton was here reviewing, through her
historical writing, the ways in which British women could participate in
the shaping of the national character.

Hamilton assumed her readers' familiarity with the events of Agrippina's
life, though modern readers are unlikely to be so conversant. Agrippina
was born in the early years of the Roman Empire. The Roman Republic
had proved itself unable to take on the responsibilities of ever-growing
new territories. The first Emperor, Augustus, stabilised the Empire
through his long reign from 31 BC to AD 14, and passed it on to his
adopted heir, the Emperor Tiberius. Agrippina was born into the imperial
house around 10 BC, educated in the last years of Augustus, and as the
representative of a rival branch of the family, spent her adult life pursued,
harassed, and persecuted by the jealousy of Tiberius. Her story was one of
many complex intrigues and struggles for power, clearly following
Tacitus' *Annals of Imperial Rome*, and Hamilton retold it for three long

volumes. Here, the setting and pattern of Agrippina's early life and marriage in Rome, her visit to the German tribes, and her imprisonment and death will be discussed.

Hamilton's first chapter was a 'philosophical' history of an empire in transition, still shaped by the legacy of the republic, yet vulnerable to increasing luxury. Contradictory forces had shaped the Roman character. The political institutions of the republic had instilled a sense of patriotism, an identification with the nation. That patriotism was reared and nourished in the home; female manners had shaped the republic. A Roman matron 'animated her mind in the instruction of her children and the regulation of her family'. Her ambition lay in 'an increase of the fame and glory of her race'. Hamilton noted that such strength and fortitude were not necessarily amiable, but that 'never, indeed does the female character appear to have been more esteemed or venerated', and that such female influence had facilitated the progress of civilisation at Rome.[28]

Yet there were weaknesses, even at the heart of the republic, and these weaknesses were the love of pride and the canker of slavery. As the republic became an empire, and Romans increasingly brought others under subjection, so patriotism became national arrogance, and an acceptance of tyranny and cruelty already nourished by slavery, for 'the degrading influence of this pernicious system operates upon the enslaver no less than upon the enslaved'.[29] The superstitious beliefs of Romans could not restrain the love of domination, or cruelty to the oppressed, even in an age of some refinement. And the surest indication of corruption at the heart of power lay in the unrestrained sexual depravity of the Empire. Roman marriage was dynastic and expedient, 'an institution of policy' from which affection was absent.[30] Under the Republic frugality and activity had preserved it, but under the Empire there were no such safeguards.

The parallels suggested with contemporary Britain, whose wealth and empire were both growing dynamically, were significant, and familiar to contemporaries. Christopher Bayly, writing of the new British Empire around 1800, has commented that for British statesmen, 'the model – both positive and negative – was the Roman empire'.[31] The movement for the abolition of slavery, to which women writers were actively contributing, had been gathering strength since the 1780s.[32]

To Hamilton, Agrippina's early life exemplified some of the positive aspects of early imperial Rome. Born into the royal house, she was exceptionally fortunate to be betrothed in infancy to Germanicus, named after his father's conquests in Germany, and to be educated in the house of one of the few remaining virtuous Roman matrons, Antonia, the mother of her future husband. Together, Agrippina and Germanicus came to know each other, and their complementary characters, his gentleness and wisdom, and her vivacity and pride. We learn that 'his gentle virtues were perhaps roused to greater energy by her superior spirit and vivacity' and 'in Germanicus were seen the dignified virtues of an ancient republican, blended with all the graces of modern politeness'.[33] Both enjoyed literature and learning, and learned much from Augustus' patronage of the arts in his last years. They read and conversed in Greek, sharing their studies. Germanicus did not consider Agrippina as inferior, but as his chosen companion, whose learning would not divert her from her serious duties.

In their home a firm but not oppressive rule among the slaves was maintained by Agrippina. Spinning and weaving were still a part of the duties of a virtuous matron. Everything was made at home. As Agrippina supervised the activity of the household, she would listen to readings from favourite authors by a young female slave educated for the purpose. But of all her duties, the care of her children was the most important, and she instructed them from the point at which they began to talk. Here Hamilton combined in her portrait of a marriage the domestic virtues of the republic with the attractions of learning, literature and sociability in the polite society of early Augustan Rome. There are echoes here of her appreciation of the advantages of that London literary world, only too evidently at the centre of an empire, to which she was introduced by her brother.

In the year of Augustus' death, AD 14, the Roman armies on the Rhine mutinied, and Germanicus, accompanied by Agrippina, was sent by the new Emperor, Tiberius, to crush the mutinies, and also the rebellious Gaulish and German peoples. In the last three chapters of Book 1, Hamilton showed her readers the reactions of Agrippina, who was clearly located in an imperial context, as wife to the representative of the empire, to the unfamiliar cultures and peoples she encountered, and in particular to the German tribes. She apologised in this section of her work for following Agrippina into scenes where historians had not placed her, yet noted that though reconstruction of her role was 'merely conjectural' it would be found to follow Tacitus so exactly, that 'the picture may be depended upon as genuine'.[34]

This, then, was 'conjectural history', and it was also an encounter with cultural difference. Agrippina was shown to draw hasty analogies and make rapid judgements of superiority over the German peoples. She had failed to reflect how recently the Romans themselves might have been in a similar state of civilisation for 'such an idea of her ancestors would have been too shocking to Agrippina to be permitted to enter her imagination'. Although she was proud of tracing her ancestry she did not take into account that 'every step she ascended brought her nearer to barbarism'.[35] Hamilton represented Agrippina as placing the Gauls very precisely –

though more 'polished' and Romanised than the Germans or Britons – they were still 'in a very early stage of civilisation'.[36] When Germanicus moved on from Gaul to the army of the Upper Rhine, Agrippina was sent away for her safety, to the German town of Ubiorum Oppidan (Cologne) to take refuge from army mutinies.

Hamilton followed Tacitus precisely in her descriptions of the clothing, the diet, the drunkenness of German men, the layout of housing in the town and the exchange of gifts at the marriage ceremony. She recorded Agrippina's arrival, and her welcome by the German chief:

> 'Our wives', said the chief in presenting his to the princess, 'our wives are unadorned except with modesty. Their treasure is the affection of their husbands and the reverence of their children. You who are a virtuous wife and happy mother will find them worthy of your protection!'
>
> Agrippina, returning a proper compliment, saluted the honourable matrons with great complacency.[37]

The word 'complacency' here is worth dwelling on; John Dwyer has traced its eighteenth-century meaning as a kind of social sensibility, an ease, agreeableness, and willingness to please, characteristic especially of the women in polite society, to whom Scottish literary figures like Henry Mackenzie addressed their novels and prescriptive works.[38] Hamilton here incorporated a dialogue, defending it as a practice of Tacitus.[39]

Although, by Roman standards, Agrippina had had a simple upbringing, yet even to her the life of the German women was frugal, domesticated, and industrious, untainted even by the relatively simple vices, drunkenness and idleness, of men. She had been allotted a house surrounded by a small enclosure, as was the German custom, but found it homely and smoky. In turn, the daughter of a German chief, attending at her toilette, commented on Agrippina's numerous servants:

> 'Is the lady lame' asked the young barbarian, 'that she requires so much assistance? … Alas that one so great should be so helpless!'
>
> The pride of the Roman was piqued at thus exciting only pity, where she expected admiration. 'And has your mother then no slaves to attend her person?' asked Agrippina.
>
> 'Oh no;' replied the girl, 'my mother is too proud to be dependent. Our slaves live in their own houses, and take care of their own families; they till the ground, and raise corn, and take care of the vineyards; but they do not come near us, we want none of their assistance'.[40]

Agrippina's meeting with the 'honourable matrons' of the German tribes showed the 'complacent' Roman, the representative of a wealthy empire whose first instinct in the encounter had been a judgement of cultural superiority, learning more about an alien people. Yet Hamilton was also, at the same time, constructing a moral contrast, between the proud matron, educated in republican values yet still dependent on her slaves, and the independence of the German domestic household.

The dialogue continued. Agrippina was invited to a German wedding, marked again by great simplicity of dress, and she witnessed the exchange of gifts between bride and groom described by Tacitus. The wife was to be her husband's 'companion in war, the partner of his toil and danger' with 'but one country and one fate', guardian of her husband's honour. The contrast drawn was with the dynastic opportunistic marriages of the Roman Empire. It was the high regard in which women were held, Hamilton suggests, which Agrippina *might* have seen − conjecture again − as the cause rather than effect of the German achievements.[41]

In these sections Hamilton herself entered the narrative, reminding us at a number of points that it was 'our German ancestors' of whom she was writing, ancestors who lacked their own historian to match a Tacitus. She commented that Agrippina herself would have been astonished 'had she been told that at the distance of nearly eighteen hundred years, her history would be written by a female descendant of the barbarians she despised'.[42] Hamilton's sympathies had shifted, and that shift was reflected in another 'conjectural' incident, though the individuals all appear in Tacitus. On the evening of the wedding, Agrippina is depicted as giving shelter to Thusnelda, wife of Arminius, the leader of the German forces, who was fleeing from her father, in alliance with the Romans, to her husband. The shelter had been unrecorded by Tacitus. Thusnelda was ultimately to be recaptured and returned to her father; even the admirable Germanicus, Hamilton suggests, had in imperial Rome no opportunity to obey 'the generous impulse of sensibility'.[43]

And it is at this point that Hamilton asked her readers to consider the consequences of empire. The Roman leader was unable to respect the spirit of liberty which Arminius and Thusnelda represented. There was thought only of the glory of Rome, of future conquests, Agrippina, though sympathetic to Thusnelda, felt 'no conscientious scruples concerning the morality of invading the territories of a free and unoffending people'.[44] The patriotism of the republic had become the pride and ambition of an empire; and the German Thusnelda was to appear as captive in Germanicus' triumphal procession through Rome.

The question posed within this narrative could be read as: what hope was there for a contemporary empire, one which sought to safeguard the spirit of liberty inherited from the German forests? Was it irretrievably flawed by the spirit of conquest and ambition? The answer to such questions was to be found in Hamilton's account of the imprisonment and ultimate death of Agrippina. She recorded, in a volume and a half, the details of Tiberius' increasingly harsh persecution of Germanicus and Agrippina, including Germanicus' death, and the deaths of two of their sons. Agrippina as a widow was represented as motivated above all by notions of honour and revenge, her pride at the foundation of her increasing misery. As Tiberius and his leading minister Sejanus destroyed her family and friends, so imperial Rome succumbed to vice and luxury.

By the year AD 30 Agrippina was imprisoned on a small island in the Mediterranean under the harshest of conditions. Ill-treated by the soldiers of the garrison, she was assaulted by the centurion in charge and lost the sight of an eye. Though she tried to starve herself to death, she was forcibly fed. Here, the writer again intervened, noting that it would be highly improper in her, as a Christian writer, not to offer an account of the events taking place elsewhere in the Roman Empire in that year, events foretold in the Book of Daniel. For it was Tiberius' minister Sejanus who had appointed the provincial governor of Judaea called Pontius Pilate, and in his name that Pontius Pilate pronounced the sentence of crucifixion on Jesus Christ.[45] Providence had chosen to make the Romans witnesses of the death of Christ, and also witnesses of his resurrection.

Unlike the triumph over death of Jesus Christ, for Agrippina there was no resurrection; she died three years later. Hamilton's concluding words suggest that though she had acted according to her ideas of virtue – 'her ideas of virtue were imperfect'.[46] Republican motherhood was flawed, flawed by personal pride, a passion incompatible with the purest virtue, and flawed by the very existence of slavery at the heart of the republic. To Hamilton only a Christian empire might aspire to overcome the divisions of culture and of race:

> Imperfectly as Christianity has operated in conquering the pride of the human heart, it has removed the barriers which before its introduction separated man from man. The mean and narrow policy of avarice and selfishness may still affect to believe in radical distinctions, and teach us that complexion ought to be the criterion of human sympathy; but these sentiments are confined to the ignorant and the interested, while the enlightened of every Christian nation consider the inhabitants of the globe as the children of one common parent.[47]

Here then was a merging of patriotic and Christian history. Hamilton's message was by no means a simple one. If in the political context of the period, of the war against Napoleonic France and the discrediting of revolution, the ideal of republican motherhood had lost its appeal, the 'complacency' and polite sensibility of Augustan Rome were not altogether to be rejected. If the origins of the British nation were to be found in the liberty, simplicity and domesticity of the lives of the women of the German forests, the German tribes nevertheless awaited the gift of Christian conversion. The Christian empire of the future needed to recast its institutions in the spirit not so much of a patriotism which sought glory and conquest, but of benevolence, a benevolence which drew its affections and its sensibility from the virtues of domestic education and inspiration.

Sadly Hamilton's book was not well reviewed. Most critics classed it under 'Novels and Romances', doubting the usefulness of 'an inconvenient confusion of fact and fiction', of mixing 'prophane history with Christian reflections'.[48] The *Scots Magazine*, however, compared her style with that of Gibbon, for 'if a little inferior in magnificence, it is in a great measure free from his bad taste'.[49] The book did not run to a second edition, and she did not continue her plan for a series of comparative biographies.

Though Hamilton wrote no more history, her political interventions continued, through her last novel, *The Cottagers of Glenburnie* (1808), set among the Scottish peasantry, and through her educational writing. In her substantially revised *Letters on the Elementary Principles of Education* (1810), she wrote of the duty of:

> the Christian and the patriot, to raise the female mind to a sense of the dignity of a situation, which enables it not only to effect the happiness or misery of individuals, but to influence the character of nations, and ameliorate the condition of the human race.[50]

She contrasted the task facing mothers in her own society with the duties of mothers in 'the first stages of civilization', and with 'the bigot mother' of 'nations pretending to civilization', but crippled by superstition.[51]

One part, then, of her contradictory political enterprise lay in the definition, in which the legacy of Tacitus played its part, of that distinctive 'Anglo-British' national character which it was to be the task of mothers to shape. Nevertheless, just as Hamilton had seen the career of Agrippina exemplifying the dangers of the pursuit of imperial glory, so she was to suggest that a love of one's country which was merely a modification of the selfish principle should be distinguished from 'genuine patriotism'.[52] That 'genuine patriotism' was to be found in maintaining the Christian imperative, indeed the Christian mission, to universal benevolence and improvement, whether to be carried to a Scottish peasantry or to other societies in earlier 'stages of development'. Hamilton was here helping to construct a different kind of faith, one to be shared by 'the enlightened of every Christian nation', in the unquestioned benefits of her own white, Christian and domestic civilisation.[53]

Notes

I should like to thank the Nuffield Foundation for support during the writing of this paper. I would also like to acknowledge how much I have learned from sharing work and conversation on Elizabeth Hamilton with Ruth Symes, and to thank Ludmilla Jordanova and Clarissa Campbell Orr for their comments and help.

1   Elizabeth Hamilton, *Memoirs of Modern Philosophers* (Bath, R. Cruttwell, for G. G. and J. Robinson, London, 1800), 3 vols, vol. I, p. 196.

2   This article was completed in draft before I was able to read Gary Kelly's *Women, Writing and Revolution, 1790–1827* (Oxford, Clarendon Press, 1993); his chapters 4 and 8 now form by far the best introduction to Hamilton's work. See also Rosalind Russell, 'Women of the Scottish Enlightenment: their importance in the history of education', Ph.D. University of Glasgow, 1988.

3   Miss [Elizabeth] Benger, *Memoirs of the late Mrs Elizabeth Hamilton: With a Selection from her Correspondence and other Unpublished Writings*, 2 vols (London, Longman, Hurst, Rees, Orme and Brown, 1818), pp. 7–8, 13. All biographical information is taken from these *Memoirs*, unless otherwise indicated.

4   *See her Letters on the Elementary Principles of Education*, 1st edition, (Vol. I, Bath, R. Cruttwell, 1801; vol. 2, Bath, R. Cruttwell, 1802), vol. I, Letters V–VI, and pp. 405–8; *Memoirs*, vol. I, p. 40.

5   See on this circle John Dwyer, *Virtuous Discourse: Sensibility and Community in Late Eighteenth-Century Scotland* (Edinburgh, John Donald, 1987).

6   On Stewart, see Knud Haakonssen, 'From moral philosophy to political economy: the contribution of Dugald Stewart', in Vincent Hope (ed.), *Philosophers of the Scottish Enlightenment* (Edinburgh, Edinburgh University Press, 1984); Stefan Collini, Donald Winch and John Burrow, *That Noble Science of Politics: A Study in Nineteenth Century Intellectual History* (Cambridge, Cambridge University Press, 1983) ch. I.

7   See the references to Stewart, in her *Letters*, vol. I, pp. 20, 29, 304–7, 403–4; vol. 2, pp. 8, 69, 186, 349, 378; *Memoirs*, vol. I, pp. 33–4.

8   *Memoirs*, vol. 2, p. 42; *Memoirs of the Life of Agrippina, the Wife of Germanicus*, 3 vols. (Bath, R. Cruttwell, 1804).

9   Peter Gay, *The Enlightenment; An Interpretation. vol 2. The Science of Freedom* (London, Weidenfeld and Nicolson, 1970), ch. 8; Ronald Meek, *Social Science and the Ignoble Savage* (Cambridge, Cambridge University Press, 1976); Stuart Hall and Bram Gieben (eds), *Formations of Modernity* (Oxford, Polity Press, 1992), pp. 309–20.

10   Stewart first used the term in print in his 'Account of the Life and Writings of Adam Smith LL.D.' [1793], reprinted in W. P. D. Wightman and J. C. Bryce (eds), *Adam Smith: Essays on Philosophical Subjects* (Oxford, Oxford University Press, 1980), p. 293.

11   Thomas Peardon, *The Transition in British Historical Writing, 1760–1830*, (New York, Columbia University Press, 1933), pp. 310–25. See also Natalie Zemon Davis, 'Gender and genre: women as historical writers, 1400–1820', in Patricia H. Labalme (ed.), *Beyond Their Sex: Learned Women of the European Past* (New York and London, New York University Press, 1984); Bonnie Smith, 'The contribution of women to modern historiography in Great Britain, France and the United States', *American Historical Review*, 89 (1984), 709–32.

12   Hannah Adams, Ellis Cornelia Knight, Deborah Norris Logan, Catherine Macaulay, Hester Piozzi, Sarah Scott, Mercy Otis Warren, Helen Maria Williams, and Mary Wollstonecraft, Janet Todd, A Dictionary of British and American Women Writers 1660–1800 (London, Methuen, 1987).

13   Isobel Grundy, 'Women's History? Writings by English nuns', in Isobel Grundy and

Susan Wiseman (eds), *Women, Writing, History 1640–1740* (London, B. T. Batsford, 1992), p. 126.

14 *Agrippina*, vol. I, pp. xxviii–xxxi.

15 *Memoirs*, vol. 2, pp. 45–63. Dugald Stewart can be clearly identified through, for instance, the reference to his biography of William Robertson.

16 Elizabeth Hamilton to George Robinson, 29 November 1803, National Library of Scotland MS 585 f. 48. She proposed in this letter that the full title of the work should be 'Memoirs of the elder Agrippina, being the commencement of a series of Comparative Biography, illustrative of the principles of the human mind'.

17 *Agrippina*, vol. I, p. xxvi. For a discussion of representations of Agrippina by Scottish artists Gavin Hamilton, Alexander Runciman, and Katherine Read, in the 1760s and 1770s, see Duncan Macmillan, 'Woman as Hero: Gavin Hamilton', in Gill Perry and Michael Rossington (eds), *Femininity and Masculinity in Eighteenth-Century Art and Culture* Manchester (Manchester University Press, 1994), pp. 84–7.

18 *Ibid.*, vol. I, pp. 41–2; *Agrippina*, vol. I, pp. xxii–viii.

19 *Memoirs*, vol. I, p. 44.

20 Howard D. Weinbrot, 'Politics, taste, and national identity: some uses of Tacitus in eighteenth-century Britain', in T. J. Luce and A. J. Woodman (eds), *Tacitus and the Tacitean Tradition* (Princeton, Princeton University Press, 1993).

21 Arthur Murphy, *The Works of Cornelius Tacitus; With an Essay on the Life and Genius of Tacitus: Notes, Supplements and Maps* 4 vols. (London, G. G. and J. Robinson, 1793), 'Dedication'.

22 See Suzanne Wemple, *Women in Frankish Society: Marriage and the Cloister 500 to 900* (Philadelphia, University of Pennsylvania Press, 1981), pp. 10–15.

23 Tacitus, *The Agricola and the Germania*, translated … by H. Mattingly … revised by S. A. Handford (Harmondsworth, Penguin, 1970).

24 See my forthcoming article, 'Tacitus engendered: "Gothic feminism" and British history'.

25 Murphy, *Works*, vol. 4, pp. 240–1.

26 On the term 'Anglo-British', see Colin Kidd, *Subverting Scotland's Past: Scottish Whig Historians and the Creation of an Anglo-British Identity, 1689–c. 1830* (Cambridge, Cambridge University Press, 1993). 'Introduction'.

27 Linda Colley, *Britons: Forging the Nation 1707–1837* (New Haven and London, Yale University Press, 1992), pp. 273–81.

28 *Agrippina*, I, pp. 18–20.

29 *Ibid.*, I, p. 28.

30 *Ibid.*, I, pp. 45–6.

31 C. A. Bayly, *Imperial Meridian: The British Empire and the World, 1780–1830*, (London, Longman, 1989), p. 160; Frank Parker, 'British Politics and the demise of the Roman Republic: 1700–1939', *Historical Journal*, 29 (1986), 577–99.

32 See Moira Ferguson, *Subject to Others: British Women Writers and Colonial Slavery, 1670–1834* (New York, Routledge, 1992); for Hamilton's views, see the *Translation of the Letters of a Hindoo Rajah…*, 2 vols (London, G. G. and J. Robinson, 1796), vol. 1, pp. 86–9, and her *Letters*, vol. 1, p. 185 note.

33 *Agrippina*, vol. I, pp. 116, 157–8.

34 *Agrippina*, vol. I, pp. 315–16 (note V).

35 *Ibid.*, vol. I, pp. 193–5.

36 *Ibid.*, vol. I, pp. 231–2.

37 *Ibid.*, vol. I, pp. 259–60.

38 Dwyer, *Virtuous Discourse*, p. 118.

39 *Agrippina*, vol. I, p. 316 (note V).

40 *Ibid.*, vol. I, pp. 260–1.
41 *Ibid.*, vol. I, pp. 272–80.
42 *Ibid.*, vol. I, p. 191, and vol. 2, p. 58.
43 *Ibid.*, vol. I, pp. 285–6, and vol. 2, p. 18.
44 *Ibid.*, vol. 2, p. 44.
45. *Ibid.*, vol. 3, pp. 277–83.
46 *Ibid.*, vol. 3, p. 342.
47 *Ibid.*, vol. 2, pp. 21–2.
48 *Annual Review*, 3 (1804), 542–4; *Monthly Review*, New series, 50 (July 1806), 274–8; *Critical Review*, 3rd series, 7 (Feb. 1806), 188–90; *Monthly Magazine*, 19, Supplementary number (July 28 1805), 660; *British Critic*, 26 (July 1805), 26–33.
49 *Scots Magazine*, 66 (December 1804), 930–5.
50 *Letters on the Elementary Principles of Education*, 5th edition, 2 vols (London, Wilkie and Robison, and G. Robinson, 1810), vol. I, p. 21.
51 *Ibid.*, vol. I, pp. 2–3.
52 Elizabeth Hamilton, *A Series of Popular Essays, Illustrative of Principles Essentially Connected with the Improvement of the Understanding, the Imagination, and the Heart* (Edinburgh, Manners and Millar, 1813), 2 vols. vol. I, p. 410.
53 See Catherine Hall, 'Missionary stories: gender and ethnicity in England in the 1830s and 1840s', in *White, Male and Middle Class: Explorations in Feminism and History* (Oxford, Polity Press, 1992), for a further discussion of these themes.

4

Politics without feminism: The Victorian political hostess

K. D. Reynolds

DUCHESSES, Martin Pugh has observed, are available at a discount for the historian.[1] Neglected by political and social historians as at best of marginal interest,[2] aristocratic women have also been largely ignored by historians of women and gender.[3] The former is regrettable, but unsurprising. For feminist historians, the aristocratic woman has been an unappealing subject in consequence of the circumstances which characterised her life: privileged but not power-ful, female but not feminist, aristocratic women are difficult to fit into the discourses of women's oppression and liberation which still dominate, albeit in disguise, so much of British women's history. The paradigm of separate spheres which has been central to our understanding of Victorian women for so long presents particular difficulties in relation to women whose most private actions carried enormous public significance, and whose public and political roles were carried out in the privacy of the domestic setting.[4] In part, this article is intended as a contribution to the debate on the validity and utility of the paradigm of the spheres, and as an attempt to demonstrate that 'the political' for Victorian women was not necessarily connected with a sense of gendered identity, nor yet derived from an incipient feminist consciousness.

Several historians have noted the irony that the organised campaigns for women's rights met with little favour among the one group of women who enjoyed a measure of political influence in pre-democratic Britain, upper-class and aristocratic women, and in particular those whom they have defined as political hostesses.[5] I have no quarrel with their conclu-sions, that such women enjoyed more influence indirectly than they could hope to gain through the ballot-box: as with their male counterparts, any dilution of the pool from which political actors was drawn restricted the power and opportunities available for the traditional ruling classes. I do take issue with their methodology and their interpretation of the meanings attached to the Victorian political hostesses. All are concerned to explain late nineteenth- and early twentieth-century phenomena – anti-feminism, the '"actual reality" of the lives of upper-class women' between 1860 and 1914,[6] and the development of popular Toryism – rather than early- and mid-Victorian political culture. Each is concerned to discover the origins of female political action, and to seek them in the political hostess. This retrospective perspective leads them to view the political hostesses as the precursors of the female parliamentarians, as (however unwilling) proto-feminists.[7] A more fruitful approach is to see them in the context of a long line of politically-active aristocratic women, as the end of one tradition rather than the beginning of another.[8] The names of Emily Palmerston, Sarah Jersey, and Frances Waldegrave fit more readily into a sequence of aristocratic Court-based politics that includes Sarah Marlborough, Abigail Masham and Georgiana Devonshire than the civic feminist tradition of Millicent Garrett Fawcett, Emmeline Pankhurst and Ellen Wilkinson – and, indeed, Mary Wollstonecraft. For this reason, this study concentrates on the first forty years of Victoria's reign, during which period the political culture of Britain retained much of its old character whilst gradually making way for the new.[9]

Virtually all aristocratic women were engaged to some degree in activities such as entertaining political connections, exercising patronage, guarding political confidences and offering advice, which were the particular speciality of the political hostess. This poses a problem for us if we wish to recognise a difference between the political hostess and the aristocratic political wife – or in more concrete terms, if we wish to highlight the differences which the Victorians themselves recognised between the parties held by say, Harriet, Duchess of Sutherland (the leading member of the Grand Whiggery in the 1840s and 1850s), and Emily Palmerston, the foremost political hostess of the same period. Jalland evades the problem by conflating the political hostess with the political wife (although admitting to differing degrees of success and competence), and arguing that the work of political entertaining was essentially an activity which could be designated as belonging to the private sphere.[10] By contrast, Pugh sets out a series of intrinsic requirements for a woman who aspired to be a political hostess – a wealthy husband, houses for entertaining, both in the country and near Westminster, and a series of personal characteristics such as beauty, charm and intelligence.[11] Such features undoubtedly were essential; they were not, however, enough. What Pugh cites as the defining characteristics of the political hostess could, with a little imaginative effort (particularly in the areas of beauty and intelligence) be applied to most of the aristocratic female population – and very few of them either aspired to be or succeeded in becoming political hostesses. For example,

Frances Anne, Lady Londonderry met all Pugh's requirements, being additionally the friend, correspondent and patron of Benjamin Disraeli; but she was not, at least in this period, a political hostess.[12]

Personal characteristics played a significant part in creating the political hostesses; the structure of Victorian politics was crucial, and explains the demise of the political hostess towards the end of the century. Family interest on the part of the landed elite remained one of the driving forces of the nineteenth-century political culture in which the aristocratic woman was required to operate. Despite the alterations made to the political structure by the first Reform Act, at the parliamentary level the political community remained predominantly a close-knit, socially cohesive and essentially aristocratic body, certainly until the Reform Act of 1867.[13] Politics, interpreted by those empowered by the political structure, was chiefly seen as the legitimate preserve of the aristocracy; one of the channels of entry into that society by outsiders was through the salons of aristocratic women.[14] It is at this interface between the social and the political that the aristocratic woman found a role in politics which, while exercising a limited impact on the content of political discourse, was of immense importance in defining its context.[15]

The intermingling of the demands of social life and government provided the first condition for the political hostess to flourish,[16] the second was the absence of highly-structured party organisations, either within or outside Parliament. There was no formal method of communication between members, between front and back benches, or between opponents; still fewer were the means of communicating with supporters outside Parliament. Moreover, for much of this period the political parties themselves were in a state of turmoil with members changing party affiliation and a rapid turnover of ideological positions. When members voted in Parliament on the basis of personal conviction or personal advancement and not in accordance with a party whip, much was to be gained by extra-parliamentary persuasion. These conditions noticeably altered during the 1880s, both in terms of the widening of 'Society' itself, and hence the diminishing hegemony of the aristocracy,[17] and in terms of the emergence of more effective parliamentary and constituency party organisations.[18] Thus it is reasonable to assert, as Lady Jeune did in 1895, that Frances Waldegrave was the last of the political hostesses, because after her death the political culture had altered to such an extent that the aristocratic political hostess was essentially redundant.[19]

Perhaps the greatest distinguishing feature of the political hostesses, of which group Ladies Palmerston, Holland, Jersey, Molesworth and Waldegrave were leading examples, was the degree of enthusiasm and perceived success which marked their endeavours, and the centrality which politics played in their lives, which lifted their activities from the general category of the political wife into that of the political hostess. For these women in particular, no distinction can be drawn between activities in a public or a private sphere. Family interest, the furtherance of careers, support for husbands and sons, were all pursuits which, in a binary world, contained both public and private elements. Organising the household, the servants, menus, decorations, and invitations, for the reception and entertainment of guests are, on one level, archetypally feminine, private, domestic activities. Carried out by a political hostess, the tasks remain the same, but the interpretation and the symbolic meaning of the work become different. The party develops a public aspect (not least because such events were frequently reported in the press for an audience beyond the charmed circle of politics), and a potential for political significance. At this point, where private actions have public meanings, where a social event is also political, the language of spheres becomes merely a rhetorical device, misleading in its attempts to clarify. Unlike Linda Kerber, however, I do not advocate the rejection of the language in its entirety – anyone who has attempted to discuss the nineteenth century without recourse to 'worlds, realms, spheres' or other territorial designations must recognise the difficulty of so doing.[20]

But we must constantly realise and emphasise that these are not literal, physical categories, and that the existence of one does not exclude the possibility of the other. An action is not *either* public *or* private in any absolute sense but rather takes its character according to context and the interpretational stance of the beholder. The Victorian world was not binary, despite the best efforts of the Victorians to define it as such: inconsistency and paradox mark real lives in ways of which historical narrative seldom takes account.

The final blow to those who would wish to see the political hostess as either the precursor of the suffrage movement, or as the inheritor of the bluestocking salons is given by the political hostesses themselves. Nowhere in the papers of Ladies Waldegrave and Palmerston have I been able to trace any discussion of themselves as women, still less as women behaving in any way unusually. They carry out their self-imposed functions as political hostesses without any reference to their gender at all.[21] Indeed, any such recognition would be an indication that these women did in fact acknowledge the reality of the separate spheres: to see themselves as acting unusually *for women* would indicate that there was a 'proper sphere' for female activity, and that they were stepping beyond it. The absence of any such recognition is the strongest recommendation (in the absence of direct evidence) for the argument that aristocratic women's political roles were assumed as a matter of class duty and expectation, and not, as middle-class women later claimed, as a right grasped in the name of gender and justice.

The one characteristic that the Victorian political hostesses shared was unorthodox social position. The Canningite Palmerston, it has been noted, 'had never been really liked or accepted by the Whigs',[22] while his wife belonged to a family new to the peerage, with distinctly impeachable moral credentials. Lady Jersey's money came from banking, Lady Holland had been divorced, Lady Molesworth took care to disguise her antecedents, but had been a professional singer for a number of seasons. Lady Waldegrave had bourgeois, theatrical, Jewish parents, and four husbands. With uniformly eccentric social or moral backgrounds, the career of political hostess gave these women the opportunity to establish themselves and their families in the highest ranks of society, from which they might well have been excluded. Brazening out indiscretion had ever been an option, as Lady Blessington demonstrated at Gore House, and as Jane Austen has Mary Crawford suggest in the case of the adulterous Mrs Rushworth: 'In some circles, we know, she would never be admitted, but with good dinners, and large parties, there will always be those who will be glad of her acquaintance'.[23]

'Good dinners and large parties' were the stock-in-trade of the political hostess: they were the arena in which she exercised her tact and authority, incurred obligations, conferred favours. They were also the mechanism through which she contributed to the maintenance of the political culture, through the provision of a specific physical location for extra-parliamentary political activity. Such provision was necessitated not only by the personal preferences of members of the aristocratic elite, but by the inadequacy of the buildings of the Houses of Parliament for social and informal contact between members. Both the Old Palace of Westminster, destroyed by fire in 1834, and the Barry palace which was used by both Houses for the first time in 1852 suffered from severe pressure on space, making alternative venues both desirable and necessary. During the almost twenty-year rebuilding programme, the difficulties were exacerbated. John Wilson Croker had described the Old Palace in 1833 as 'notoriously imperfect, very crazy as buildings, and extremely incommodious in their local distribution.'[24] Sir Charles Barry's replacement building met the original specification for a House of Commons dining-room to seat thirty, illustrating in bricks and mortar the expectation that the majority of members would either own town houses or be in receipt of sufficient invitations to dine as to render a larger facility in Westminster redundant. However, the historian of the buildings, Michael Port, offers the information that in the opening session of 1867, some 6,412 dinners were served, which figure represents more than two hundred members dining on some evenings.[25] Under such circumstances, the close proximity of a number of hostesses offering invitations to dine, or to spend the evening in the company of other political persons (without the embargo on politics which mixed company often entailed) and the possibility of access to men with powers of patronage and political advancement, was of more than mere gastronomic or social benefit. Lady Palmerston's comment on the value of Holland House after the death of its master in 1840 sums up the vital role of these alternative physical locations: 'he is a great loss privately and publickly, for his House kept the Party together, and was of much use as a place of meeting, and had great effect upon literary people, and the second class of politicians'.[26] The 'second class of politicians' were precisely those who had to be wooed and cajoled in a political system without formal party machinery, and it was they who were often the targets of the political hostesses' hospitality.[27]

In basic format, the entertainments remained essentially similar throughout the period. They usually took place in a town house, close to the political centre of Westminster – Lady Palmerston entertained at Carlton House Terrace, and later at Cambridge House, Piccadilly, Lady Waldegrave's house was also in Carlton Gardens, Lady Jersey in Berkeley Square, Lady Molesworth in Eaton Place. Only Holland House was removed from this centre, in Kensington, but it ceased to be an important centre after Holland's death in 1840. As transport improved, the weekend retreat on the outskirts of London became a viable alternative: Frances Waldegrave used her Twickenham residence, Strawberry Hill, to great advantage in this way. One of her guests noted that her husband could go to London daily for the meetings of parliament, and return in time for dinner in the evening, enabling him to fulfil both his political and his social duties.[28]

The hostesses tended to specialise in slightly different forms of party, with different constituencies of guests. Ladies Holland and Jersey usually gave small dinner parties, with allegiance to political party providing the unifying factor among their guests. Lady Palmerston took the evening reception or 'drum' as her principal forum, and invited a broad spectrum of political opinion, while Lady Molesworth was renowned for her dinner parties for a wide range of guests. Lady Waldegrave also gave evening parties in Carlton Gardens, and introduced the idea of the 'Saturday to Monday' party at Strawberry Hill.[29] Her guests were of a far broader social and professional mix than those of any of her predecessors.

These differences reflect changes in the structure of politics and the altering status of political parties. While Lady Holland and Lady Jersey were in their heyday, between say, 1810 and 1845, political allegiances

were relatively well defined, and firmly maintained, with opinion polar-
ising around specific issues – Reform, Catholic Emancipation, the Corn
Laws – with the social implication of separate-party entertaining. Lady
Jersey entertained in a deeply partisan spirit for the Tories and high aristocracy.[30] She claimed to be in the confidence of the Duke of Wellington,
and hence to have access to the latest political information, which provided her salons with appeal to those who sought such knowledge. Her
ties with the Tory leadership were strengthened by the marriage in 1841
of her eldest son with Sir Robert Peel's daughter. Sceptics such as Greville
doubted the extent and accuracy of her information, while Disraeli (who
was one of her protégés) satirised her in his novels as the self-important
but ineffectual Lady St Julians.[31] Lady Holland entertained in a similar
spirit for the Whigs, although her guest-list was affected to some degree
by her social ostracism. The drawbacks, for the hostess at least, of such an
exclusive, political party-based social life were summed up in 1821, by
Lady Cowper (the future Lady Palmerston), who wrote to her brother:

> We had a large dinner on Wednesday for Lady Holland which was uncom-
> monly agreeable because she begged to have a mixed dinner – 'some of the
> company not her daily bread', meaning the big Whigs. I thought her wise for her
> declaration. The same political set at dinner every day must be tiresome in the
> long run – & people of our party call her shabby for not wishing like Ly R.
> Spencer that there should be a deep pit between her and all Tories.[32]

Emily Cowper's willingness to entertain a variety of political opinions
distinguished her from many of her contemporaries. Peter Mandler has
observed that she entertained across the party lines, particularly during
the crisis of Canning's ministry, maintaining 'an atmosphere in which
people of fashion could mingle without letting politics come between
them'.[33] This experience was to prove invaluable during the politically
unstable years from 1846 until Palmerston's death in 1865, during which
time Lady Palmerston's parties came to reflect the shifting coalitions that
made up the governments of the day. Still socially exclusive, the reception
allowed a much broader spectrum of political opinion to be invited,
solicited, cajoled and rewarded than the more intimate dinner parties of
the earlier years. For example, a party was held in Carlton Gardens on
Saturday 28 February 1852, following the collapse of Russell's ministry as
a result of Palmerston's manoeuvrings. Present were a large proportion of
the diplomatic corps and some two hundred and seventy other named
guests, including three members of Derby's newly-formed Tory cabinet,
and/or their wives, and four members of the outgoing administration
and/or their wives – although notably no Russells. Also present were
three members of the Cabinet which Aberdeen was to form in the

following December. This range of political opinion and allegiance was reflected in the backbench MPs attending, some forty-two in number, who came from all shades of the political spectrum.[34] The broad range of political opinion encompassed by Lady Palmerston's parties reflected the instability of the political world of the 1850s and 1860s, whilst the continued dominance of the aristocracy was reinforced by the social exclusivity which limited entry to Cambridge House.

Lady Waldegrave's parties in the later 1860s and 1870s embody a further change in the social structure of politics. The passing of the second Reform Act had broadened the political base, and the authority of aristo-cratic political culture was diminished by the concurrent redistribution of power. Arno J. Mayer's comment that the function of the hostesses was 'to serve as catalysts for the ongoing fusion of the old nobility ... with the new magnates ... on terms favourable to the aristocratic element'[35] holds particularly true under the inexorably changing political circumstances of the post-Reform decade. Frances Waldegrave's background and connec-tions ideally suited her for this more inclusive entertaining. Lady Waldegrave's credentials with the traditional aristocracy were enhanced by her connections through her third husband, George Granville Harcourt, to the Whig grandees, and by her status as the preferred hostess of the deposed French Orleanist royal family.[36] At the same, her theatrical family background gave her connections with the cultural and artistic worlds, whom she introduced into high political society for the first time.[37]

> Lady Waldegrave ... received opponents as well as friends. ... her reception
> rooms were open to Whigs, Tories, and Radicals, as well as to representatives
> of art, science, and literature. She broke away the last barriers of exclusive-
> ness, and socially helped more than anyone to destroy the lines of cleavage.
> She softened the asperities of political life.[38]

Moreover, it was Lady Waldegrave who, following her time in Dublin as wife of the Chief Secretary under successive Liberal governments between 1865 and 1870, first introduced the Irish Home Rule members into society.[39]

If this represents fairly the changing character of the entertainments given by Victorian political hostesses, what did the hostesses aim to achieve by them, and what degree of success attended their efforts? The influence of hostesses has generally been discussed in terms of their positive effect on their husbands' careers, and, indeed, usually dismissed on those grounds.[40] Palmerston would undoubtedly have been Prime Minister without his wife's efforts, and Chichester Fortescue never rose above the mediocre despite the best efforts of Frances Waldegrave.[41] Moreover, many of the most successful politicians were not blessed with political hostesses for wives: Catherine Gladstone's antipathy to the rigours and forms of political entertaining has been frequently noted, whilst Emma, Lady Derby's, efforts in that direction were described by Lord Redesdale as being 'of a dullness as depressing as a London fog'.[42] Because the political hostess has been viewed so extensively in the light of her influence on her husband's career, it has been easy to dismiss her as serious player in the Victorian political game and to reject the idea of her influence.[43]

'Influence' is a particularly difficult feature of the political scene to trace. In the first instance, it was seldom exercised in writing, leaving few quantifiable traces for the historian.[44] There is no study which examines the political effect on potential supporters or opponents of governments and measures, of an invitation to dine, or of the opportunity to be present at a grand reception, and it is doubtful that such a study could be written.[45] Nonetheless, the fact remains that contemporaries certainly believed that such methods were efficacious, as their recorded comments show, and as their eager attendance at such events appears to confirm. Emily Palmerston is quoted as greeting the need for votes to support her husband's ministry with the rallying cry, "Stay! we will have a party."[46] One commentator on her influence suggests that her utility to Palmerston was that 'she cemented his friendships, attracted the waverers, and disarmed many of his political opponents!',[47] while another noted that : 'No political hostess in England ever held the same sway as Lady Palmerston at Cambridge House. ... It was always said that an invitation to her parties had determined many a wavering vote'.[48]

If we attempt to elucidate the actions of Victorian political hostesses, and to explain their contribution to political culture, it is not necessary to quantify or 'prove' that political hostesses in fact exercised political influence: it is enough to show that they believed they did, and that the political culture in which they operated also acted in accordance with that belief. Thus one of the reasons for the declining possibilities for political hostesses after the death of Lady Waldegrave was the result of a diminishing belief in the influence of the hostesses. This can perhaps be linked to the increasing dominance of the domestic ideology (but not, of course its reality), which certainly had an impact on sections of the aristocracy, and in accordance with which, political activity by women, regardless of class, demonstrated unwomanliness. As early as 1842, Anne, Lady Cowper (daughter-in-law to Lady Palmerston) had commented that 'the less a woman has to do with eager, ardent, virulent politics, the better', while Lady John Russell inveighed against the 'regular hardened lady politicians'.[49] Increasing doubts about the propriety of female engagement with politics as hostesses can also be seen in Anthony Trollope's novels of political life in the 1860s. The two fictional hostesses, Lady Laura

Kennedy and Glencora, Duchess of Omnium, are painted in equivocal colours – they behave in accordance with traditional female aristocratic practice, but that practice is itself portrayed as increasingly inappropriate to the political age, and both characters are seriously flawed in terms of the feminine ideal.[50] Frances Waldegrave's jubilant note of 1875 after Hartington had fought off Forster's challenge and become leader of the Liberals in the Commons indicates both her perception of the influence she wielded, and the contrary view: 'Do you remember the *Times* saying the *Salons* had *no* influence now? That *put my back up* & I am *very* glad we came to town in time to be of use'.[51]

While Lady Waldegrave lived, her firm conviction of her influence, and the large circle of her admirers kept the influence of the hostesses (or at least of this particular hostess) going. She had no successor. It is important to note that there was really only one hostess at a time, although Lady Holland and Lady Palmerston coincided for a few year, as did Ladies Palmerston and Waldegrave, each entertaining a slightly different generation of the party. As I hope this chapter shows, this is because these women were the 'official' hostesses not so much to their husbands but to their political party. There was no room, nor any need for more than one such hostess at a time, because the primary function of the entertainments was to enable the members of the party to gather for the transfer of information, for the bestowal and seeking of patronage, and the drumming up of support for measures and men. If more than one hostess entertained for the party, these functions would be diluted and less efficiently carried out. There was also the danger of internal factions meeting at different houses, as to some extent occurred in the 1870s, when Frances Waldegrave increasingly supported the anti-Gladstonian sections of the Liberal Party, leaving Gladstone to the tender mercies of his female relatives' entertaining. The necessity for a single and agreed place where men of differing views could meet was particularly acute in the 1840s and 1850s, as Lady Palmerston recognised: 'The wonderful political events of the last few months have made everybody glad to have some talks, and this has answered particularly now, since all parties meet willingly in our House'.[52]

The political hostesses recognised their activities for what they were – service to the party, and they carried out their self-imposed tasks from a sense of duty as much as from any pleasure in the activity. Shortly after her marriage to Palmerston, Lady Palmerston listed the benefits of her new house, which she considered 'so suited to reception', which were to be able to 'gratify' the diplomatic corps (Palmerston was, of course, Foreign Minister at this time), to 'give our party advantage in many ways', and finally, as something of an afterthought, to 'amuse Fanny', her younger, unmarried daughter.[53] Emily Palmerston clearly did not regard her entertaining primarily in the light suggested by Leonore Davidoff, as a mechanism for regulating 'Society' and the marriage market,[54] but rather as a tool of party politics. In 1849, confronted with the contentious repeal of the Navigation Acts in Parliament, Emily Palmerston wrote to her husband: 'When is the Navigation in the Lords? If the 28th is coming on to that time perhaps *I had better have* [my italics] a party on the 28th. It tends to give a Spirit and to keep the party together & induces our people to meet'.[55] This is as clear a statement of the self-perceived functions of the entertainments given by political hostesses as one could hope to find. Similarly, Frances Waldegrave, in an undated letter concerning a 'hateful' bill in Parliament, mentioned that: 'I am very busy sending out cards for a Party tomorrow night. I had not intended to receive, but but [sic] I think it as well to try to get people together before Thursday'.[56]

More important are her comments on the suggestion that Fortescue might be returned to Ireland as Chief Secretary in 1870:

I never said that I would not go to Ireland *at all*, but that I could only be there during the times it was absolutely necessary for Chichester to carry out his work, & that I should not be such a fool again, as to put my whole heart and soul in the business of making the Govt popular there et cta as I had done last year with as you must know from O Hagan & others great success.[57]

It was not Fortescue whom she had sought to make popular, but the Government: party interest had taken precedence over personal wishes. Of course, this same letter implies that, as the party had not rewarded Fortescue in a suitable manner, Frances would in future place her family interests before those of the party, going to Ireland to support her husband, but not actively to enhance the image of the Liberal Government there. This is a timely reminder that just as the attempt to define all female activity as private is mistaken, it is an error of equal magnitude to swing the other way, and define all female activity as political and to ignore the imperatives of personal ambitions and relationships.

Notes

I have to thank the Trustees of the Broadlands Archives and the Hon. Mrs Crispin Gascoigne for permission to quote from, respectively, the Palmerston Papers and the Harcourt Mss. The staff of the Bodleian Library, the Hartley Library and the Somerset Archive and Record Service were uniformly helpful. Tim Barringer, Michelle Cale, Colin Matthew and Clarissa Campbell Orr all commented on drafts of this paper, for which, my thanks.

1 Martin Pugh, *The Tories and the People 1880–1935* (Oxford, Basil Blackwell, 1985), p. 43.
2 Among those who have touched on the subject of the aristocratic woman are F. M. L. Thompson, *English Landed Society in the Nineteenth Century* (London, Routledge and Kegan Paul, 1963, paperback, 1971) and Peter Mandler, *Aristocratic Government in the Age of Reform: Whigs and Liberals, 1830–1852* (Oxford, Oxford University Press, 1990).

A more common attitude is that of David Cannadine, *The Decline and Fall of the British Aristocracy* (New Haven, Yale University Press, 1990). He explains the absence of women from his book thus: '[It] is concerned with wealth, status, power, and class consciousness, which in this period were preponderantly masculine assets and attributes.' (p. 7).

3 Notable exceptions are Leonore Davidoff's brief sociology of the London Season, *The Best Circles: Society Etiquette and the Season* (London, Croom Helm, 1973, reprinted in The Cresset Library, 1986); Judith Schneid Lewis's examination of aristocratic women and childbirth, *In the Family Way: Childbearing in the British Aristocracy, 1760–1860* (New Brunswick, Rutgers University Press, 1986) and parts of Pat Jalland's *Women, Marriage and Politics 1860–1914* (Oxford, Oxford University Press 1986, paperback, 1988). M. Jeanne Peterson, *Family, Love and Work in the Lives of Victorian Gentlewomen* (Bloomington, Indiana University Press, 1989) examines upper-middle-class women.

4 For instance, marriage in the aristocracy involved the transmission of property, as did child-bearing, and were treated as events of public, if local, importance. See for example, Thompson, *Landed Society*, pp. 76–80; Lewis, *In the Family Way*, chs 1–2. This article discusses the political hostesses, but they are not the unique expression of this duality of meaning for aristocratic women: for example, ladies-in-waiting at Court held public (paid) office, but the setting was overwhelmingly domestic. See my forthcoming D.Phil. thesis, '"Thorough gentlemen"': gender, politics and the Victorian aristocratic woman' (Oxford University).

5 Brian Harrison, *Separate Spheres: The Opposition to Women's Suffrage in Britain* (London, Croom Helm, 1978) pp. 81–3; Pat Jalland, *Women, Marriage and Politics*, pp. 190–95; Martin Pugh, *The Tories and the People*, pp. 43–7.

6 Jalland, *Women, Marriage and Politics*, p. 2.

7 Consider, for example, Jalland's juxtaposition of Lady Palmerston (1787–1869) with Margot Asquith (1864–1945), *Women, Marriage and Politics*, ch. 7.

8 See, for example, Linda Colley's discussion of Georgiana, Duchess of Devonshire in *Britons: Forging the Nation 1707–1837* (New Haven, Yale University Press, 1992) pp. 242–8.

9 There is an extensive literature on continuity in Victorian political culture – see for example, Arno J. Mayer, *The Persistence of the Old Regime: Europe to the Great War* (London, Croom Helm, 1981) and Mandler, *Aristocratic Government*.

10 Jalland, *Women, Marriage and Politics*, especially pp. 198–204.

11 Pugh, *Tories and the People*, p. 44.

12 Edith Vane-Tempest-Stuart, Marchioness of Londonderry, *Frances Anne: The Life and Times of Frances Anne Marchioness of Londonderry* (London, Macmillan, 1958).

13 See, for example, David Cannadine, *Decline and Fall*; Lawrence and Jeanne Fawtier Stone, *An Open Elite?* (Oxford, Oxford University Press, 1984); J. V. Beckett, *The Aristocracy in England 1660–1914* (Basil Blackwell, Oxford, 1986, paperback 1988). The argument that political society remained impervious to outsiders is clearly overstated: new men clearly did enter the political realm. The important point is that assimilation into the dominant culture was virtually essential for political success.

14 An outstanding case was that of W. E. Gladstone, who through his friendship with Harriet, Duchess of Sutherland made important connections with the Whigs. See H. C. G. Matthew, *Gladstone 1809–1874* (Oxford, Oxford University Press, 1986) pp. 49–50.

15 David Cannadine and Simon Price, eds, *Rituals of Royalty: Power and Government in Traditional Societies* (Cambridge, Cambridge University Press, 1987) suggest that the 'theatre of power', in which politics have not only a content, but a form and a context,

deserves greater consideration. It is here that the political hostess finds her place. 'Introduction', pp. 1–2.

16 That the social 'Season' was co-terminous with the meetings of Parliament was no coincidence. Davidoff, *Best Circles*, ch. 2.

17 Cannadine, *Decline and Fall*, ch. 8; Nancy Ellenberger, 'The Transformation of London "Society" at the end of Victoria's Reign: Evidence from the Court Presentation Records', *Albion* 22 (Winter 1990), 633–53.

18 H. J. Hanham, *Elections and Party Management: Politics in the Age of Disraeli and Gladstone* (London, Longmans, 1959); John Vincent, *The Formation of the British Liberal Party* (New York, Charles Scribner's Sons, 1966), especially pp. 82–96.

19 Mary, Lady Jeune, 'Political Great Ladies', *The Realm* 5 April 1895, p. 785, column a. John Vincent, *Formation*, pp. 22–3, suggests that the demise of Palmerston and the Whigs and the emergence of a new, apolitical 'high society' around the Prince and Princess of Wales at Marlborough House marked the end of the power of the hostess.

20 Linda Kerber, 'Separate Spheres, Female Worlds, Women's Place: The Rhetoric of Women's History', *Journal of American History*, 75 (1988), 9–39. Amanda Vickery, 'Golden Age to Separate Spheres? A Review on the Categories and Chronology of English Women's History', *Historical Journal*, 36:2 (1993), 383–414 carries an extensive debate on the origins and anomalies of the use of the separate spheres paradigm. It seems to me significant that Vickery does not propose an alternative language, beyond a call for research into 'intertextuality' (p. 414).

21 I have found this to be true of virtually all the aristocratic women I have studied, not just political hostesses. The one exception is Lady Charlotte Guest, whose downwardly-mobile social status distinguishes here from the rest. See Angela V. John and Revel Guest, *Lady Charlotte: A Biography of the Nineteenth Century* (London, Weidenfeld & Nicolson, 1989).

22 Mabell Ogilvie, Countess of Airlie, *Lady Palmerston and her Times* (London, Hodder and Stoughton, 1922), vol. 2, p. 121.

23 Jane Austen, *Mansfield Park* (London, Penguin English Library, 1966), p. 443.

24 Quoted in Michael Port, (ed.), *The Houses of Parliament* (New Haven, Yale University Press, 1976) 'Introduction', p. 5.

25 Port, *Houses of Parliament*, pp. 184–5.

26 Lady Palmerston to Frederick Lamb, 23 Oct. 1840. University of Southampton Library, Broadlands Archives BR30.

27 Ralph Nevill, *The Life and Letters of Lady Dorothy Nevill* (London, Methuen, 1919) p. 145, 'No one better than [Palmerston] knew the value of shaking hands in the lobby with members likely to give trouble, and of asking their wives to Saturday soirées.'

28 Laura Palmer, Countess of Selborne to Frances Waldegrave, 31 Dec. 1866, Somerset County Record Office, Strachey Mss, DD/SH C/1189 G283. A study of the *Royal Blue Book and Court Guide* for the period demonstates vividly the proximity in which the political classes live to each other.

29 Lady Waldegrave noted the popularity of her innovation: 'People seem quite wild to come to the Saturday to Monday parties at Strawberry.' Frances Waldegrave to Constance Braham, Lady Strachey, 6 June 1874, Strachey Mss, DD/SH C/1189 D17.

30 Sir William Gregory, *An Autobiography* (London, John Murray, 1894) p. 77, commented approvingly on Lady Jersey's exclusivity: she declined to be introduced to the banker Baron Lionel Rothschild 'as of course [she] could not receive him'.

31 Greville is quoted by Margaret E. Child-Villiers, Countess of Jersey, *Records of the Family of Villiers, Earls of Jersey* (London, privately printed, 1924) p. 52; Benjamin Disraeli, *Sybil; or the Two Nations* (1845), ch. 4.

32 Ogilvie, *Lady Palmerston*, p. 87.

33   Mandler, *Aristocratic Government*, p. 54.

34   *Morning Post*, 1 March 1852, p. 5, col. f.

35   Mayer, *Persistence of the Old Regime*, pp. 91–2.

36   Osbert Wyndham Hewett, *Strawberry Fair: A Biography of Frances, Countess Waldegrave, 1821–1879* (London, John Murray, 1956).

37   Some aristocratic women held literary and artistic salons, but their guests were not admitted to 'Society', and were generally restricted to the patron–client relationship. Davidoff, *Best Circles*, p. 78. The widening of the social boundaries universally was not welcomed – see Ralph Nevill (ed.), *The Reminiscences of Lady Dorothy Nevill* (London, Edward Arnold, 1906).

38   Mary, Lady Jeune, 'Political Great Ladies', *The Realm* 5 April 1895, p. 785, column a.

39   Previously they had been courted by ministers when convenient, but not generally admitted into Society. Hence we find Lady Palmerston giving a dinner exclusively for thirty-one Irish members in 1862. Broadlands Archives BR22(ii)/19.

40   Jalland, *Women, Marriage and Politics*, p. 195: 'An accomplished political hostess could oil the wheels of her husband's career … But having a good political hostess for a wife was not a major determinant of political success.'

41   Opinion as to the positive benefits of Lady Waldegrave's influence were not universal. Lord Kimberley commented 'What a prodigious amount of harm that woman [Lady Waldegrave] does poor Fortescue, who is an excellent fellow if she wd. only leave him alone.' Ethel Drus, ed., John, First Earl of Kimberley, 'A Journal of Events during the Gladstone Ministry, 1868–74', *Camden Miscellany* vol. XXI, Camden Third Series, Vol. XC, 1958, p. 16.

42   Lucy Masterman (ed.), *Mary Gladstone (Mrs Drew): Her Diaries and Letters* (London, Methuen, 1930), pp. 74, 197; Lord Redesdale, *Memories* (London, Hutchinson, 1915) p. 534. It was frequently noted at the time that the Conservatives were without successful political hostesses after the decline of Lady Jersey. See Redesdale, *Memories*, p. 534 and Disraeli to Frances Anne Londonderry, 7 Aug. 1854: 'There never was an aggregation of human beings, who exercised less social influence.' Edith Vane-Tempest-Stuart (ed.), *Letters from Benjamin Disraeli to Frances Anne Marchioness of Londonderry, 1837–1861* (London, Macmillan, 1938) pp. 130–2.

43   The other way in which the political hostess is denigrated is by suggesting that her influence extended 'only' to personalities and patronage, not to the arena of political decision-making and ideology. This, of course, reflects the historical pecking-order, whereby the 'hard' subject of politics and ideology are predicated over the 'soft' subject of social action, in which women are constantly relegated to the 'soft', and thereby less significant realm both as historical actors and as historical subjects. Personalities and patronage were of primary importance to the individuals attempting to make careers for themselves in the Victorian political world.

44   David Roberts, *Paternalism in Early Victorian Britain* (New Brunswick, Rutgers University Press, 1979) has a similar difficulty.

45   Sophisticated studies of the operation of patronage exist for other countries and periods. See, for example, Norbert Elias, *The Court Society*, translated by Edmund Jephcott (Oxford, Basil Blackwell, 1983; first published 1969); Roger Mettam, *Power and Faction in Louis XIV's France* (Oxford, Basil Blackwell, 1988), especially ch. 2; Jennifer C. Ward, *English Noblewomen in the Later Middle Ages* (Harlow, Longman, 1992) especially ch. 7.

46   Ogilvie, *Lady Palmerston*, vol. 2, pp. 42–3.

47   R. C. Lucas, sculptor, 'Continuation of the Enquiries of Artist, Clericus, Scalpel and Baggs', May-Day 1878, Broadlands Archives, BR28/10.

48   Mary, Lady Jeune, 'Political Great Ladies', *The Realm* 5 April 1895, p. 785, column a.

49 Quoted in Jalland, *Women, Marriage and Politics*, p. 196.

50 Anthony Trollope, *The Prime Minister* (Oxford, Oxford University Press, 1983. Originally published 1876), vol. 1, pp. 265–6: "'I almost think,' said Phineas, "that the time has gone by for what one may call drawing-room influences. They used to be very great. ... But the spirit of the world has changed since then."'

51 Frances Waldegrave to Lady Strachey, Feb. 1874, quoted in Hewett, *Strawberry Fair*, p. 244.

52 Emily Palmerston to Mrs Huskisson, 19 March 1846, Tresham Lever, *The Letters of Lady Palmerston* (London, John Murray, 1957), p. 273.

53 Emily Palmerston to Margaret de Flahault, 15 March 1840, Lever, *Letters*, p. 225.

54 Davidoff, *Best Circles*, pp. 49–58.

55 Emily Palmerston to Palmerston, 17 April 1849, Broadlands Archives, BR30.

56 Frances Waldegrave to William Vernon Harcourt, Tuesday, n.d., Bodleian Library, MS Harcourt dep. 93 ff. 41–2.

57 Frances Waldegrave to William Vernon Harcourt, 2 Oct. 1870, MS Harcourt dep. 93 ff. 43–8.

5

Woman supportive or woman manipulative? The 'Mrs Ellis' woman

Henrietta Twycross-Martin

RECENT debate among cultural historians as to the viability of 'separate spheres' as a defining ideology for the nineteenth-century middle class has opened up the whole question of nineteenth-century class-formation, with particular emphasis on women's role in families of the 'middling sort'. On the one hand, Hall and Davidoff[1] see 'separate spheres' as an integral element in nineteenth-century middle-class self-identity, and stress the increasingly domestic role lived by women of this class, which they suggest represented a diminution of such women's economic activity. Taking a different line, Vickery[2] has recently called into question the usefulness as a historical category of the concept of 'separate spheres', and in an important article argues that a separation of gender roles is scarcely a nineteenth-century phenomenon, and is not a concept which it is particularly useful to link with either the rise of the middle classes or with any idea that it represented a limitation of female opportunity or activity. Vickery takes exception to the methodology that would read directly from literature to life, and disputes the conclusions of those historians who, using as their sources 'the sanctimonious novels and sermons of Evangelicals like Hannah More, Mrs Sherwood, and Mrs Trimmer, the didactic manuals of Sarah Stickney Ellis and her ilk ... told essentially the same story ... that a new ideology of ultra-femininity and domesticity had triumphed by the mid-Victorian period'. On the contrary, she argues that prescriptive advice manuals may have been popular precisely because more comfortably-off women were doing more outside the home than seemed desirable to certain sections of the community.

With the concept of 'separate spheres' questioned in this way, it is important that historians should be aware of the varieties of domestic ideology represented by specific writers, whose nuances may support or subvert generalisations about gender roles. The wide-ranging debate that emerged in the early and mid nineteenth century around the function of women in the family and society has become known as the 'woman question debate',[3] and was particularly characteristic of writers and novelists of the 1840s and 1850s. Sarah Stickney Ellis, a Quaker who became a Congregationalist on marriage to the missionary William Ellis, was one of the first and certainly one of the most influential contributors to this debate, but it is misleading to see her advocacy of domesticity for women as in any sense simple, or as similar in its nuances to other prescriptive writers, or as unproblematic in her own period.

Born in 1799 into a comfortable Yorkshire tenant-farming family of semi-gentry status, when her father lost money Sarah Stickney deliberately launched herself on a varied literary career, editing journals, writing moral fiction and non-fiction, and finally running a school in tandem with her writing.[4] She published her first conduct book, *The Women of England, Their Social Duties and Domestic Habits*, in 1839, to instant acclaim, in the same year that also saw the publication of Sarah Lewis's *Woman's Mission*,[5] but while Sarah Lewis and Mrs Ellis were both important contributors to the women question debate, it is Mrs Ellis who seems to have become identified in the public mind with promoting a serious, Christian and moral discourse in support of a specifically middle-class domestic ideology. This is presumably partly because she followed the runaway success of *The Women of England* with three sequels: *The Daughters of England, Their Position in Society, Character and Responsibilities*, was published in 1842, and *The Wives of England, Their Relative Duties, Domestic Influence, and Social Obligations*, and *The Mothers of England, Their Influence and Responsibility* both followed in 1843.[6]

Although she came from the kind of family in which women's domestic role had, as Vickery suggests, long pre-dated the rise of the Victorian middle class, in her own conduct books Mrs Ellis targeted women from families with a wider social base: she assumes of her readership a background in which income is earned, and is sufficient to support at least two or three servants. In other words, the nineteenth-century middle class. Thus Mrs Ellis's domestic ideology (whether we take it to be descriptive or prescriptive) is clearly associated *in her books* with a particular class, and it seems that the class at which it was aimed recognised itself, either as it was or as it liked to think of itself, since her books sold particularly well during the 1840s.

Although more women may have been more comfortably-off than ever before, irrespective of whether a woman contributed to family finances through her own efforts, or via the capital she contributed through her dowry, upon marriage she entered a patriarchal institution that denied her any legal or financial autonomy.[7] Once married, all a woman possessed became her husband's, as did anything she earned or inherited during her married life; her husband could not even gift property to her, since anything she was given remained his. If a woman left her husband, for whatever reason, she had no means of support: it was not until the Divorce Act of 1857 that a married woman could claim alimony and a divorced one maintenance, nor was it until the Married Women's Property Acts of 1870 and 1882 that married women were able to have their own property secured to them during marriage. Hence in the early nineteenth century the role of the married middle-class woman could seem almost as problematic as that of a spinster without family support: completely dependent upon her husband, with servants to help run her house, and debarred by convention from paid employment, what exactly was her function? A consistent subtext in Mrs Ellis's writing, present overtly in her temperance stories and more covertly in her conduct books is the vulnerability of women because of their financial dependence upon men, and it is this awareness that gives such an ambiguous edge to her writings.

Mrs Ellis's contribution to the ideological debate surrounding women's domestic role is very difficult to assess, since at times she supports and at times subverts the subordination of women to men sanctioned by legal and financial custom. So ambiguous can she seem that the most recent bibliographical notices of Mrs Ellis still present sharply polarised views of her work, suggesting either that she 'saw women as supportive, loving, uncomplaining wives and mothers',[8] or that she 'is offering a handbook for survival',[9] and 'did maintain women's interests were best served by ministering to men'.[10] It has not before been noticed that Mrs Ellis's reception in her own time polarised along the same lines as the recent notices cited above: if problematic now, she was not less so then. It seems that in her emphasis on the domestic role for women, she aimed to enhance its significance by encouraging women to capitalise on the only power she felt they could properly exploit, that of affectionate moral authority within marriage and the family.

Precisely because Mrs Ellis saw male superiority as an inherent fact of social and legal life, she regarded marriage as often hard for women to adapt to: in *The Wives of England* she warned any woman contemplating marriage that she would have to accept:

> the superiority of your husband, simply as a man. It is quite possible you may have more talent, with higher attainments, and you may also have been more generally admired; but this has nothing whatever to do with your position as a woman, which is, and must be, inferior to his as a man.

But within this apparently rigid structure of superiority and subordination, Mrs Ellis had two important reservations: on the practical level, she insisted that a wife should be given complete authority to run the domestic side as she saw fit, and she also asserted the complete moral autonomy of men and women. Her conduct books and fiction show that she did not have a particularly high opinion of most men,[11] brought up with arrogant assumptions of dominance and hardened by competition in the savage world of nineteenth-century capitalism. Women, however, benefited from being brought up to accept secondary status and could avoid contamination by 'the world' because of their domestic seclusion. Hence the individual woman might often be morally superior to her husband, and had the Christian duty of exerting a beneficial influence upon him, provided she could preserve the proprieties by doing so without jeopardising her subordinate status as wife.[12] By stressing the moral imperative as she does, Mrs Ellis implies that the balancing of overt male power by covert female influence is inherent in God's plan for social organisation, and such influence, refined by domestic retirement, testifies to the importance of women's domestic lives and precludes any possibility that such women could be conceptualised by themselves or others as idle ladies.

Given Mrs Ellis's view of men in general, any moral influence a wife could exert would benefit not only her husband and through him society in general, but would also secure her own status and authority within the family. Hence when Mrs Ellis stresses a wife's duty of uncomplaining self-sacrificial domestic service the implications can be decidedly ambiguous. Domestic duties become elided with the influence a woman is able to exert through the affection they invoke, and it is entirely possible to read Mrs Ellis as implicitly supporting profoundly covert and manipulative tendencies in women.[13] What *The Wives of England* in particular makes unambiguous is that within marriage and the family as then constituted, a woman without such influence might be very vulnerable indeed.

Evidence that Mrs Ellis's paradoxical attitude was noticed in her own time comes from an unexpected source: the writers and cartoonists of *Punch* seem to have had a running joke at her expense throughout much of the 1840s as they targeted various aspects of the woman question. *Punch* started in 1841, and the markedly satirical, topical and often political contents combined with the somewhat self-consciously chauvinist persona of 'Mr Punch' the leader-writer, gave this periodical a defining masculinity of perspective; thus when Mrs Ellis or her ideas are mocked, the subtext assumption is that this is done man to man, satirist to reader.

Although initially *Punch* satirists mocked Mrs Ellis for copiousness and tediousness, they soon developed an eye for the implicit battle of the sexes suggested by her view that although men were socially and legally dominant in marriage, women often had the moral advantage. *Punch* also spotted the manipulative tendencies latent in this view of male and female roles, and its satirists gleefully suggested this was motivated by a female love of power. In this respect, *Punch* is in sharp contrast to the favourable reception Mrs Ellis's works were usually given in the more serious reviews of the 1840s, which tended to read her as entirely supportive of a domestic role for women that emphasised their service to others. S. Austin Allibone's[14] 1854 bibliography, for example, cites several eulogistic notices of Mrs Ellis's works. Among these *The British Magazine* noticed *The Wives of England* thus:

> It is a comfort to think that in all things we are not retrograding. The talents which made Hannah More and Madame D'Arblay the idols of the literary world in their generation, would now secure them but a slender share of homage. The cultivation of the female mind has certainly advanced; and we greatly doubt if any woman of the last century *could* have written The Wives of England.

The *London Methodist Magazine* even asserted:

> We know no volume better calculated to exercise a powerful, lasting, and beneficial influence. If we could have our own way, every family should order a copy of The Women of England. Husbands, especially young Husbands, should buy it for their Wives; Fathers, for their Daughters; Brothers, for their Sisters.

This could be read as a hint that men may need to be guided by their female relatives; if so, this would be quite consistent with what Mrs Ellis actually says, but clearly no hint of undue female influence or of covert ambiguities over power relations has troubled the reviewer.

The *London Spectator* saw the same volume as promoting a domestic role in which self-interest of any kind was entirely absent:

> At a time when women are becoming anxious to shine in other spheres than that humble but holiest of all – home, to inculcate the truth that the paramount and peculiar duties of woman consist in ministering to the wants, comforts, and happiness of her fellow-creatures, especially those of her own family circle, is a salutary task; this Mrs. Ellis has accomplished in a way to bring conviction to the minds of mothers and daughters – the teachers and the taught.

An unattributed notice in Allibone even commended Mrs Ellis for the 'meek and modest spirit' in which she wrote.

So how was this 'meek and modest spirit' perceived by *Punch*? The first notice of Mrs Ellis's conduct books, a mock review of *The Grandmothers of England*,[15] followed by an advertisement for similar works on the Babies, Cooks, Washerwomen, Charwomen, Applewomen and Bathing women of England, appeared in 1843 and accuses her of nothing worse than stating the obvious and profiting from it. By 1844 *Punch* was targeting the pretensions of female moral crusaders, in a full-page article called *Woman and her Interrogatives*,[16] the theme of which is 'Can woman regenerate society?' *Punch* is graciously disposed to allow her the chance, and suggests likely targets, among which are the law-courts:

> Woman may next step over to the Courts of Law; and if it be proved that she can morally regenerate anything therein, why *Punch* will grant her all she asks; and to shew his sincerity will buy all Mrs. Ellis's *Women*, from the *Wives of England* to *England's Stepmothers*. More: as a further penance for his scoffing, he will bind himself to read them.

So far *Punch* merely ridicules Mrs Ellis as tedious, with the added suggestion that she has written too much, presumably to exploit her popularity; and the same point is reiterated in *The Literary Cemetery*[17] where *Punch* laments over the number of books destined for oblivion, and celebrates the founding of a literary cemetery to give such works fitting interment:

> Mrs. Ellis has, it will be seen, a very chaste design, for her *Women of England*. It is full of talent and sensibility. The bosom of that man is not a bosom, but a paving-stone, who could pass the monument insensible of the erection! The *Mothers and Daughters*, with the *Grandmothers, Mothers, Aunts*, and *Cousins*, descended from the aforesaid *Women of England*, will, in due time, be chronicled on the same cenotaph. May no rude hand disturb their memory!

This passage is illustrated with a drawing of the tomb, on which is inscribed 'To The Memory Of The Women Of England', flanked by two weeping, bonneted figures, and surmounted by an urn supporting an umbrella.

As *The Literary Cemetery* shows, although Mrs Ellis was a topical figure in 1844 *Punch* had not as yet specifically begun to target implications of manipulation apparent in her representation of male and female relationships. By 1845 all this has changed, with a half-page column called *The Whole Duty Of Woman. By a pupil of Mrs. Ellis*,[18] in which an old and experienced woman gives a young one the benefit of sound advice:

> Now, in order to get married, my love, you must learn to manage yourself; and, after you have got married, to manage your husband: and both together is what I call the Whole Duty of Woman.

This article reads as a very clever and well-informed parody of *The Wives of England*, in which Mrs Ellis's ambiguities over power are shown up as female self-seeking, and moral influence for the mutual benefit of husband and wife is replaced by cunning manipulation. During courtship, the woman is advised to conceal her faults:

> If anybody is attached to you, never contradict him, dear, but fall in with all his little wishes and whims, however unreasonable. In short, devote yourself

to him entirely; your turn will come. When you are married, you should pursue another course altogether. The object of all husbands is, to put upon their wives as much as they can, by making perfect slaves of them, and stinting them in their pleasures and enjoyments so as to have the more to lay out upon themselves.

Since this is so, the wife should use her domestic autonomy to fiddle her accounts, and provide herself with luxuries, while if her husband displeases her in any way: 'in that case, dear, there are plenty of ways to bring a man to reason. His buttons may not be sewn on; his dinner kept waiting; pickles or potatoes not provided.'

After this, direct references to Mrs Ellis tail off in *Punch*, although the harridan Mrs Caudle, Douglas Jerrold's popular anti-heroine of the series 'Mrs. Caudle's Curtain Lectures',[19] should certainly be included in the sequence of jokes *Punch* had been running about Mrs Ellis and the domestic role of women: by 1845 even when neither Mrs Ellis nor her conduct books are mentioned, they provide the unmistakable context for comedy.

When Punch does mention Mrs Ellis by name, it allows such satire to be associated directly with discussion about her view of women's domestic role, but, as with the Curtain Lectures, alongside the *Punch* articles that specifically mention Mrs Ellis, there are a number of articles running through 1843–4 that play variations on the Mrs Ellis theme, although no actual allusion to her or to her conduct books appears. It is in these articles that suggestions of manipulation and exploitation first appear; *Letter XXXV* in *Punch's Complete Letter-Writer series, From a Matron to a Newly Married Young Lady, on the Treatment Of A Husband*,[20] details example after example of how a wife may manage her husband so as to ensure her dominance over him, and shows close knowledge of *The Wives of England* in at least one such example, although a specific link between Mrs Ellis's works and advocacy of deceptive manipulation is not made until 1845 with *The Whole Duty of Woman*.

In these two articles *Punch* satirists of 1844 and 1845 seem to be invoking the bogey of an independent female tradition in which women pass down from generation to generation information on how to subvert accepted patriarchal power structures. While this is a travesty of what Mrs Ellis in fact advocated it also represents very shrewd comment on her subtext. In the 1830s and 1840s Evangelical and Nonconformist circles were interested in social reform through a gradual extension of serious, respectable domesticity as a personal ideal for men as well as women, and Mrs Ellis does suggest a powerful female agenda in support of this reformation in manners. Whatever was thought of her agenda, her means for bringing it about undoubtedly did lay her open to suggestions that her writings can be read as licensing manipulation.

Thackeray, who worked on *Punch* throughout the period in which it was indulging in jokes at Mrs Ellis's expense, and who made two direct allusions to her in his *Book of Snobs* [21] series, certainly hints that once one has grasped the implications of her advice to married women, legal reform may seem preferable to continuing with the present system. In 1849 *Punch* ran one of Thackeray's series *Mr. Brown's Letters To A Young Man About Town*,[22] subtitled *Love, Marriage, Men and Women*, in which Thackeray gives what amounts to a sustained portrait of a 'Mrs Ellis' woman:

> you see a demure-looking woman perfect in all her duties, constant in house-bills and shirt-buttons, obedient to her lord, and anxious to please him in all things; silent, when you and he talk politics. Benighted idiot! She has long ago taken your measure and your friends'; she knows your weaknesses and ministers to them in a thousand artful ways. Every woman manages her husband; every person who manages another is a hypocrite. Her smiles, her submission, her good-humour, for all which we value her, – what are they but admirable duplicity? We expect falseness from her, and order and educate her to be dishonest. ... and it is we who made the laws for women, who we are in the habit of saying are not so clever as we are.

Thackeray's reaction to Mrs Ellis may well have influenced his novel *Vanity Fair*, on which he was engaged between 1845 and 1846, while also working for *Punch*. Amelia and Becky in the story seem to explore twin 'Mrs Ellis' possibilities: Amelia, for whom Thackeray's narrating voice shows both admiration and contempt, is the domestic paragon, defining herself only in relation to the men in her life. The narrator feels similarly ambivalent about Becky Sharp, for inverse reasons: her wit and intelligence command respect, but Becky's view of the relations between the sexes certainly hinges on overt and covert power, with the balance coming down heavily on the latter. The novel's last view of her shows Becky triumphant, a pillar of Evangelical piety: 'Her name is in all the charity lists.'

Thackeray and the *Punch* satirists are not alone in pointing out the problems inherent in Mrs Ellis's attempt to empower the domestic role of women while leaving existing patriarchal power structures securely in place. It is clear that Geraldine Jewsbury, novelist, *Athenaeum* reviewer, and friend and confidante of Jane Carlyle, did not like Mrs Ellis's views either; in an undated letter,[23] probably of 1849, she wrote to Jane Carlyle:

> But will you lay your hand on your heart, and say that, in your 'fifteen years' long illness, as you call your life, you have not both felt and shown qualities infinitely higher and nobler than all the 'Mrs. Ellis-code' can dream of? ... A 'Mrs. Ellis' woman is developed to the extreme of her little possibility; but I can see there is a precious mine of a species of womanhood yet undreamed of by the professors and essayists on female education.

It seems that Jewsbury was interested in challenging Mrs Ellis's ideas in print, for in another letter,[24] dated 22 November 1849, she writes:

> some day I hope to be able to have a 'say' at Mrs. Ellis and all her school, and develop my own theory more at length. We only want to be let alone, and then we shall neither be 'strong-minded' women nor yet dolls.

It was not until 1860, when reviewing Mrs Ellis's *Chapters on Wives* for the *Athenaeum* [25] that Jewsbury voiced her objections to Mrs. Ellis's morality most clearly, and her objections are remarkably close to Thackeray's reservations about the 'demure looking woman perfect in all her duties', although Thackeray's *Punch* article antedates the *Athenaeum* review by eleven years. That Jewsbury still felt Mrs Ellis merited a lengthy article in 1860 is remarkable testimony to the latter's popularity twenty-one years after she published her first conduct book; it is no less striking evidence of the depth of Jewsbury's dislike of Mrs Ellis's view of marital relationships. *Chapters on Wives* consists of a series of exemplary tales illustrating virtuous wifely conduct, which Jewsbury subjects to a scathing critique:

> In 'Forest Farm' ... the qualities (the wife) brings to bear show a power of intrigue ... a power of using everybody and gaining them over to her own purpose, that is somewhat startling. All the model women painted by Mrs. Ellis have this power of design ... (her) leading idea of a model wife is that of one who dextrously manages her husband, leading him to think and do whatever she thinks right ... she must be always on the watch not to give offense, always careful never to do or say anything except what may please or soothe her master. But the husband must be always more or less of a dupe. He must never know exactly, when his wife brings him his warm slippers, what she wants to effect by the act; only it would be absurd and gratuitous for him to fancy that the desire to make him comfortable is all she aims at. A model wife ... never indulges in the luxury of a spontaneous, unpremeditated, impulse ... nor can a man become anything but a well-managed tyrant: his selfishness developed and exploited.

Jewsbury's *Athenaeum* review is worth quoting at length because it is the most perceptive as well as the most damning account ever given of the 'Mrs Ellis' woman. Perhaps Jewsbury's dislike of Mrs Ellis was fuelled by a certain similarity between them: they were both professional writers, in that they needed the money writing brought them, and both contributed, from different perspectives, to the woman question debates of the 1840s. It is possible to see Jewsbury's novel *The Half-Sisters*, which came out in 1848, as in some sense a rebuttal of Mrs Ellis's views. The two heroines of this novel represent different views of the possibilities open to women: Alice, the submissive, childless wife is driven to the brink of elopement by chronic boredom; her half-sister Bianca earns her own living on the stage, and develops maturity and force of personality before retiring to make a titled match. Jewsbury may have detested the 'Mrs Ellis' woman, preferring to campaign for an open rather than an insidious recognition of women's capacities, yet in her own way she also was ambivalent about the female role. Although Jewsbury shows Alice as being without resources, someone for whom a sound education or a career before marriage might have worked wonders, the novel ends with Bianca giving up her career when she makes her splendid marriage, and neither she nor her creator seem to regret that she has done so. The overt power of being self-supporting is one thing, marriage is another, even for a Jewsbury heroine.

In deciding to write about the domestic role actually lived by the majority of middle-class women, Mrs Ellis chose to write for a large middle-class market whose basic assumptions about the social and legal subordination of women to men she never challenges. Her acceptance of the *status quo* may have been because she believed in the divine origin of such hierarchy, or it may have been a tactical device to secure wide hearing. Either way, Mrs Ellis's contribution to the competing voices that make up mid nineteenth-century discourses on domestic ideology remains ambiguous. Certainly she promoted a 'separate sphere' for middle-class women, but in her eyes this may have represented a real expansion of their power: at a time when a married woman had no independent rights, she argued for a wife's autonomy in running her house, and gave women the responsibility for the moral health of their husbands, their family, and the nation. Domestic organisation and moral order belong together, since the home fosters both: in these two areas men are dependent upon women, and in this way Mrs Ellis sought to redress the imbalance of women's legal and financial dependence on men.

Notes

1 See L. Davidoff and C. Hall, *Family Fortunes* (London, Hutchinson, 1987), pp. 148–92. Also C. Hall, *White, Male and Middle Class* (Cambridge and Oxford, Polity Press, 1992), pp. 75–93.

2 See A. Vickery, 'Historiographical Review: Golden Age to Separate Spheres? A Review Of The Categories And Chronology Of English Women's History', *The Historical Journal*, 36:2 (1993), 383–414.

3 See E. Helsinger, R. Sheets and W. Veeder (eds), *The Woman Question: Society and Literature in Britain and America 1837–1883* (Manchester, Manchester University Press, 1983).

4 The only detailed source for information about Mrs Ellis's life comes from *The Home Life and Letters of Mrs. Ellis Edited by her Nieces* (London, J. Nisbet and Co., 1893). This is not as informative as it might be since it contains no index, and there is little explanation of family relationships. The letters selected are clearly intended to serve a hagiographical function and have been heavily edited.

5 Sarah Lewis's *Women's Mission* (London, J. W. Parker, 1839) was a part-translation and part-adaptation of Louise Aimé Martin's *De l'éducation des mères de famille, ou la civilisa-*

tion du genre humain par les femmes (1834). Although Mrs Ellis cannot have known of Sarah Lewis's book while writing *The Women of England*, it is clear from an allusion in *The Mothers of England* that she had read her before she wrote the latter book.

6 Mrs Ellis's conduct books were published as follows: *The Women of England, Their Social Duties, and Domestic Habits* (London. Fisher, Son and Co., 1839); *The Daughters of England, Their Position in Society, Character and Responsibilities* (London, Fisher, Son and Co., 1842); *The Wives of England, Their Relative Duties, Domestic Influence, and Social Obligations* (London, Fisher, Son and Co., 1843), and *The Mothers of England, Their Influence and Responsibility* (London, Fisher, Son and Co., 1843). All references to The Wives of England are to the first edition. Since Mrs Ellis's writings insist on the moral importance of the female role, the term 'conduct book' is perhaps preferable to the more neutral alternative, 'advice manual'.

7 A good account of the legal position of women during the nineteenth-century, and of how this was affected by the Divorce Act and The Married Women's Property Acts, can be found in L. Holcombe, *Wives and Property: Reform of the Married Women's Property Law in Nineteenth Century England* (Oxford, Martin Robertson, 1983)

8 See V. Blain, P. Clements and I. Grundy, *The Feminist Companion to Literature in English* (London, Batsford, 1990), p. 340.

9 See G. Plain's entry on Sarah Stickney Ellis in J. Todd (ed.), *Dictionary of British Women Writers* (London, Routledge, 1989), p. 221.

10 See P. Schlueter and J. Schlueter, *An Encyclopedia of British Women Writers* (New York and London, Garland Publishing, 1988), p. 157.

11 A similar recognition of Mrs Ellis's ambiguity is found in Davidoff and Hall, *Family Fortunes*, p. 183. The most perceptive discussion to date of the tensions inherent in Mrs. Ellis's views of gender relations is found in A. J. Hammerton, *Cruelty and Companionship* (London and New York, Routledge, 1992), pp. 75-7. However, Hammerton underestimates the degree to which Mrs Ellis's construct of masculinity justifies both separate spheres and female empowerment by decidedly manipulative means: as Thackeray and Jewsbury both suggested.

11 See, for example, *The Wives of England*, pp. 16-17, 65-6, 69-70, 106-7, 176-8, 199-200.

12 For the difficulties involved in such a balancing act, see *The Wives of England*, pp. 105-8.

13 See *The Wives of England*, pp. 77, 95-6, 118-19 for examples of manipulative behaviour.

14 See S. Austin Allibone, *A Critical Dictionary of English Literature, and British and American Authors, Living and Deceased, From The Earliest Accounts To The Middle Of The Nineteenth Century* (Philadelphia, Childs and Peterson; London, Trubner and Co., 1859), pp. 553-4.

15 See *Punch*, vol. 5 (1843), p. 258.

16 See *Punch*, vol. 6 (1844), p. 128.

17 See *Punch*, vol. 7 (1844), p. 235.

18 See *Punch*, vol. 8 (1845), p. 78.

19 See *Mrs. Caudle's Curtain Lectures, Punch*, vols. 8 and 9, (1845-46). R. Kelly, 'Mrs. Caudle: A Victorian Curtain Lecturer', *University of Toronto Quarterly*, 38:3 (1969), makes the connection between Mrs. Ellis's manuals and Mrs. Caudle's lectures, but says nothing about the many other *Punch* jokes at Mrs. Ellis's expense.

Douglas Jerrold followed *Mrs. Caudle's Curtain Lectures* with a series called *Capiscum House*, that started in volume 12 of *Punch* and ran through 1847. This series chronicles the fortunes of proprietress and pupils at a girls' boarding-school, where the girls are given a culinary and domestic education. R. Kelly, in *Douglas Jerrold* (New York, Twayne Publishers Inc., 1972) pp. 103-7, points out that Mrs. Ellis is mentioned in *Capiscum House*, and therefore connects this series with her conduct books. However, it is an *a priori* possibility that *Capiscum House* was modelled on Mrs Ellis's Rawdon House School, which offered a specifically domestic as well as academic training.

Capiscum House contains a number of jokes about male drunkenness, recipes for rum-punch etc, and Jerrold seems to have been satirising Mrs. Ellis as teacher and temperance worker as well as writer of conduct books.

20 See *Punch*, vol. 7, (1844), p. 199. Letter XXXV cites (among other irritating habits) a husband's infuriating tendency to rattle fire-irons, which may be an echo of *The Wives of England*, p. 170–1. On a more serious level, Mrs Ellis saw female influence as essential for the alteration of male behaviour even in the most brutal instances. She was writing *Family Secrets Or Hints To Those Who Would Make Home Happy*, a series of anti-alcoholism moral tales, at the same time that she was writing *The Wives of England*, and these stories show men as liable to drunkenness and at times to an astonishing tendency to violence, from which faults only their female relatives' moral influence can save them. For male violence, see particularly *Fireside Recollections*, in *Family Secrets Or Hints To Those Who Would Make Home Happy*, vol. 3 (London, Fisher, Son and Co., 1842).

21 See *Punch*, vol. 10 (1846) pp. 115, 137.

22 See *Punch*, vol. 17 (1849), p. 13.

23 See Mrs. Alexander Ireland (ed.), *Selections from the Letters of Geraldine E. Jewsbury to Jane Welsh Carlyle* (London, Longmans, Green and Co., 1892), pp. 348–9.

24 See Ireland, *Letters*, p. 321. N. Clarke has a useful account of Geraldine Jewsbury's life and career in *Ambitious Heights, Writing, Friendship, Love – The Jewsbury Sisters, Felicia Hemans and Jane Carlyle* (London, Routledge, 1990), but makes no mention of Geraldine's antipathy to the 'Mrs Ellis' woman. This antipathy, based as it is on the latter's preference for manipulation rather than open encounter, may have revealing implications for Geraldine Jewsbury's view of the Carlyle's marriage, to the inner workings of which she was privy for so many years.

25 See *The Athenaeum*, No. 1707, (14 July 1860), pp. 52–3. The editor's marked file shows that the reviewer for Mrs Ellis's *Chapters on Wives* was Geraldine Jewsbury, and I am grateful to Dr Micheline Handcock Beaulieu, cataloguer of *The Athenaeum*, for access to this information.

6

Mary Wollstonecraft and Flora Tristan: one pariah redeems another

Máire Fedelma Cross

MARY WOLLSTONECRAFT and Flora Tristan have both become latter-day saints in the feminist canon, not before suffering derision and ostracism from the Left and the Right. The posthumous vilification of Mary Wollstonecraft, 'the hyena in petticoats', was not altogether as widespread as some historians would have us believe.[1] Flora Tristan, once dubbed in a similar fashion 'O'Connell in petticoats' (a reference to Daniel O'Connell who led a mass movement in Ireland to achieve Catholic Emancipation in 1829) was one of the first to recognise the value of Wollstonecraft's achievements and was in a modest way responsible for rescuing the reputation of Britain's pioneer champion of female emancipation. In this chapter the link between the two pariahs shall be used as a basis for presenting the lesser-known but equally interesting historical figure for modern feminism, Flora Tristan, the self-declared pariah. First the similarity of their circumstances will be explained; then we shall see the manner in which Flora Tristan exemplified her predecessor; third, the achievements of this French radical will demonstrate the further development of another brand of feminism and at the same time illustrate reasons for Flora Tristan's own vilification and neglect.

The most obvious similarity lies in the comparable sets of circumstances in which Mary Wollstonecraft and Flora Tristan developed their awareness of gender inequality. Both were highly intelligent and strong willed, autodidactic, frustrated by parental neglect, unhappy in love affairs, impoverished, having to survive in a labour market which was very restrictive for women outside the family enterprise. Both were employed in their early career as ladies' companions and witnessed the privileged lifestyles of the upper classes from that perspective. Both women travelled extensively, both lived by their pen and both died tragically, in their prime, one at thirty-eight the other at forty-one. They had a horror of idleness and of the waste of female talent, and especially of the inappropriate education for young girls. Both were keenly interested in public life, in politics, in art and in events outside their own country and managed to thwart the restrictions on females of their time to study, write and socialise with the leading radicals of the capital cities of both sides of the Channel. In both cases unhappy personal circumstances led them to campaign on behalf of a larger group. They were able to theorise from the personal to the general.

We have looked briefly at the commonalty of circumstances.[2] Let us examine the similarities of ideas to answer the question of whether Flora Tristan could be said to be a disciple of Mary Wollstonecraft.

Flora Tristan was born six years after the death of Mary Wollstonecraft. While there were many other momentous changes in the socio-economic and political structures in the two countries, one event over-shadowed the writing of both women: the upheaval of 1789. From this they each inherited a strongly developed sense of egalitarianism and libertarianism. Both Flora Tristan and Mary Wollstonecraft analysed the French Revolution, and in so doing they were thrust into the heart of the debate about the new and old orders, and the changing values regulating the public sphere. They both insisted that women were entitled to play a role in public affairs.

After she had achieved success as a writer and as a member of the Parisian radical milieu, Flora Tristan went further into the public sphere of politics and sought to carry out this principle. During the last year of her life much of her energy was devoted to preaching a plan of campaign to implement her scheme for a workers' union which would unite women with the working class and thus redeem humanity, a rather ambitious act, and one which would lead to her demise.

Mary Wollstonecraft's exceptionality is matched by that of Flora Tristan, although the latter was part of a generation of women and men who recognised the need for female emancipation. Flora Tristan's exceptionality lay in her deliberate choice of a socialist agenda to further the cause of women. After the failure of the women participants in the events following the 1789 Revolution and the imposition of a legal definition of rights and duties of men and women in the form of the *Code Civil*, there was a certain reorientation of feminist thinking in the search for emancipation. Among some feminists of the July Monarchy, direct involvement and action by women in the public sphere were not con-sidered desirable; when they commented about the nature of love and motherhood, as many such as George Sand (the male pseudonym of the feminist novelist Aurore Dupin) were to do, they willingly kept women within their allotted domestic sphere. It is true that they wanted legal reforms to improve the position of women within society: to have their roles and duties relating to motherhood recognised and given civic value. But these aspirations merely reinforced gender divisions between the public and private spheres, limited the nature of the debate and enclosed women in a very restricted political agenda with little opportunity to escape. Moreover, the Code Civil devised and imposed during the reign of Napoleon legitimised the division between public and private sphere giving women no legal forum for contributing to public life. They were however allowed to write petitions to Parliament.

Flora Tristan began her writing career with such petitions, one for divorce to be restored as it had been implemented after 1789 but abolished under the Restoration Monarchy, and one for the abolition of the death penalty, shortly after being shot and wounded by her estranged husband.

The importance of the distinction between civil and civic rights was for a long time considered to be an all-important demarcation point between feminists of different political persuasions. Mary Wollstonecraft, in demanding political and civil equality as a natural right, wished to see an end to women being confined to domesticity, whereas although Flora Tristan did not take up Mary Wollstonecraft's agenda for equal political and civil rights as entirely as one might have wished, she had her own plans for releasing women from the domestic sphere by thrusting them into the socialist agenda, and by using the Saint-Simonian image of the female messiah. This is a significant difference in their interpretation of female oppression and one which would hook Mary Wollstonecraft into the liberal feminist tradition and Flora Tristan into the socialist feminist tradition. However, I would suggest that these labels or boundaries are sometimes less than helpful. Recently attempts have been made to examine historical figures in a more fluid manner. Modern interpretations of Mary Wollstonecraft's feminism vary quite considerably; the same goes for her disciple.[3]

Flora Tristan's life and work contained a complex blend of rational and religious arguments, egalitarian and hierarchical notions, together with a variety of social and economic insights into the working of the new order of capitalism. However, she did not pursue the matter of political equality since she was convinced that democratic opposition groups under the July Monarchy were doomed to failure. She campaigned for the right of association for the working class, to have one appointed representative only to sit in Parliament, funded by a collection from all workers.[4] This was a political agenda which left her vulnerable to criticism: 'O'Connell en jupons' was how she was described in scathing ironic tones by a paper which was normally sympathetic to the cause of the working class and to that of Catholic Emancipation, but which mockingly derided her attempts to form a workers' union:

While we were preoccupied with Ireland where important and big events are about to take place through the dedication of O'Connell and the national association, we scarcely imagined for one moment that we are about to be provided with a parody of all that: yet we are going to have our own Union, our O'Connell, our meetings, our cheering. ... However, never let it be said that we would want to raise a storm in order to destroy Madame Flora Tristan's project. ... Yes, Madame Flora is perhaps our O'Connell, O'Connell in petticoats; ... the O'Connell of France could well be Madame Flora. We would just love to see her up on the hustings platform, one hand across her chest, the other raised in a clenched fist with eyes ablaze, frowning and making us all cheer.[5]

Like her predecessor, Flora Tristan was subject to severe criticism simply by being a woman wishing to engage in the political process.

Although we can see the making of a critique of capitalism in Mary Wollstonecraft's work, it must be said that Flora Tristan developed it much further. Of course capitalism was older by three decades then, and although the industrial capacity of Britain was greatly admired by Flora Tristan, the ravages of fierce competition and brutal exploitation of the labour force were all too visible to her. As a result Flora Tristan went beyond the question of oppression of women within the family to a class analysis of gender oppression, which in turn led her to socialism. Before going further with Flora Tristan's class analysis, consideration should be given to where and how Flora Tristan portrays her predecessor.

Flora Tristan discovered Mary Wollstonecraft in the course of her study of Britain in the 1830s. It was the writer she extolled, as the symbol of female freedom. It is hardly surprising then for us to note that it is from *Vindication of the Rights of Woman* that Flora Tristan quotes extensively and comments on in her own work, *Promenades dans Londres* published in 1840 and again in 1842. This book was a major achievement for Flora Tristan and continued the tradition of cross-Channel observations to which Wollstonecraft had contributed. *Promenades dans Londres* is a series of sketches on political social and economic aspects of London as she had seen first hand during the late 1830s. Although there are frequent references to women throughout the work there are only two chapters directly on the subject of women, one on *Filles Publiques* and one on *Les Femmes Anglaises*, by which she means upper-class English women, that is women who do not work outside the home, whom Tristan considered to be doubly exploited, by the marriage laws which kept them in the confines of the home and by double standards of morality. It is in this chapter that Flora Tristan quotes from Wollstonecraft's dedication to Talleyrand where she had argued that essentially women had an equal capacity to reason, that political tyranny would not be overthrown if men were to continue their tyrannical behaviour towards women, that women had natural civic and political rights, and that to deprive women of a sound education would be to hinder the progress of knowledge and virtue of humanity.[6] These are indeed the main precepts of early egalitarian feminists, with which Flora Tristan was entirely in sympathy. What is equally important is that Flora Tristan was very much aware of the historical link between Mary Wollstonecraft and her own generation. She begins by praising her for tackling the received ideas of her day. She points out that she attacked Rousseau:

> Mary Wollstonecraft protested against the writers who considered woman as a creature with a subordinate nature, destined to please man. On this subject, she made a very accurate criticism of Rousseau, who asserts that woman must be weak and passive, man active and strong, that woman is made to be subject to man, and finally that it is the duty of woman to be agreeable and obey her master and that such is the reason for her existence.[7]

The general theme of this chapter is Flora Tristan's strong condemnation of the servility of marriage but it is also a tribute to the importance of Mary Wollstonecraft's doctrines. Not only does she acknowledge her place in the history of ideas:

> In 1792 Mary Wollstonecraft published the same principles that Saint Simon preached later, and which spread so quickly after the 1830 revolution. Her critique is admirable; she brings out in their true light the difficulties resulting from the present organisation of family life; and the strength of her argument leaves the contradictors without an answer.[8]

but she pays her a backhanded compliment[9] by expressing astonishment that so many women authors are flourishing – she mentions others in name only – and that Mary Wollstonecraft managed to produce the *Vindication of the Rights of Woman* in such a repressive society: 'What a revolting contrast there is in England between the extreme servility of women and the intellectual superiority of women authors!'[10] Herein lies one element of Flora Tristan's feminism which, although never stated explicitly, was hinted at on several occasions and which has been taken up by feminists later, namely the superiority of women, because of or in spite of their oppression. Whilst it could be argued that this is not a central issue in Flora Tristan's attempt to fuse feminist and socialist ideas and action, it is useful to refer to a recent work which develops this point.[11]

Without going further into their similarities and differences we can clearly establish a link between Mary Wollstonecraft and Flora Tristan. However, it would be too simplistic to assume that there is a natural progression of feminist ideas, with one generation taking up where the other left off. What we can safely say is that Flora Tristan took on board

the egalitarian and libertarian principles propounded by Mary Wollstonecraft and rescued her from oblivion by extolling her achievements.
Just how far she tried to emulate her is more difficult to assess and can
only be speculative.

To continue with an analysis of Flora Tristan's socialist feminism, it
must be recognised that feminism is almost impossible to define in the
early nineteenth century in France, such is the range of literary, artistic
and philosophical outpourings. That century also witnessed the growth
of the human sciences where women often feature as a subject for discussion in the debate about the family and its role in society. In that she
dabbled in art, literature and philosophy and can also be considered to be
a precursor of modern sociology, Flora Tristan was very much a woman
of her time.[12]

Flora Tristan was influenced by the discoveries of the early socialists in
France and in Britain that capitalism had created a new form of serfdom.
Economic freedom for capitalists guaranteed by the sweeping reforms of
the Revolution, was criticised as it inflicted misery on the lower classes.
Hence the development of a new body of thought to which Flora Tristan
contributed, which devised schemes to eliminate the imperfections of the
new economic and social order. The Revolutionary language of rights
was used by Flora Tristan to demand an end to economic serfdom:

> These three rights obviously correspond to the three words uttered to make
> the revolution of 89: 1 – equality – first right to work, 2 – liberty – second
> right to bread, 3 – fraternity third right to education. – Because in order to be
> equal everyone must work – to be free everyone must be able to live – and to
> be brothers everyone must have received the same education in order to be
> able to get on well with one another.[13]

Within Flora Tristan's demand for these three rights was the implicit
assumption that women would be entitled to that equality. She is specific
in her demands for gender economic equality; she addresses men and women
workers separately; she deplored the practice of unequal wages; economic
equality was to be made possible through equal access to education:

> Start by realising, you men who are scandalised before you even want to
> consider the question, why am I demanding rights for woman? – why would
> I like to have her on an absolutely equal footing with man in society, and as
> a result, to have her enjoy legal rights which is everyone's birthright? I am
> demanding rights for woman because I am convinced that all the world's
> misfortunes originate from the neglect and contempt with which the natural
> and imprescriptible rights of a woman have been treated until now. – I am
> demanding rights for woman because it is the only way to look after her
> education, and on woman's education depends man's in general, and common
> man's in particular. – I am demanding rights for woman because it is the only

way to obtain her rehabilitation before the Church, the law and before society and that this rehabilitation is conditional before the workers themselves can be rehabilitated.[14]

Often during her campaign, class issues became more explicit and feminism more implicit. In spite of a hostile reception by the labour aristocracy in Paris, her loyalty to that class deepened as she discovered the extent of its oppression. She was so appalled by the extent of poverty and alienation among workers that she had to resort to simplifying her message by every means possible to encourage a reaction. She found herself adopting the simplistic religious language of the Saint-Simonians and the banner headlines of liberty equality and fraternity.

Although Flora Tristan recognised that women were exploited according to their class, she consistently called upon all women to overcome class hostilities and join in the struggle for freedom. She believed that the proletariat had been freed from serfdom by the overthrow of the old regime and that as beneficiaries the workers should continue the work of the 1789 Revolution by granting all women their emancipation:

> Workers in 91 your fathers proclaimed the immortal declaration of the RIGHTS OF MAN and it is thanks to this solemn declaration that today you are free and equal men before the law. – Honour to your fathers for this great work! – But proletarians, there remains for you, men of 1843, a task no less important to accomplish. – In your turn, enfranchise the last remaining slaves in French society, proclaim the RIGHTS OF WOMAN.[15]

However, by setting such great store on the enthusiasm of workers to be willing liberators of women from all classes, Flora Tristan was to be sorely disappointed. Although she specifically mentioned the duty of the workers to free their oppressed sisters, her call was simply ignored. Why did she choose this form of action?

By the time she came to her tour of French towns Flora Tristan had already tried to develop her theories in other ways, each time finding it impossible to carry on. What is so relevant to her case is that she encapsulates so many of the dilemmas still faced by modern feminists.[16]

Flora Tristan's egalitarian phase was when she called for immediate specific reforms so that women could be as free as men. In her *Nécessité de faire bon accueil aux femmes étrangères* and *Pérégrinations d'une Paria* and in her petitions she declared that women should be allowed to divorce and travel. When these calls fell on deaf ears, she then tried using art as a medium for her message where she developed her theory of messianic feminism in her novel *Méphis*. Unlike the Saint-Simonians' female messiah who was to be part of a couple, Flora Tristan's woman messiah was alone in leading humanity to salvation. In this way she could resolve the two greatest evils, class conflict and gender oppression. Once she had discovered the extent of class and gender oppression in advanced countries such as Britain and France, and in a New World country recently freed from colonial rule, Flora Tristan became more and more impatient with her fellow radical intellectuals; she was determined to act as a militant, as a leader. She frequently condemned her contemporary socialists for being too passive, too idealistic in their model communities and too removed from those who were in need of redemption. Her determination to get close to the oppressed led her to dedicate her 1842 second edition of *Promenades dans Londres* to the workers in France:

> Men workers and you, women workers, who, until now have never counted for anything in human society, I cordially shake your hand. I am united with you for the common cause; I live in you through love, and I am your sister in humanity, Flora Tristan.[17]

The next step was to call for the creation of a self-help organisation for the working class. She would not simply talk about the working class, she would talk to men and women directly. This was easier said than done, but by 1843 nothing daunted Flora Tristan in her burning ambition to carry out what she considered to be her divine mission to save the human race. In 1843 she published by subscription her feminist socialist programme: *Union Ouvrière*. Her plan was based on the assumption that the working class was ready to act. After all there was a tradition of insurrection in France as she so proudly reminded the French workers. Furthermore they had a duty to combat oppression:

> Do you believe that if the English people had been raised in the principles of liberty and equality, if they had learnt to consider that resistance to oppression is not only the natural *right* of man but that on the contrary, when the people are oppressed, insurrection becomes a *sacred duty*.[18]

At this stage Flora Tristan had a highly optimistic view of the readiness of the French working class for action and their capacity for taking her ideas on board. Although she had visited the working-class districts of English cities she was not familiar with French provincial cities and towns. Indeed we can see from her remarks in her journal that she was not prepared for the equally appalling living conditions in France.

Faced with the insurmountable problems of indifference and lack of comprehension of the downtrodden masses, Flora Tristan began to relate back to the notion of a female messiah as her role model. This was an essential means of breaking down class and gender barriers. This was the gendered symbol of liberation for women, for the working class and for humanity. It was a symbol of mobility for Flora Tristan to penetrate a milieu which could have been hostile and which was certainly alien to her. Where she obtained the greatest following was through the message of love of humanity from the female messiah. The workers could associate with the project of the *femme de lettres* by referring to the mother figure; it was gender-specific; it made it easier for her to surmount the difficulties of breaking into new territory.

Flora Tristan chose this course of action just as other contemporary militants did. She was not alone in her choice of travelling around French cities. One remark of Proudhon is very revealing:

> I see very few people and keep as far away as possible from public meetings. Cabet is here just now. This good fellow has already designated me as his successor to the apostolat, and I will nominate as my successor whoever will give me a cup of coffee. At the moment I don't know how many gospels are being preached, gospel according to Buchez, gospel according to Pierre Leroux, gospel according to Lamennais, Considérant, Mme George Sand, Mme Flora Tristan, gospel according to Pecquer and many more still. I don't wish to add to the number of these lunatics; also I have a fantastic effect on those who see me for the first time when they realise that I have common sense.[19]

Proudhon's cynical view exaggerates the number of proselytisers, but from the correspondence it engendered it was obviously a highly successful venture for Flora Tristan as it enabled her to meet those to whom she had no direct access otherwise. The period was highly significant for her class analysis. In delving further and further into the class question, Flora Tristan began to revise her opinion about the possibility of class collaboration. She had been keen to get the enlightened members of the bourgeoisie involved in the new association, but towards the end of her tour she was convinced that the working class must liberate itself. The exclusion of the enlightened bourgeois as members of the *cercles* was one of the most contentious issues she had to deal with as she campaigned.

Excluding the bourgeoisie reduced the possibility of female participation from other classes. Had she lived longer, Flora Tristan would have come across the dilemma of gender and class conflicts in the 1848 struggles, a time of another revolution. The 1789 Revolution is however the one to which feminists refer more readily. The link between Mary Wollstonecraft and Flora Tristan is strengthened by the way the term 'revolution' was fundamental to their interpretations of oppression. The idea of completing what was begun in 1789 by granting women a place in the new order was also taken up with enthusiasm by the new wave of 1848 feminist socialists, including Jeanne Deroin, Eugénie Niboyet, Pauline Roland and Désirée Gay, who highlighted the contradiction between universality and the exclusion of women from the concept. Demands for freedom for women were for all women; be it for civil or for civic rights, there was a universality in feminist demands, regardless of class, which was being denied to them just when the meaning of universality was being transformed by becoming male gendered in France:

> In spite of the repeated calls from republican women, far more numerous than is thought at the time, to add women's enfranchisement to that of the people, convinced as they were that it was not possible without, republican men did not hear this feminine reasoning: they attributed a restricted meaning to the notion of liberty, believing it to be the right one.[20]

In 1848 the newspaper to which these same women belonged, La Voix des Femmes, was asked to publish a biographical article on Flora Tristan.[21]

This period is highly ambiguous for the gender question in nascent socialist theory. On the one hand the radical thinkers such as Fourier and the Saint-Simonians called for a rethinking of family values and rejected the widespread insistence on separate spheres. There were sexual differences, they argued, but womanly qualities were a necessary balance to masculine qualities. However, many of Fourier's theories were considered to be too revolutionary and were quietly dropped by Victor Considérant, the social philosopher, and the phalanstérians to whom Flora Tristan referred in her writing. While the Saint-Simonians were preaching their new religion of the rehabilitation of woman's place in society leading to redemption of the whole of humanity, Proudhon was arguing for traditional roles for women to be maintained:

> I consider all our daydreaming about the emancipation of woman to be harmful and stupid; I deny her any kind of political action; I think that for woman, freedom and happiness lie solely in marriage, motherhood, domestic cares, faithfulness of the husband, chastity and quiet.[22]

We know that it was Proudhon's ideal of family life rather than more libertarian views which became part of working class aspirations.

Flora Tristan's campaign for a workers' union incorporated demands for new family relationships but side-stepped the issue of universal suffrage. Her writings include a very vivid picture of the double exploitation of women within the working class. She describes the vicious circle of poverty and ignorance in the life of a woman in her earlier novel Méphis and in her book Union Ouvrière. The educated Paris workers objected strongly to her condemnation of male behaviour on the grounds that it would give them a bad reputation outside their own class.

The only gender-specific references Flora Tristan could salvage from the experience of a woman preaching directly to the workers were the uses of mother, sister, angel. As she became more and more exhausted by her trip, she fed on her reserves of nervous energy, which seemed to take comfort in the adulation and praise she was receiving and which began to feed her illusion of becoming the woman messiah. All the while, she was coming to the realisation of just how remote the chances were of achieving her ambitions: that the working class was far from ready to associate into a vast self-help organisation, that the misery of the new poor in industrial France was matched only by the callousness of the property-owning class, and that she would be lucky to be able to form her Union *cercles* at all, such was the lack of resources of the workers and the strength of police and bourgeois repression. This served to strengthen her conviction that it was all the more vital to exclude members of the bourgeoisie from the self-help programme of the proletariat.

Flora Tristan developed a critique of colonial and class exploitation and alienation in her study of French and British capitalism and is ac-knowledged to be in advance of the Saint-Simonians in this respect. This did not prevent her from using the religious terminology of the Saint-Simonians whose passivity she despised, to galvanise the workers into action. In Flora Tristan's scheme a love of humanity, the great new moral force of the Utopian socialists was to unite women and workers.

In part one the similarities between Mary Wollstonecraft and Flora Tristan were explained. They inherited a political terminology from the 1789 Revolution which they applied to gender oppression. Flora Tristan identified with her predecessor as a writer and as a champion of female emancipation. Flora Tristan went in search of a solution by becoming a political activist; she defied gender norms by engaging in socialist poli-tics. In part two I showed that at each stage of Flora Tristan's develop-ment she strove to overcome the contradictions she had discovered and tried to find a way of combining theory with action. The most important part of her legacy is that her short career as a militant illustrates many of the dilemmas faced by feminist socialists which are still unresolved.

In part three I have shown that the domestic sphere and the demand for democracy were rejected by Flora Tristan as foundations on which to base her demand for female emancipation. She pinned all her hopes on a class-based organisation. The dilemmas she encountered would re-surface much later after women found themselves betrayed by the republican cause and be thrown back into the bosom of the patriarchal family whose structures were considerably strengthened in all classes. By the time femi-nists were able to re-emerge in the socialist debate in France at the end of the nineteenth century, the 'goal posts' had been moved, as Madeleine Pelletier was to discover.[23]

By way of a general conclusion about the nature of nineteenth-century feminism we can see that in terms of actions it was highly individualistic, but individuals desperately sought an outlet, a form of identity in the public domain. In the case of Mary Wollstonecraft and Flora Tristan, an ability to comment on and participate in spectacular and turbulent events provided them with a powerful vehicle to come out and be noticed. The frustrations arose when they were condemned with such ferocity for wishing to destabilise society by attacking so-called fundamental values as this made their incursions into the public domain all the more difficult. Without the support of a collective movement, individual thinkers, such as Mary Wollstonecraft and more particularly Flora Tristan, were often driven to channel their feminism into broader non-specific gender areas. Because of the nature of the gender power structure, as long as these individuals were portrayed as freaks they could not pose a threat.

Flora Tristan was part of the movement in France which saw opportunities in the new social order that the 1789 Revolution had failed to address. She contributed to the rescue of Mary Wollstonecraft. She had a sense of historical continuity of ideas. It was thanks to those who followed her with the same notion of the importance of past ideas that Flora Tristan herself was rescued from oblivion.

Notes

1 See Bonnie S. Anderson and Judith P. Zinsser, *A History of Their Own: Women in Europe from Prehistory to the Present*, 2 vols (Harmondsworth, Penguin, 1988), vol. 2, p. 125.

2 For further biographical details of Flora Tristan see Máire Cross and Tim Gray, *The Feminism of Flora Tristan* (Oxford, Berg, 1992); Sandra Dijkstra, *Flora Tristan: Feminism in the Age of George Sand* (London, Pluto Press, 1992); Susan Grogan, *French Socialism and Sexual Difference* (London, Macmillan, 1992). I would also refer to a recent article by Margaret Talbot, 'An emancipated voice: Flora Tristan and utopian allegory' *Feminist Studies*, 7: 2 (summer 1991), 219–39.

3 For revised studies of Wollstonecraft's feminism see Jane Grimshaw, 'Mary Wollstoncraft and the tensions in feminist philosophy' in Sean Sayers and Peter Osborne, *Socialism, Feminism and Philosophy* (London, Routledge, 1990); Barbara Taylor, 'Mary Wollstonecraft and the wild wish of early feminism' *History Workshop Journal*, 33 (1992), 197–219; Moira Gatens, *Feminism and Philosophy: Perspectives on Difference and Equality* (Cambridge, Polity Press, 1991).

4 For a discussion of the question of schemes for working-class representation contemporary to Flora Tristan see Daniel Armogathe and Jacques Grandjonc, *Introduction* to their new edition of Flora Tristan's *Union Ouvrière* (Paris, Editions Des Femmes, 1986), pp. 34–44.

5 'Pendant que nous nous occupons de l'Irlande, où de graves et grands événements se préparent par les soins d'O'Connell et de l'association nationale, nous ne nous doutons guère que l'on se prépare ici à nous donner une parodie de tout cela: nous allons cependant avoir notre Union, notre O'Connell, nos meetings, nos hourra. ... Cependant, que l'on n'aille pas nous accuser de vouloir exciter une tempête pour détruire le projet de madame Flora Tristan. ... Oui madame Flora est peut-être bien notre O'Connell, O'Connell en jupons; ... l'O'Connell de la France sera peut-être madame Flora. Nous aimerons la voir montée sur des hustings, une main dans la poitrine, et de l'autre montrant le poing, l'oeil en feu, le sourcil froncé, et nous faisant à tous crier hourra.' *L'Atelier*, Deuxième Année, 9 (mai 1843) 71.

6 Flora Tristan, *Promenades dans Londres ou l'aristocratie et les prolétaires anglais,* Edition établie et commentée présentée par François Bédarida (Paris, Maspéro, 1978), pp. 273–4.

7 Mary Wollstonecraft s'élève contre les écrivains qui considèrent la femme comme un être d'une nature subordonnée et destinée aux plaisirs de l'homme. A ce sujet, elle fait une critique très juste de Rousseau, qui établit que la femme doit être faible et passive, l'homme actif et fort; que la femme a été formée pour être assujettie à l'homme, et enfin que la femme doit se rendre agréable et obéir à son maître et que tel est le but de son existence. *Promenades dans Londres,* p. 275.

8 Mary Wollstonecraft publiait en 1792, les mêmes principes que Saint Simon a répandus plus tard, et qui se propagèrent avec tant de rapidité à la suite de la révolution de 1830. Sa critique est admirable; elle fait ressortir dans toutes leurs vérités les maux provenant de l'organisation actuelle de la famille; et la force de sa logique laisse les contradicteurs sans réplique. *Promenades dans Londres,* p. 276.

9 This chapter like the rest of the book is full of Anglophobic remarks – a tendency to which Flora Tristan was more than a little prone.

10 Quelle révoltant contraste en Angleterre que l'extrême servitude des femmes et la supériorité intellectuelle des femmes auteurs! *Promenades dans Londres,* p. 262.

11 See Grogan, note 2.

12 For an assessment of these aspects on Flora Tristan see Stéphane Michaud (ed.), *Actes du Colloque Un Fabuleux destin: Flora Tristan* (Dijon, Editions Universitaires de Dijon, 1985).

13 Ces trois droits correspondent évidemment aux trois mots prononcés pour faire la révolution de 89: 1 – l'égalité – premier droit au travail, 2 – liberté – deuxième droit au pain – 3 fraternité – troisième droit à l'instruction. – Car pour être égaux il faut que tous travaillent – pour être libres il faut que tous puissent vivre – pour être frères il faut que tous aient reçu la même instruction afin de pouvoir sympathiser entre eux. *Le Tour de France* (Paris, Maspéro, 1980) Tome 2, p. 192.

14 'Commencez-vous à comprendre, vous, hommes qui crient au scandale avant de vouloir examiner la question, pourquoi je réclame des droits pour la femme? – pourquoi je voudrais qu'elle fût placée dans la société sur un pied d'égalité absolue avec l'homme, et qu'elle en jouît en vertu du droit légal que tout être apporte en naissant? Je réclame des droits pour la femme, parce que je suis convaincue que tous les malheurs au monde proviennent de cet oubli et mépris qu'on a fait jusqu'ici des droits naturels et imprescriptibles de l'être femme – Je rélame des droits pour la femme parce que c'est l'unique moyen qu'on s'occupe de son éducation et que de l'éducation de la femme dépend celle de l'homme en général, et particulièrement celle de l'homme du peuple. – Je réclame des droits pour la femme parce que c'est le seul moyen d'obtenir sa réhabilitation devant l'Eglise, devant la loi et devant la société et qu'il faut cette réhabilitation préalable pour que les ouvriers soient eux-mêmes réhabilités.' *Union Ouvrière* (Paris, Editions Des Femmes, 1986), pp. 204–5.

15 'Ouvriers en 91 vos pères ont proclamé l'immortelle déclaration des DROITS DE L'HOMME et c'est à cette solonelle déclaration que vous devez d'être aujourd'hui des hommes libres et égaux en droit devant la loi. – Honneur à vos pères pour cette grande oeuvre! – Mais prolétaires, il vous reste à vous, hommes de 1843, une oeuvre non moins grande à accomplir. – A votre tour, affranchissez les dernières esclaves qui restent encore dans la société française, proclamez les DROITS DE LA FEMME.' *Union Ouvrière,* p. 212.

16 For some of the many dimensions of this question see Valerie Bryson, *Feminist Political Theory, An Introduction* (London, Macmillan, 1992); R. W. Connell, *Gender and Power* (Oxford, Polity Press, 1987); Denise Riley, *Am I that name? Feminism and the Category of*

Women in History (London, Macmillan, 1988); Harriet B. Applewhite and Darline G. Levy (eds), *Women and Politics in the Age of the Democratic Revolution* (Ann Arbor, The University of Michigan Press, 1990); Kessler Harris, 'Gender Class and Conflict' *Gender and History* 5:1 (spring 1993).

17 'Travailleurs, et vous, travailleuses, que jusqu'ici n'avez encore compté pour rien dans les sociétés humaines, je vous serre cordialement la main. Je m'unis à vous pour la tâche commune; je vis en vous par l'amour, et suis votre soeur en l'humanité, Flora Tristan.' *Promenades dans Londres*, p. 55.

18 'Croyez-vous que, si le peuple anglais avait été élevé dans les principes de liberté et d'égalité, s'il avait appris à considérer que la résistance à l'oppression est non seulement le *droit* naturel de l'homme, mais que, bien plus, lorsque le peuple est opprimé, l'insurrection devient un *devoir sacré.'* *Promenades dans Londres*, p. 50.

19 'Je vois peu de monde et m'éloigne autant que je puis des réunions publiques. Cabet est ici en ce moment. Ce brave homme me désigne déjà comme son successeur à l'apostolat, et je cède la succession à qui me donnera une tasse de café. Il se prêche en ce moment je ne sais combien d'évangiles nouveaux, évangile selon Buchez, évangile selon Pierre Leroux, évangile selon Lammenais, Considérant, Mme George Sand, Mme Flora Tristan, évangile selon Pecqueur et encore bien d'autres. Je n'ai pas envie d'augmenter le nombre de ces fous; aussi je produis un effet mirobolant sur ceux qui me voient pour la première fois quand ils viennent à s'apercevoir que j'ai le sens commun.' Cited in Jules L. Puech, *La Vie et l'Oeuvre de Flora Tristan* (Paris, Marcel Rivière, 1925), p. 204.

20 Malgré les appels pressantes des républicaines, plus nombreuses qu'on ne le pense à l'époque, les exhortant à joindre l'affranchissement des femmes à celui des peuples, persuadées que sans elles il ne sera pas, les hommes répubicains n'entendent pas cette raison féminine: ils donnent une sens restrictif au concept de liberté en croyant lui donner son sens vrai.' See Michèle Riot-Sarcey, 'La liberté des femmes dans les années 1830', in *Les femmes et le révolution française*, Tome 3, *L'effet 89* (Toulouse, Presses Universitaires du Mirail, 1991), p. 168.

21 According to Armogathe and Grandjonc, these same women turned down the article on Flora Tristan's life on the grounds that they did not approve of her private life. See their Introduction to *Union Ouvrière*, p. 80. Michaud claims that they did publish it on 15 April 1848. See his Introduction to her correspondence, *Lettres* (Paris, Editions du Seuil, 1980), p. 16.

22 'Je regarde comme funestes et stupides toutes nos rêveries d'émancipation de la femme; je lui refuse toute espèce de droit et d'initiative politique; je crois que pour la femme, la liberté et le bien-être consistent uniquement dans le mariage, la maternité, les soins domestiques, la fidelité de l'époux, la chastité et la retraite.' Cited in Edouard Dolléans, *Proudhon*, 2ᵉ édition (Paris, Gallimard, 1948), p. 101.

23 Differences and arguments among feminists in France during the latter half of the nineteenth century are covered in Laurence Klejman and Florence Rochefort, *L'Egalité en marche* (Paris, Des Femmes, 1989). See also Felicia Gordon, *The Integral Feminist: Madeleine Pelletier 1874–1939* (Cambridge, Polity Press 1990); and Charles Sowerwine, *Sisters or Citizens: Women and Socialism in France since 1876* (translation of *Les Femmes et le socialisme* (Paris, Press Nationales des Sciences Politiques, 1978, Cambridge, Cambridge University Press, 1982).

7

'Saintes soeurs' and 'femme fortes'; alternative accounts of the route to womanly civic virtue, and the history of French feminism

Hazel Mills

IN her famous and passionate defence of the 'rights of woman' in 1792 Mary Wollstonecraft offered her readers an account of the 'inferiority of woman, according to the present appearance of things'. She gave detail to this image by describing the common faults of women: they were generally weak, cunning, vain and selfish, a prey to prejudice, foolishly delicate, too filled with sensibility, devoted to pleasure, and the slaves of their feelings. For this sorry state of affairs Wollstonecraft blamed above all the education women received. She championed the establishment of public day-schools where boys and girls would be educated together. Thus, she argued, would women 'become enlightened citizens'. 'Let woman share the rights, and she will emulate the virtues of man', she proclaimed.[1]

Wollstonecraft looked forward to an era when woman would be the civil and political equal of man. Visits to Portugal and France provided material for some of her texts, and consciously or unconsciously a frame of comparison for the condition of women within different cultures.[2] In some respects she admired French women, arguing that, 'they (had) acquired a portion of taste and knowledge rarely to be found in the women of other countries'.[3] Elsewhere, however, she made it clear that she regretted the influence of Catholicism in both France and Portugal. In her *Vindication of the Rights of Woman*, she commented:

> In France boys and girls, particularly the latter, are only educated to please, to manage their persons, and regulate the exterior behaviour; and their minds are corrupted, at a very early age, by the wordly and pious cautions they receive to guard them against immodesty.[4]

However, it is my contention that in contrast with Wollstonecraft's opinion (and those of many Anglo-American feminists, perhaps reared in a tradition profoundly influenced by the sort of assumptions about the differences between Protestant and Catholic cultures exemplified in Wollstonecraft's work), nineteenth-century French Catholicism permitted certain groups of women real power within the community, as well as the means to negotiate dominant and restrictive images of the 'unpolitical' sex. Further, the quintessentially 'public' activity of these women gave them a sense of civic responsibility and membership of the local, if not the national polity.[5] Some of these women were nuns, '*saintes soeurs*' who devoted their lives to prayer and extensive charitable and nursing activity. Others were lay women – single or married – members of charitable associations who ran soup kitchens, schools for the daughters of the urban and rural poor; visited prisoners, assisted prostitutes, and much more besides. '*Femmes fortes*',[6] they were often in command of considerable funds, and fought to defend their independence from encroaching external authority, both religious and secular.

These are the women of my title; women whose history is as yet barely uncovered, and whose activities may cause us to rethink the categories of analysis constructed by Mary Wollstonecraft and subsequent writers. Their history, I would argue, informed the later experience of French feminism, and the contours of emerging political identities of French women. That French feminism was to be, across the nineteenth and twentieth centuries, very different from the English model (and indeed from that of the United States), was in part a result of the profound cultural legacy of Catholicism in France.

Wollstonecraft's most famous work, the *Vindication of the Rights of Woman*, can be set within a number of frames. First, it was part of a wider corpus of texts written by English authors at the end of the eighteenth, and beginning of the nineteenth centuries, responding to contemporary events in France, and commenting on a radical and dissenting agenda within England. Each of these texts drew meaning from that context, and from each other.[7] It can also be read alongside Wollstonecraft's other works, including her fiction. Beyond that, it is useful to site it within an eighteenth-century tradition of educational writings, to which Wollstonecraft explicitly responded,[8] and an overlapping body of French texts on women's roles in society. Among this latter group, the work of Rousseau was pre-eminent.[9] Wollstonecraft was clearly incensed by much of his writing, particularly *Emile*, with its representation of Sophie, a woman trained to be passive, agreeable, dependent upon man, mild, and submissive. Sophie's sphere of operation was utterly domestic, but even within that realm Wollstonecraft took issue with Rousseau's prescriptions for the education and character of the virtuous woman:'how grossly do they insult us who thus advise us only to render ourselves gentle, domestic brutes'.[10]

For this, and for its general tone and subject, the *Vindication of the Rights of Woman* has been claimed as an early feminist text, rediscovered at the end of the nineteenth century, and now firmly placed within the canon.[11] Certainly, the book marked a notable attempt to place the unequal treatment of men and women on the English radical agenda, and sections read today as precociously modern.

However, when she addresses the question of the extent of a virtuous woman's influence and participation in society, Wollstonecraft's writing is somewhat contradictory. She stresses that a woman's first duty is within the family, above all as a mother: 'the care of children in their infancy is one of the grand duties annexed to the female character by nature'.[12] She contrasts Rousseau's Sophie with a vigorous, rational woman, yet one surrounded by a brood of children,[13] and later describes a possible future society in which a woman will be 'intent to manage her family, educate her children, and assist her neighbours'.[14] However, for Wollstonecraft, this educated, rational mother-figure is also a *citizen*, and an active one at that.[15] She should, crucially, be independent of her husband, or any man: 'it is vain to expect virtue from women until they are in some degree independent of men'.[16] A proper education will equip her for this independence, which will be rooted in her ability to earn a living in 'respectable stations' in society.[17] Proclaiming, 'in order to render their private virtue a public benefit, they must have a civil existence in the state, married or single',[18] Wollstonecraft also hints that she believes that women, properly educated, would be qualified for political rights.[19]

If education was the path to female virtue and future civic status, what contributed to the present unhappy situation, according to Wollstonecraft, were social institutions – bodies of men who had acquired their power in the distant past by force, and now sought to organise society hierarchically, insisting upon complete obedience from all.[20] This suspicion of institutions appears in all of her writing. In her analysis of the French Revolution, she depicts aristocracies, monarchs, and established churches as common blocks to progress; producing a French character 'depraved by the inveterate despotism of ages'.[21] Raised an Anglican, Wollstonecraft's writings reveal a profound distrust of institutionalised religion, especially of Churches connected to the State:

> Religion, pure source of comfort in this vale of tears! how has thy clear stream been muddied by the dabblers, who have presumptuously endeavoured to confine in one narrow channel, the living waters that ever flow towards God.[22]

On many occasions Wollstonecraft declared her affiliation to religion as consolation in times of trouble.[23] In *Thoughts on the Education of Daughters* (1787), she argued in favour of teaching girls 'fixed principles of religion'.[24] Hers was, however, a very refined God; a rational deity whose existence could be deduced from the evidence of the ordered universe.[25] Here we can see, at least in part, the influence upon Wollstonecraft of the Dissenting circles she joined in London, first at Newington Green, and later at St Paul's churchyard.[26]

However, hardly an avowed supporter of the Anglican Church, Wollstonecraft was especially hostile to Catholicism. Of the Portuguese, she proclaimed:

> the gross ritual of Romish ceremonies is all they can comprehend; they can do penance, but not conquer their revenge, or lust. Religion, or love, has never humanised their hearts; they want the vital part; the mere body worships. Taste is unknown; Gothic finery, and unnatural decorations, which they term ornaments, are conspicuous in their churches and dress.[27]

Similarly, chief among the causes of the 'depraved and volatile' national character of France were the institution and personnel of the Catholic Church.[28] In fine Dissenting tradition, Wollstonecraft reviled monks: 'the canker-worms that lurked behind monastic walls ... leeches of the kingdom', who had contributed nothing to the nation from their vast wealth while 'ostensibly boasting of their charity'. Their lives were 'a mockery of the doctrines, which they taught, and pretended to reverence'.[29] She defended the Revolutionary seizure of church property, which had been 'accumulated by the most abominable violation of every sentiment of justice and piety.'[30] England did not escape her scorn. She decried 'the relics of Popery retained in our colleges', and the 'Romish customs' which still had 'the most baneful effect on the morals of our clergy'.[31] For Wollstonecraft, Catholicism's myriad faults were barely concealed beneath 'Gothic drapery'[32] and 'the pestiferous purple'.[33]

While she seems to have felt that religion was a necessary part of a young woman's education, Wollstonecraft was particularly hostile to a convent education. In her highly autobiographical novel, *Mary, a Fiction* (1788), the heroine of the novel visited several convents, finding them full of 'unhappy individuals ... discontented, prejudiced':

> Wrapped up in themselves, the nuns thought only of inferior gratifications ... In short, when they could be neither wives nor mothers, they aimed at being superiors, and became the most selfish creatures in the world.[34]

In sum, although in some respects she admired French women, it seems likely that Wollstonecraft felt that the Catholic Church was one of the factors blocking the achievement of 'virtue' by that nation's female population. And of course, by 'virtue' she meant a status wherein the individual was rational, educated, independent of mind and spirit, and free from 'superstition'.[35] If men would but help women break the chains restraining them, they would find women, she asserted, 'in a word – better citizens'.[36]

If we now turn to France in the first half of the nineteenth century, a somewhat different picture of the role the Catholic Church could play in women's lives emerges from the archives. To take the example of one diocese, that of Besançon in old Franche-Comté,[37] civil and ecclesiastical records for this period allow the partial reconstruction of a dense and fascinating map of female activism, conducted under a religious aegis, but extending far beyond the confines of the convent or parish church.

The nineteenth century in France could be labelled 'the era of the nun'.[38] The female religious life bloomed dramatically in the period from the end of the Revolution of 1789, until the 1870s, and even thereafter remained popular and full of vitality: in 1808 there were at least 13,900 nuns and novices in France; 66,000 in 1850, and 127,000 in 1878. As a consequence, while on the eve of the Revolution the male hierarchy of the church had out-numbered the female by at least two to one, by 1861 women comprised 54.5 per cent of its personnel.[39]

However, it is important to note that the vast majority of these women were not nuns on the medieval, contemplative, model – les religieuses, cloistered, silent, with eyes downcast. Rather, they belonged to a newer form of the female religious order – the congrégation – and as soeurs they took only simple annual vows. Most significantly, they did not live their lives behind convent walls, but spent the majority of their time in the community, teaching poor girls in charity schools, tending to the sick in hospitals or their own homes.[40] They were easily recognised in their black, brown or grey habits, presenting a traditional, yet curiously transformed image to their many viewers, and coming to be highly esteemed.

In the diocese of Besançon at the end of the eighteenth century there had been some sixty-one houses of religious women, linked to eleven different Orders, and in addition, seventeen communities of semi-independent nursing sisters. With eleven communities, the Ursulines were the most successful Order in the diocese. All sixty-one communities were located in towns of two thousand or more inhabitants; most had been founded in the seventeenth or eighteenth centuries.[41] The great majority (as across France) were also, by 1789, essentially enclosed houses, a result of the suspicion of female activism within the clerical hierarchy in that era.[42]

The history of female religious communities in the Franche-Comté in the first half of the nineteenth century is one of early reappearance, expansion and success. After the most anti-clerical phase of the Revolution passed, women were among the first religious people to regroup, or form new communities. Full *congrégations* emerged gradually from groupings of like-minded pious women, including ex-nuns. These groups only gradually took on the full trappings of the religious life. Initially they appeared in Besançon itself,[43] and from around 1806 were to be found across the diocese. Due to ambiguities in the sources it is impossible to give a definitive total for the number of female religious communities in Franche-Comté between *c.* 1798 and 1850.[44] However, there were at least one hundred and fifty-eight such groupings, linked to twenty-three different female Orders, plus sixteen semi-autonomous communities of *soeurs hospitalières* affiliated to one of three general rules. A 'community' could be as few as one or two sisters permanently living and working at a considerable distance from their mother-house, or as many as sixty women at the same location.

Of the twenty-three Orders represented in this period in the diocese only two were purely contemplative,[45] and two were particularly prolific, having respectively around thirty, and around seventeen communities in the three *départements* by 1850.[46] The most successful took in women with very small dowries or with no dowry at all, and accepted large numbers from the poorer ranks of society. By 1850 there was a total of over 930 women living and working as sisters in the diocese – around 500 in the *département* of the Doubs, of whom about 350 were in the city of Besançon itself; roughly 340 in the Jura, and approximately 90 in the Haute-Saône.[47]

To examine the opportunities that could present themselves to members of these Orders we have only to consider briefly the life-story of one particularly dynamic Bisontin *soeur*, who founded an Order of women in the last years of the Revolution, and vigorously and confidently defended the autonomy and prerogatives of that community as it grew into the most successful congregation in the diocese.

Jeanne-Antide Thouret was born in 1765 in the village of Sancey in the Doubs, the daughter of a farm labourer. Aged twenty-two, and against her father's wishes, she entered the novice-house of the *Filles de Charité* in Paris. Founded in 1633, this was the oldest and most venerable of the nursing communities which emerged from the Counter-Reformation.[48] She was in the mother-house of the congregation in July 1790 when it was attacked during a grain riot. By 1792 she was in Amiens, once again working in a hospital staffed by her community, but in October 1793, again in Paris, she had to leave for Besançon when the Convention prescribed the immediate dissolution of all religious associations.[49]

It is at this point that Jeanne-Antide's story becomes remarkable. Officially forbidden from living and working as a nun, she did not return to her family, or enter the secular life. Instead, Jeanne-Antide continued to practise what she saw as her 'ministry', both in the city of Besançon and in the surrounding countryside. At moments of resurgent anti-clericalism she went into semi-hiding in Sancey. Even there, however, she taught the girls of the village their catechism. In 1795 she became an exile in Switzerland. Returning to Besançon once the political climate was more tolerant, on 11 April 1799 she gathered around her a small group of like-minded women and together they opened a free school for the poor girls of the city, and set up a *centre de soins* where free meals were distributed to the indigent and the old. The group became known in the city as the *Soeurs de Bouillon et des Petites Ecoles* or the 'Grey Sisters', from their manner of dress. From this beginning Jeanne-Antide and her followers soon opened a second school in the poorest district of the city. Recruits to the association now called themselves *soeur*.[50]

From that point on, Sister Jeanne-Antide faced three related challenges. First, she sought official sanction for her community, which was finally obtained from the ecclesiastical authorities in 1807, and from the Government in 1810.[51] Her second task was to retain control of the new Order against encroachments from male clerics and to protect it from attempts to subordinate it to the re-formed *Filles de Charité* in Paris. In successful pursuit of this goal she appealed to the Prefect of the Doubs in 1804:

> The sisters of our Association are not remotely disposed to become attached to the House of Charity in Paris. They have told me that they would rather die and be thrown into boiling water; that is their reply.[52]

Jeanne-Antide's third task was to see the congregation spread throughout the diocese and beyond. She achieved this goal as well, but in so doing profoundly alienated herself from the local ecclesiastical hierarchy. In pursuit of security, she travelled to Rome after 1815 to seek explicit papal protection for her Order, arousing the antagonism of the new Archbishop of Besançon, Courtois de Pressigny. He stirred dissent in the Besançon communities during her absence, and by complicated local manoeuvring succeeded both in ensuring that Jeanne-Antide remained in Rome until her death, and also that the Italian communities of the Order were con-stitutionally separated from those in France.[53] Nevertheless, the French congregation flourished and grew very much along the lines envisaged by Jeanne-Antide. By 1847, in addition to the central community, there were 105 other houses, spread over seven *départements* of France, gathering a total of over 400 full sisters.[54]

This, then, was a particularly successful woman, whose charisma, determination and ambition is strikingly evident in her writings. The congregations of the nineteenth century, however, offered most of their thousands of members a very active, highly esteemed life, despite the restrictions of the vows of poverty and obedience, and the sacrifice of 'normal' family life.

   For those reluctant or unable to devote their entire lives to the Church, there was an alternative pattern of religious association available to women in early nineteenth-century French towns and cities. This was the *confraternité*, or voluntary association of lay men or women who met regularly for certain 'pious' ends, or whose affiliation was at least defined in religious terms. While the male confraternity is generally held to be in decline in this era, its female equivalent was undergoing a renaissance in the early to mid-nineteenth century. The diocese of Besançon witnessed the appearance or re-appearance of dozens of female confraternities in the period immediately following the French Revolution.[55] In particular, most major towns in the region, seventeen in all, quickly saw the formation of associations of women taking the name *Dames de Charité*. In addition, other similar groups took the names *Dames de Charité Maternelle* and *Dames de Sainte Anne*. Many had pre-Revolutionary antecedents; all welcomed both married and unmarried women as members. Those whose existence can be traced back to the eighteenth or seventeenth centuries[56] appear to have disbanded between 1789 and 1793, and then re-grouped from 1798. The first to reappear was the Besançon *Dames de Charité*. In 1814 the city's *Bureau de Bienfaisance* noted that:

> It was only in the Year 8 that the Prefect ... provisionally authorised these Ladies to reunite their society for different works of charity, and particularly in order to collect money in the parishes of the city.[57]

   Some of these societies were clearly formed as the result of the initiative, or enthusiasm of a particular cleric. However, this was not always the case. The *Dames de Charité* of Arbois, for instance, independently came together to re-form their association, and in the first years of its existence had to defend themselves against the determined hostility of the *Curé* of the town.[58] After they were established, most such associations were allocated a clerical *Directeur*. Once again, however, this was not always the pattern, and the association in Arbois provides an example of a society that operated, in their case into the 1830s, without clerical (or for that matter any other male) supervision.[59]

   What was common to all these societies was their social make-up: they grouped women from the most prosperous strata of the community. Wherever membership lists survive they permit a glimpse of this pattern of recruitment. To take only the example of the city of Besançon itself – here there were several bourgeois associations whose memberships overlapped. The officers of the *Dames de Charité de Besançon* in 1811 included Mme Daclin, the *Présidente*, Mme Chifflet, *Secrétaire*, the elder Mlle Domet,

Trésurière, and her sister, Marie-Anne Domet. Mmes Daclin and Chifflet were married to men prominent in Besançon society – landowners and office-holders, they were on the boards of the local hospitals and, after 1814, electors in national politics. M. Daclin was the Mayor of Besançon.[60] Similarly, among the members of the *Société de la Charité Maternelle*, (active during the first Empire) was the Duchess of Conegliano, wife of the *Premier Inspecteur Général de la Gendarmerie Impériale*. As *Présidente* of the society, she donated a thousand francs to its coffers in 1810, and agreed to provide a similar amount each year thereafter. The *Vice-Présidente*, and the woman who effectively ran the society was Félicité DeBry, the wife of the Prefect of the Doubs. She donated an initial sum of five hundred francs, and promised to repeat that amount every year. Two other women made significant donations in 1810 – Mme Gabrielle de Grammont, a member of one of the most eminent families in the city, which had provided an archbishop of the diocese in the eighteenth century, and Mme la Baronne de Marulaz. In addition, nine other women became members of the new society's governing council, of whom four were also members of the *Dames de Charité*.[61]

This overlap of membership was far from coincidental, however. In 1810 the Prefect of the Doubs wrote requesting information on deserving families in the city from the *Présidente* of the *Dames de Charité*, and a list of names of *Dames Charitables* who would be willing to aid the new *Société de Charité Maternelle* in its activities. The *Dames de Charité* nominated Mlle Domet for this task, and she then provided six further names to the council of the new association. One woman so invited declined, however, giving as her reason her inability to contribute to the society's coffers.[62]

Something similar occurred in April 1824 when the Widow Lemoine was invited to join the *Dames de Charité*. In her reply to the *Présidente*, Mme Chifflet, Mme Lemoine said that although very flattered by the invitation to 'work with you in the relief of poverty and distress', she felt herself unable to accept the honour, citing her lack of the necessary 'leisure' to take on such responsibility.[63]

What then did these women, combining under a religious aegis, be they nuns, or bourgeois *Dames de Charité*, actually do? How much did they contribute to the communities in which they lived, and to what degree, in their behaviour, did they appear to accept the contemporary, oft re-stated prescription of predominantly private powers and responsibilities for women?

Once again, a focus on Besançon is instructive. The city had a vast wealth of regular communities, in addition to its two or more bourgeois confraternities. The activities undertaken by such groups of women can be placed in four categories: education (both of fee-paying and poor children); nursing and care of the sick (in hospitals and in their own homes); poor relief via soup kitchens and food distribution; and the care of indigent and vulnerable members of the community, such as orphans or unmarried mothers. This does not, however, really do full justice to the range of female charity in a French city such as Besançon. It does not properly cover, for example, the work of the *Charité de Maternité de Sainte Anne* which provided *layettes* and the costs of a midwife for poor working women in the lower-class districts of the city; nor the *atelier* run by the *Soeurs de St Joseph* for young women who were taught to sew, iron, and spin. It does not provide a neat space for the house for 'fallen women' run by the *Soeurs de Notre-Dame de Charité du Refuge* from 1839 in the centre of the city; nor for the *asile* for the long-term care of the indigent elderly founded and run by the *Petites Soeurs des Pauvres* from 1849.[64]

However, in each of these four categories we can glimpse something of the impact such women had on the communities of which they were a part. In Besançon the *Dames de Charité* and the *Soeurs de la Sainte Famille* co-operated in the funding and running of three schools for poor girls in the city and its suburbs. In 1807 seven sisters and four postulants taught some forty-two paying pupils, (twenty of whom were supported by the *Dames de Charité*), and at least thirty-six poor girls for no charge.[65] In 1824, 134 sisters were teaching some 2,800 free pupils and 5,700 who paid fees in schools in the city, and in twenty-five further houses elsewhere in the diocese; by 1877 there were over 150 pupils in the city schools alone.[66] In addition, from 1816 the congregation set up a school to train pupil *soeur* school-mistresses for the countryside. As well as teaching girls to read, to write their names, and to do a little basic arithmetic, the Mayor reported in 1807 that they gave instruction to their pupils, 'according to their dispositions, in the skills of dress-maker, laundress, embroiderer, knitter and seamstress'.[67] From the 1820s they also took fee-paying pupils from better-off families, subsidising the poor schools with the profits from this *pension*. Their aim, according to their statutes was:

> to procure a christian and civil education and instruction for poor and indigent young girls, to train them in the principles of virtue and the catholic religion ... and to train for the countryside fine school mistresses who will be useful to their pupils.[68]

The *Soeurs de Charité* were also involved in education in the city, principally of poor girls. By 1819 they were running four schools in different parishes of Besançon, educating over 240 pupils. This had increased to seven schools with around 550 pupils in 1832, and to twelve schools and two *asiles* in 1838.[69] In addition, however, this congregation was also dedicated to the care of the sick and indigent in the *Maison de Refuge*, or poor-house, and to visiting the ill in their own homes. In 1824 they estimated they had 120 patients in institutions, but regularly aided a further 600 at home.[70] Their members also staffed two charitable hospices for the elderly and indigent in Besançon, the *Depôt de Mendicité*, and the military hospital in this garrison city. Further nursing services were provided by the *Hospitalières de Notre-Dame des Sept Douleurs*, in the main hospital, St Jacques. In 1808 they numbered seventeen nuns and two novices, and had in their care over 350 patients. By 1819 these numbers had risen to twenty-seven (plus twenty-five women at varying stages of their training) and seven hundred respectively, although over three hundred of these 'patients' were *enfants de la charité* – orphans placed with willing families and wet-nurses wherever possible.[71]

This narrative could be much longer, but the broad picture is clear. In the city of Besançon, as in many towns in the diocese, and indeed in similar settings throughout France, women acting in groups defined by a loose, or explicit religious identity were central to the provision of the welfare services of the community. Their very ubiquity makes them easy to overlook, but is at the heart of the importance of the associations they formed. They provided fundamental public services, and were seen by the wider community and the civil authorities as competent in these areas. Their wide-ranging activities were by no means only small-scale, amateur, or part-time. Through them, cohorts of women acquired important administrative, managerial and negotiating skills. They often came into conflict with civil and religious authorities. For example, in Besançon in 1821 there was a disagreement between the *Dames de Charité* and the *Bureau de Bienfaisance*, over who should control a donation made to the confraternity for distribution to the city's poor, a sum which the civil body felt should rightly fall within its perview. Both sides wrote to the Prefect, making their case. Ultimately he decided that 'The bequest shall ... be given to the Bureau de Bienfaisance for their disposal, but they must consult the Ladies of Charity as to the most deserving cases at the present time'.[72]

Between them, these Catholic associations – the congregation, and the confraternity – offered active involvement in events in the public spaces of the community to women from a variety of social backgrounds. This activity gave women *de facto* careers outside the home, and an outlet for sociability – opportunities moreover, not on offer elsewhere in that period. That this activity was not explicitly theorised as 'political' (and certainly not 'feminist') by the women involved is significant, but perhaps ought not to stop modern readers labelling it as such.

Thus, I would argue that during the first half of the nineteenth century religious associations of women were one of the most characteristic forms of female religiosity, and of female organisational practice in France, certainly outside the capital. Their formation and activities offer an excellent opportunity to examine 'ordinary' women's perceptions of their roles in society outside the home, particularly in the urban community. From the archival records, it is clear that Catholicism was not, necessarily, or in a straightforward sense, the limiting factor to the experience of women it is often assumed to have been. However, in so permitting certain forms of female activism, patterns of Catholic association had profound implications for the nature and boundaries of many subsequent generations of French women's political identities; for their sense of themselves as actual or potential political actors. As such, the complex heritage of Catholicism had a very considerable impact in the later nineteenth and twentieth centuries on the shape of French feminism, with its small numerical base, legalism, and ambiguity surrounding the issue of suffrage. It is thus at the heart of the problems that varieties of feminist organisations were to face in attracting significant support from among middle and working-class women, for what were by then *explicitly* political ends.[73]

In addition, this evidence suggests we must reject analyses of nineteenth-century France which rest upon an over-simplistic division of society between a womanly, superstitious, emotional, sentimental, and unintellectual piety, and a manly, vigorous, 'modern' and rational secularity.[74] The motivation behind these patterns of female associative activity was undoubtedly complex. However, we should retain a place, in that picture, for the affiliation felt to Catholicism by women experiencing, in a mental and bodily sense, the nineteenth-century family, with its attendant restrictions, power relations and physical dangers. What we should not do is relegate such historical experience to a 'less modern', non-rational frame. Biology might not be a sufficient explanation of religious destiny, but the histories of marriage, sexuality and obstetrics may have played their part in the choices women made.[75] We eschew the history of the lived reality of the body at our peril.

Thus, Mary Wollstonecraft would have been wrong, had indeed, as the evidence suggests, she believed that women attracted to the rituals and associations of the Catholic Church were simply the victims of a superstitious, restrictive institution, veiled in 'Gothic drapery'. This was in many cases a positive relationship which gave fulfilment and meaning to many women's lives. Paradoxically, for some French women the thing Wollstonecraft explicitly longed for, the 'road upon which (women) can pursue more extensive plans of usefulness and independence'[76] was provided by Catholicism.

Notes

1   Mary Wollstonecraft, *Vindication of the Rights of Woman with Strictures on Political and Moral Subjects* [1792], ed. M. B. Kramnick (London, Penguin, 1982) (hereafter *Vindication*), pp. 105–6, 119, 130, 145, 169, 202, 253, 280–3, 286–7, 319.

2   For Wollstonecraft's early life see C. Tomalin, *The Life and Death of Mary Wollstonecraft* (London, Penguin, 1992), pp. 11–109.

3   *An Historical and Moral View of the Origin and Progress of the French Revolution and the Effect it has Produced in Europe* [1794], J. Todd and M. Butler (eds), *The Works of Mary Wollstonecraft*, 7 vols (London, Pickering, 1989), (hereafter *Works*), vol. 6, p. 148.

4   *Vindication*, p. 177.

5   Although I am using the language of 'political identity' in examining the behaviour of these 'ordinary women', I doubt any of them would have thought of themselves as feminists, always supposing, as seems unlikely, that by the middle decades of the century that term would have been available to many of their number. Nor did any of them, at least in the groups I have looked at, articulate a desire for political rights on the same basis as men. This point is crucial to my conclusion to this article.

6   For the rhetorical construction, in sermons of this era, of the *femme forte*, see H. Mills, 'Negotiating the divide: women, philanthropy and the "public sphere" in nineteenth-century France', in F. Tallett and N. Atkin (eds), *Religion, Society and Politics in France since 1789* (London, Hambledon Press, 1991), pp. 29–54.

7   M. Butler, *Burke, Paine, Godwin and the Revolutionary Controversy* (Cambridge, Cambridge University Press, 1984), p. 2.

8   *Works*, vol. 1, pp. 13–14; *Vindication*, pp. 173–218.

9   *Vindication*, partic. pp. 173–91.

10   *Ibid.*, p. 101.

11   See Tomalin, *Life and Death*, pp. 284–314.

12   *Vindication*, p. 265.

13   *Vindication*, pp. 138–9.

14   *Ibid.*, p. 259.

15   'It is plain from the history of all nations, that women cannot be confined to merely domestic pursuits, for they will not fulfil family duties unless their minds take a wider range'. *Vindication*, p. 294.

16   *Ibid.*, pp. 252–3. See also p. 259.

17   *Ibid.*, pp. 100, 105–7, 259, 261–2.

18   *Ibid.*, p. 262.

19   *Ibid.*, pp. 259–60.

20   *Ibid.*, pp. 98–9.

21   *An Historical and Moral View of the Origin and Progress of the French Revolution and the Effect it has Produced in Europe* (London, 1794), *Works*, vol. 6, p. 162.

22   *Vindication*, p. 277.

23   e.g., *Thoughts on the Education of Daughters, with Reflections on Female Conduct in the More Important Duties of Life*, (London, 1787), *Works*, vol. 4, pp. 33–5, 41; *The Female Reader, Or Miscellaneous Pieces, in Prose and Verse*, (London, 1789), *Ibid.*, p. 56.

24   *Works*, vol. 4, p. 33.

25   *Vindication*, pp. 132, 135, 218. See also, *Original Stories from Real Life, with Conversations calculated to regulate the Affections and forms the Mind to Truth and Goodness* (London, 1788), *Works*, vol 4, p. 360.

26   Tomalin, *Life and Death*, pp. 21, 46–63, 90–105.

27   *Mary, A Fiction*, (London, 1788), *Works*, vol. 1, p. 36.

28   *An Historical and Moral View of the Origins and Progress of the French Revolution and the*

Effect it has Produced in Europe (London, 1794), *Works*, vol. 6, pp. 161, 231.
29 *Ibid.*, p. 51.
30 *Works*, vol. 5, p. 48.
31 *Vindication*, p. 276.
32 *Works*, vol. 5, p. 48.
33 *Vindication*, p. 99.
34 *Works*, vol. 1, p. 34–5.
35 *Vindication*, pp. 107, 126, 283.
36 *Ibid.*, p. 263.
37 This chapter is based upon research carried out for a larger study – 'Women and the Catholic Church in France, 1800–1850' (Oxford D. Phil., in preparation), which takes the diocese of Besançon as a case-study. For more on this area's religious history see M. Rey (ed.), *Histoire des diocèses de Besançon et St-Claude* (Paris, Beauchesne, 1977).
38 C. Langlois, *Le Catholicisme au féminin: les congrégations françaises à supérieure générale au XIXe siècle* (Paris, Editions du Cerf, 1984); O. Arnold, *Le corps et l'âme: La vie des réligieuses au XIXe siècle* (Paris, Seuil, 1984).
39 C. Langlois, 'Les effectifs des congrégations féminines au XIXe siècle: de l'enquête statistique à l'histoire quantitative', *Revue d'Histoire de l'Eglise de France*, 60 (1974), 44–63.
40 The *congrégation* was based on the seventeenth-century model of Louise de Marillac and Vincent de Paul's 'Filles de Charité'. Members lived in small communities linked to a 'maison mère'. Their annual promises did not have any legal weight. See C. Jones, 'Sisters of Charity and the Ailing Poor', *Social History of Medicine*, 19 (1989), 339–48; O. Hufton and F. Tallett, 'Communities of women, the religious life and public service in eighteenth-century France', M. J. Boxer and J. H. Quataert (eds), *Connecting Spheres: Women in the Western World, 1500 to the Present* (Oxford, Oxford University Press, 1987), pp. 75–85.
41 J. de Trevillers, *Sequania Monistica: Dictionnaire des abbayes, prieures, couvents, collèges, hôpitaux conventuels et ermitages de Franche-Comté et du diocèse de Besançon antérieures à 1790*, 2 vols., (Vesoul, 1950–55), vol. 1, pp. 218–38, 227–35.
42 The only large community nationally that escaped this process of re-enclosure – the 'Filles de Charité' – was not represented in the eighteenth-century diocese of Besançon. For more on this subject, and on the one exception to re-enclosure in the diocese – the *Retraite Chrétienne*, see H. Mills, *Women and the Catholic Church*, chapter 4.
43 Namely, in 1798 the group that was to become the *Soeurs de la Sainte Famille*; in 1799, the group that was to become the *Soeurs de Charité de Besançon*.
44 Much depends upon the way a group was labelled by contemporaries, the importance attached to official authorisation, and how many 'sitings' in the documents establish a community's existence. For example, civil and ecclesiastical reports of 1808 mention nine pre-revolutionary Ursulines running a primary school for young girls who were requesting civil authorisation, and in 1809 the *Anciennes Religieuses de Salins* were mentioned in a letter from the Archbishop of Besançon, to Paris. Neither group reappears. Archives Nationales, (hereafter A.N.), *F19.6295*.
45 The *Bernadines*, (*Cisterciennes Reformées*) (Besançon, 1841), and the *Carmelites Déchaussées* (1843). *Archiepiscopal Archives, Besançon* (hereafter A.A.B.), *Fonds Congréganistes – Bernadines*, and *Fonds Congréganistes – Carmélites*.
46 The *Soeurs de Charité de Besançon* and the *Soeurs de la Sainte Famille*.
47 Archives Departmental (hereafter A.D.), (Doubs), *38.V.1–5*; A.D. (Jura) *7.V.1–10*; A.D. (Haute-Saône), *2.V.8, 4.V.1*; Archives Municipales (hereafter A.M.) Besançon, *R.1:1, 1:2, 1:25*; A.A.B, *Fonds Congréganistes*.
48 see C. Jones, 'Sisters of Charity'.

49 F. Trochu, *Sainte Jeanne-Antide Thouret* (Besançon, Imprimérie Gemo, 1933), pp. 15–210; G. Bordet, 'Jeanne-Antide Thouret, 1765–1826: une chrétienne en période révolutionnaire', *Eglise de Besançon*, 10 (May 1976), pp. 176–9; A.A.B, *Fonds Congréganistes – Soeurs de Charité*.

50 A.A.B. *Fonds Congréganistes – Soeurs de Charité*.

51 A.D. (Doubs), *38.v.4*, letters from Thouret to Prefect, Year 13 and 1808; Prefectoral Report 1808; A.N. *F19.6295*, report from Archbishop Lecoz to Paris, 1809.

52 A.D. (Doubs), *38.v.4*, letter of 26 Pluviose, Year 13. In the same year Lecoz also took up the case, writing to the authorities in Paris that in entering the Besançon community, novices showed that they wished to remain in the diocese, to work for its good, and to die on its soil; Pr. Roussel (ed.), *Corréspondence de Lecoz*, 2 vols (Paris, Alphonse Picard et Fils, 1900–03), vol. 2, pp. 196–201.

53 Trochu, pp. 369–425; A.D. (Doubs), *38.V.1*, reports on the congregation, Year 13–1840.

54 A.N. *F19.6348, Etats* of 1847.

55 See letter from the Prefect of the Doubs to the Minister of Cults, 20 Thermidor, Year 12, talking of female confraternities 'throughout the department'; A.D. (Doubs), *38.V.5*. Also H. Mills, *Women and the Catholic Church*, chapter 6.

56 Eg. the *Dames de Charité* of Orgelet and Arbois (Jura), and those of Besançon itself. The first lay grouping taking this title had been established by Vincent de Paul and Louise de Marillac in the early seventeenth century.

57 A.D. (Doubs), *38.V.4*, minutes of meeting of *Bureau de Bienfaisance*, 7 November 1814.

58 'Régistre des Deliberations de l'Association des Dames de la Charité', A.M. (Arbois), *Archives des Dames de Charité*, (hereafter *D.C.*).

59 *Ibid.*

60 A.D. (Doubs), notarial, tax, and poor-relief records.

61 A.D. (Doubs), *X.216, X.574, X.575*, 'Société de Charité Maternelle'.

62 The 'Société de Charité Maternelle' was clearly the result of a national civil initiative, following a decree from Napoleon himself in May 1810, seeking to establish such institutions. In Besançon it disappears from the records in 1815, but is later somewhat replaced by the explicitly more religious 'Société de Charité maternelle de sainte Anne'. A.D. (Doubs), *X.575*, Règlement pour la Société de Charité Maternelle, Paris, 1811'; *X.216*.

63 A.M (Besançon) *Q2.5*.

64 A.D. (Doubs), *X.575*, A.A.B., *Fonds Congréganistes – Saint Joseph, Etat du Diocèse de Besançon*, (Besançon, 1855); A.D. (Doubs), *38.V.2*, letter from Archbishop Mathieu, 6 November 1854.

65 A.D. (Doubs), *38.V.3*, Report of Mayor, 1807.

66 A.D. (Doubs), *38.V.1*, Etat of 1824; B.M.A., *R.1.2*.

67 A.D. (Doubs), *38.V.3*, Mayor's report, 1807.

68 *Ibid.*, statutes of congregation, 1826.

69 A.D. (Doubs), *38.V.1*, Prefectural Report of 1819; A.M. (Besançon), *R.1.25*, minutes of council meeting, 1838.

70 A.D. (Doubs), *38.V.1*.

71 A.A.B., *Fonds congréganistes – Hospitalières Saint-Jacques*; A.D. (Doubs), *38.V.1*, prefectoral reports of 1808 and 1819.

72 A.N. *F15.638* Decision of Prefect, 1821. Dossier on bequests by Sr and Widow Bichet.

73 I make this argument at greater length in Mills, 'Negotiating the divide', pp. 52–4. As McMillan reminds us 'the Catholic women's suffrage movement converted more women to suffragism that all other feminist groups combined', 'Women and Social Catholicism in Late Nineteenth & Early Twentieth-Century France' in *The Church and Women: Studies in Church History*, xxvii (Oxford, Basil Blackwell, 1990). On Catholic

feminism see also, S. Hause and A. Kenney, 'The Development of the Catholic Wom-
en's Suffrage Movement in France, 1896–1922', *Catholic Historical Review*, 68 (1981),
11–30; J. F. McMillan, 'Women, Religion and Politics: The Case of the Ligue
Patriotique des Françaises' in *Proceedings of the Annual Meeting of the Western Society for
French History*, 15 (Flagstaff, Arizona 1988), ed. W. Rosen, pp. 355–64; and McMillan's
chapter in this book.

74 Here I heartily concur with McMillan, 'Religion and Gender in Modern France: Some
Reflections', in F. Tallett and N. Atkin, *Religion, Society and Politics in France since 1789*,
pp. 55–66. See also Mills, 'Negotiating the Divide'.

75 Ironically, we have only to remember Wollstonecraft's own painful death after the
birth of her second baby.

76 *Vindication*, p. 259.

8

Maria Rye: the primrose path

Marion Diamond

THE *Dictionary of National Biography*, that great work of Victorian scholarship and Victorian values, contains few women of a feminist persuasion. While women such as Bessie Rayner Parkes and Harriet Taylor are missing, Maria Rye appears in an entry that stresses her role as a philanthropist, while largely ignoring her feminism.[1] The disparity between Rye's public reputation, which today is negligible, and her recognition in the official Victorian pantheon, as defined by the *Dictionary of National Biography*, requires some explanation. At a time when the concept of separate spheres confined so many women to the home, Rye lived a very public life, and the accolades she received were equally public.

It is a bowdlerised interpretation of that public life that forms the subject of her *Biography* entry. The author, W. B. Owens, recorded her long involvement with the emigration of women and children, an activity that he had no difficulty, in 1910, in categorising as philanthropic work. He included no reference to her work as a journalist, nor to her association with the liberal feminists of Langham Place, and while he acknowledged her work with the Society for Promoting the Employment of Women, he was wrong when he claimed that she 'disapprov[ed] of the women's franchise movement'.[2] Perhaps, as an old lady, Maria Rye preferred to be remembered primarily as a philanthropist, but it was not a true reflection of her life. She first became a public figure through her involvement with feminist, not philanthropic, causes. Increasing age and financial security drew her away from women's issues yet, despite her innate social and political conservatism, a feminist core remained.

Maria Susan Rye was born in 1829 in Chelsea, the eldest of nine children of a London solicitor, Edward Rye. Her father was a bibliophile, who saw to it that his daughters received a good education, but several disastrous business decisions meant there was no money for their dowries. Whether for that or other reasons, she failed to marry. Maria Rye was thus one of that large, amorphous category of 'surplus women' who so preoccupied the Victorians. All her activities depended on this primary fact, first in her own life, then in that of her sisters and friends, and above all, as the justification for her work promoting women's employment and female emigration.

In her mid-twenties, Rye began writing for *The Englishwoman's Domestic Magazine*. This journal, begun by Sam and Isabella Beeton in 1852, was a fascinating and highly profitable mix of items of general news, dress patterns, recipes, correspondence, and fairly uncontroversial articles dealing with 'women's issues'. By 1855, Rye was writing regularly for the Beetons, and seems to have earned at least a bare income from her pen. While most of her writing was descriptive and historical, she also addressed specifically women's issues. In late 1856, for instance, she addressed the question of 'The Property of Married Women'. She summarised the Law Amendment Society's draft for a proposed new law, and included, in full, the text of a petition calling for a change in the law which had been presented to Parliament the previous March. This petition, she noted approvingly, came 'from the pen of a lady already well known as the author of "A Brief Summary of the most important Laws concerning Women"'.[3] That woman was Barbara Leigh Smith, later Madame Bodichon.

The article brought Rye to the attention of other women involved in a variety of feminist issues, collectively known as the Langham Place group[4] including Barbara Leigh Smith Bodichon, Bessie Rayner Parkes, Jessie Boucherett and Emily Faithfull. In 1859, these middle-class women established the *English Woman's Journal*, dedicated to feminist issues. Registered as a co-operative under the Companies Act, Bodichon and Parkes contributed most of the capital, but there were also a number of smaller shareholders, including Maria Rye, who held one share.

During the next few years, Maria Rye wrote concurrently for *The Englishwoman's Domestic Magazine*, which paid her, and the *English Woman's Journal*, which could not. While the *English Woman's Journal*, by its very nature, preached to the converted and never attracted a large readership, the popularity of *The Englishwoman's Domestic Magazine* was unquestionable. It was half the price of the *Journal*, and the correspondents' page shows that its readership included women of all ages, married and single, employers and servants. Maria Rye's articles reached a much wider audience through *The Englishwoman's Domestic Magazine* than through the *Journal*, and through its pages she succeeded in bridging the gap between the Langham Place group and the generality of women who might otherwise have been unaware of, or untouched by, the issues that aroused such agitation in the *English Woman's Journal*.

Maria Rye's particular interests were religion, history, philanthropy and feminism. These interests coalesced in her articles. Her interest in history led her to write about the history of women, and her interpretation of history, as well as her religious faith, gave her an optimistic belief in an inevitable progress towards a more just society. This faith in progress is evident in her 1856 article on married women's property, for instance, where she tempered her outrage at the present condition of women with the assurance that change must come, for 'it is a monstrous absurdity to imagine, that while every generation beholds women shaking off those chains which have held them so long in vassalage, and while every year sees them approach nearer and nearer towards independence and equality with men ... it is ridiculous to believe they will much longer submit to be tied and bound by laws which, even in their primary institution, were a disgrace to the makers and an insult to our sex'.

Maria Rye's assessment of the position of women in her society was measured and cautious. Her characteristic brand of feminism developed gradually, and was never strident. She accepted the difference of the sexes as God-given, but difference should not mean inferiority. Her articles on philanthropy show that she believed strongly in women's superior altruism. This made her uneasy about women entering certain male professions that might compromise the distinctive virtues of woman-hood. Dr Elizabeth Blackwell, for instance, trained in America as a doctor, and was widely admired by many in the Langham Place circle. For Maria Rye, however, the practice of medicine was unsuited to women, for it would be hard 'to persuade the world that a woman, whose hands not unfrequently reek with gore, whose eyes are continually prying into the secrets of disease, who can dissect, i.e. cut up, without scruple, the sucking child or the hoary-headed matron, can possibly, by any stretch of imagination or charity ... possessed of the same nature or feelings as the generality of women. Clever the female physician may, nay, must be; gentle and sympathetic she dare not be. Do you say this argument will apply equally to man? Nay, he is coarser, harder, firmer by nature.'[5]

Similarly she was uneasy about women entering the political world, which was also coarse, hard and masculine, and she initially opposed women's suffrage as an encroachment into the public, masculine sphere. But she believed strongly that the law should treat women equally with men, and that she and other single women should not be disadvantaged by convention or the law in their efforts to achieve financial independence.

Religion played an important part in shaping Maria Rye's ideas in all areas of life, including feminism. At Chelsea she had come under the influence of the Reverend Charles Kingsley, vicar of the local parish, his wife Mary, who actually ran it, and through them, their son, Charles Kingsley, the novelist and Christian socialist, ten years her elder. The Ryes were practising members of the Church of England, but the family was more deeply religious than mere convention dictated. Maria Rye developed an intense evangelical faith in her girlhood, at a time when deep controversies were reshaping the Church of England.

The practice of religion offered a social and emotional outlet for many Victorian women. Religion could engage their untapped physical and mental energies, and participation in charitable work offered them a real taste of power, as well as a sense of practical usefulness otherwise missing from their lives. Religious controversy also offered women a substitute for the engagement in political debate from which they were excluded, for women, as well as men, participated in the debates that divided the Church of England during this period.

There can be no doubt that Evangelical Christianity, a religious faith based on a personal conviction of salvation, was a constant theme of Maria Rye's life. She never wavered from that faith, and it permeated every aspect of her behaviour. At its best Evangelicalism found an outlet in active philanthropy, but it could also find expression in a bigoted anti-Catholicism. In 1859, for instance, she wrote to A. C. Tait, the Bishop of London, to complain about alleged Papist tendencies at the Church of St Barnabas in Pimlico.[6] Uniquely in this letter, she signed herself not 'Maria S. Rye', but 'M. S. Rye', thereby concealing from the bishop that she was a woman. She introduced herself instead to Tait only as a Sunday school teacher at St Luke's, Chelsea.

Through her essays in *The Englishwoman's Domestic Magazine,* Maria Rye has left a vivid picture of the variety of philanthropic work that engaged women like herself. Writing of Louisa Twining's Workhouse Visiting Society, she assured her readers that 'the actual presence of a Christian woman among the morally or the physically sick carries with it a weight and a worth that no gold can purchase, no man measure'.[7] Her point of view has lost its appeal in a more secular age, but the visits of middle-class women amongst the poor served not just to ameliorate present conditions, but to bridge the gap of knowledge between rich and poor. Only with a knowledge of what conditions in the workhouses were like, would those with the power to make changes take the effort to bring about reform. The reports of lady visitors told people about conditions amongst the poor. Maria Rye was passionately aware of the need for radical change, rather than mere amelioration, as she harangued her comfortable readers in *The Englishwoman's Domestic Magazine* with descriptions of the horrors of workhouse life: 'I am troubling you with much unpleasant matter – 'tis a huge, unpleasant, sore that is being exposed – but, by all that is true and holy, the old rags must be torn off, and the place thoroughly cleansed; for these houses, that might be the glory of this land, are, as they stand now, a foul disgrace, where corruption breeds corruption, and every hateful thing.'

Her chief concern was the fate of women and children, and the cycle of poverty that the workhouse perpetuated. 'In one workhouse, which shall be nameless, 200 out of 309 were returned upon the parish in a deplorable state; and out of 326 from another house, 110 were known to have been subsequently led into vice and infamy! Two-thirds out of 300 girls returning to be wretched mothers of wretched infants, swelling the mass of destitute inmates, and adding to the parish expenses!'[8] Rye warned that such instances of social decay could lead to social break-down, unless those with the power and the purpose to intervene, chose to do so: 'The working classes, as a body, *are already* as discontented on this head as it is possible to be without breaking out into rebellion.'[9] None the less, her solutions were essentially personal rather than political, for she had greater faith in self-help than in state intervention.

Such practical small-scale philanthropies as sewing circles and reading classes were of direct benefit to the people they reached, but they also offered more intangible psychological advantages to the people who administered them. Philanthropic activities gave middle-class women a sense of usefulness, the opportunity to assert control over others, to parti-cipate in the public sphere in ways otherwise denied them. At their worst, charitable ladies could become officious; at their best, they could bring about social change only at the margins, and often they were sadly ineffectual when faced with problems too great to solve through their personal intervention. Charitable work was seen as acceptable and fulfill-ing work for women, but women, even middle-class women, were powerless in the political domain where the real social ills of Victorian Britain could be addressed most effectively. As long as women remained marginalised, their spheres of activity, including their work among the poor, would be marginalised too.

The *English Woman's Journal* acted as a focal point for the meeting of many like-minded women. At a time when little *public* space was available to women, the Reading Room acted as a gathering place and informal club for like-minded women. It served the same function, for women venturing beyond the confines of their homes, as the gentlemen's clubs that played such a central part in the lives of their brothers and fathers. Subscriptions to the Reading Room, set at one guinea per annum, defined the middle-class nature of the Langham Place group.

Within the Reading Room at Langham Place, members discussed a wide variety of feminist issues, such as the need for better women's edu-cation, and the political and legal rights of women. Maria Rye's particular interest was the lack of appropriate 'white-collar' employment for women, and the consequent financial difficulties faced by single women unable either to marry or to earn a decent living. The 1851 census had uncovered an apparent demographic anomaly in Britain, a surplus in the number of women over men that made it impossible for every woman to find a husband. A certain proportion of the female population therefore inevitably faced a single life, but middle-class Victorian society was based on the premise of the family, comprising male breadwinner and dependent wife and children. There was no clear role for unmarried adult daughters within this framework, yet the census warned that there was bound to be a shortfall in the number of men available for them to marry.

Male, middle-class commentators[10] saw the problem as less serious amongst the working class, since single women of this class worked, and were less likely to be a burden on their families. Indeed, a surplus of potential domestic servants was a positive advantage to the middle class, since it drove down the cost of employing them.

Amongst middle-class families, several factors exacerbated the problem. Middle-class men tended to marry late, delaying their marriage until they could meet the considerable cost of establishing a middle-class household, and the expansion of the British Empire meant that a disproportionate number of young men left Britain, either permanently or temporarily, to seek their fortunes in the colonies or the armed services. This left society with a problem, for the conventional dependence of daughters meant that they were doomed to a life of boredom and uselessness, and to the resentment of their fathers and brothers who would have to pay for their upkeep.

Perilously close to being a poor relation herself, Maria Rye confronted the issue of 'surplus women' with bitter irony in *The Englishwoman's Domestic Magazine* in 1858. In recent years, she said, 'poor (female) relations have multiplied and not replenished, but impoverished, the earth exceedingly'. Like many active and intelligent women, she was less than sympathetic to those dependent women who were too delicate to be useful, and 'who are contented to feed in youth upon the windy food of modern accomplishments, and sit under the shadow of that deadly Upas, "waiting-to-be married!"' Yet she recognised that the problem was not of their making, for 'a very large proportion of young girls are now being taught that, to sit still and look pretty, is one of the highest recommendations of a gentlewoman'.

The heart of the problem, she said, lay in the impoverished nature of much women's education. Boys' education set out 'to brace the mind [and] produce accuracy of judgment'; girls were offered nothing so rigorous, but only empty 'accomplishments'. With such poor preparation, it was little wonder that women found themselves unqualified for paid employment when the need arose, but it was a dreadful irony that 'a notion has been carried abroad ... that no occupation is so fitted for woman in general, and for broken-down gentlewomen in particular, as that of teaching'. The upshot was that the governess market was over-stocked and poorly paid, and incompetent governesses passed on an inadequate education to a new generation of girls. A comparable level of incompetence would be intolerable amongst dressmakers' apprentices, but 'ladies are decidedly more fastidious about the fashioning of their dresses than they are about the cultivation of their children's brains, or the direction given to their characters and tempers'.[11]

On the initiative of Jessie Boucherett, and with the support of the National Association for the Promotion of Social Science and the *English Woman's Journal*, the Society for Promoting the Employment of Women was formed in response to the problem of finding work for women. The Society recognised two requirements, if middle-class women were to find remunerative employment: first, they must receive an adequate training, not in traditional 'accomplishments', but in marketable skills; and second, the range of respectable employments must be widened into new areas, to relieve pressure on the 'over-stocked and' – consequently – 'poorly paid' governess market. To this end, the Society sponsored several initiatives in women's employment, including the Victoria Press, run by Emily Faithfull, and a law-copying office in Lincoln's Inn, to offer training and employment to women.

Maria Rye ran the law-copying office and stationer's shop that opened at 12 Portugal St., Lincoln's Inn Fields, early in 1860. Many clerical work-ers worked at the business of copying documents, especially by lawyers, those great generators of paper in all ages. Legal copying was a skilled occupation, for accuracy and legibility were essential, and copyists used special 'legal hand' to produce legal documents. Within a generation, typewriters, carbon copies, and more rapid printing processes would challenge this traditional occupation, but for the present, it was the sort of trade that suited the objectives of the Society for Promoting the Employment of Women. It was a 'still lighter and more suitable employ-ment' than the work of Emily Faithfull's compositors at the Victoria Press, for women could work as copyists outside the public gaze. They could sit rather than stand – always a preoccupation to those concerned with women's ailments. The skills to be acquired were especially appropriate for women, for good handwriting was one of the 'accomplishments' of educated women, and could be adapted to legal copying without great difficulty. A woman could earn more as a copyist than as, for instance, a telegraph clerk: in 1877, the *Victoria Magazine* estimated that payment for a law-copyist was from 30 shillings to £2 a week, compared with between 8 and 30 shillings as a telegraph clerk.[12]

In June 1860, Rye reported to a *soirée* at Langham Place that the law-copying office was proving a success. Eight trained writers, and two pupils, were working there, and during the past week they had copied two 'very long manuscripts', forty circular letters, and a variety of leases, affidavits and briefs.[13] During 1863, the office gained 'a very large and valuable job'[14] from the India Office, possibly through the patronage of Florence Nightingale. There was a considerable turnover of staff at Portugal Street. Of sixteen women admitted during the first year, only five stayed there for the whole year,[15] partly because of shortage of work, but also because of Rye's intolerance of her workers' inadequacies. Rye was authoritarian, and her religious scruples led to her refusal to employ a Catholic in the office, 'tho' the individual was a harmless one by birth; not a convert, & not particularly religious.'[16]

As pioneering ventures, the law-copying office and the Victoria Press both aroused the interest of the general public, and various people visited out of curiosity. Arthur Munby went there in 1863:

> a young girl showed me into a dull back office, where a young woman sat at a table examining a number of big ledgerlike folios. She was Miss Francies the deputy manager: a plainly-drest quiet feminine person, under thirty; looking like a governess. On one side, among the ledgers and briefs and business apparatus, was a little basket of woman's work, and a thimble and scissors: a quaint & touching juxtaposition.
>
> She was very civil and gentle, & by no means hard or 'strongminded': she gave me her list of charges, which are cheap enough; and said they have eight female copyists employed; all young, and nearly all persons of some education of the nursery-governess kind.
>
> There was a glass door between the manager's room and the clerks'. Through it, as we passed, Miss Francies showed me her employées at work: six or eight girls and young women, each seated at a desk and busy writing, in a dull office, the window of which was papered up to a height of five or six feet. They were all silent and laborious.[17]

Maria Rye's law-copying office illustrated how middle-class women could earn a living by respectable work. In truth, however, the office had only a limited impact on women's employment opportunities. Six women worked regularly at Portugal Street, with a few casuals employed during busy periods. Other women paid one guinea for three months' training at the office, hoping to work independently, and a handful set up offices in provincial centres with apparent success. But these were few in number.

There were two major problems, and one minor one. The minor problem, which would loom large in later years, was changing technology. The typewriter was several decades away, but already printing was beginning to take some business from the law-copyists. One speaker at the Society's annual meeting in Glasgow pointed out that in Scotland, most legal documents were now printed, rather than engrossed in the time-honoured manner. Women were therefore entering the law-copying business at a time of contracting employment, which helps to explain the more immediate problem they encountered, resentment from, and competition with, male copyists. As the *Alexandra Magazine* pointed out, women had difficulties gaining employment with established law-stationers because 'the usual obstacle is in the way, viz., the jealousy of men already engaged in the profession. The law-copyists of London form a sort of close corporation or guild, into which none are admitted without having served a seven years' apprenticeship.'

Women were outside the guild, both formally and informally, and represented a threat, according to the *Alexandra Magazine*, both because of their greater 'steadiness and sobriety', and because they took work under poorer conditions, 'deferring holiday-making until slack times arrived, and content, withal, to accept lower wages than could possibly suffice men having a family to maintain'. Faced with such competition, male clerks were understandably hostile to women and, 'should a law-stationer engage a female clerk, it is at the risk of all the men in his employ instantly leaving him.'[18]

The second problem was that there were many more women looking for employment, than there was work available to them. Only a handful could find permanent work at the office in Portugal Street. Rye spent a large part of her time turning away applicants. This was equally true of the other projects initiated by the Society for Promoting the Employment of Women. Rye claimed in 1861 that all the Society's projects were over-whelmed by applications: 'A short time since, 810 women applied for one situation of £15 per annum; still later, (only ten days ago,) 250 women applied for another vacancy worth only £12 a year; (the daughters of many professional men being among the numbers,) and ... 120 women applied in ONE DAY [to another registry office], only to find that there was literally *not one situation for any one of them*.'[19] There were clearly too few jobs for the number of women wanting work, and the Society's initiatives seemed to be only ameliorative.

Rye began to see emigration to the colonies as an alternative way to deal with the problem of impoverished middle-class women. In 1860 she suggested 'four great ways of bettering the condition of the working women of this country': through 'a better, a more practical, a more real education, by means of which they may secure those higher wages and shorter hours which fall to the portion of skilled labour'; 'by the opening of new professions and trades'; 'by withdrawing from the labour market, all those workers who have husbands and fathers, from whom the means of subsistence *ought* to be obtained', and 'by emigration, which is most wonderfully overlooked as a preventive against trouble, misery, despair, and ruin'.[20]

In 1861 she repeated her call for the emigration of women in a paper for the Dublin meeting of the National Association for the Promotion of Social Science.[21] Her argument was simple – and simplistic. There was a marked sex imbalance in the colonies, and a dearth of educated women, either for employment as teachers, nurses and governesses, or as wives for middle-class colonial men. She repeated her argument, in a paper on 'Female Middle Class Emigration', at the National Association for the Advancement of Social Science meeting in London in June 1862. With support from associates, both feminist and philanthropic, she founded the Female Middle Class Emigration Society in May 1862.[22]

Maria Rye saw emigration as a means of improving women's chances in the labour market, both abroad and at home, for if a portion of women were to move to the colonies, they would not only improve their own chances of finding work, but would reduce the number of women competing for the limited opportunities at home. Most people believed that the colonies offered better job prospects to women, as they certainly did to men, but women were usually too poor to pay the costs of emigration, and were generally ignorant of the procedures involved. Moreover the process of emigration was particularly hazardous to single women. The problem was to manage the transfer of women from England to the empire so as to guarantee both their physical security and comfort, and their reputations. A 'good character' was essential to any woman's future prospects of work and of marriage, whether she was a domestic servant or a governess, but her character could easily be tarnished by hints of shipboard profligacy, or by the suspicion that single women who emigrated alone to an area where men outnumbered women were nothing but shameless husband-hunters.

Rye set out to learn about the mechanics of women's emigration. She read the reports of the government emigration commissioners, visited emigrant ships, and contacted ex-colonists living in England.[23] She also wrote to key figures in the colonies, such as Frederic Barker, the Bishop of Sydney, hoping to elicit support for her plan to encourage the education of middle-class women.[24] Like many other private emigration schemes, the plan of the Female Middle Class Emigration Society was to provide interest-free loans to suitable applicants to pay for their fares to the colonies. The women were to pay off these loans within two years and four months of their arrival in the colony, from the allegedly high salaries they could earn there. During the next twenty years, the Society helped about three hundred middle-class women to migrate to Australia, New Zealand, Canada and South Africa.[25]

Maria Rye, however, quickly moved beyond the middle-class focus of the Society. In the early 1860s, the crisis in the cotton industry caused by the American Civil War threw many working-class women out of work. The colonies were eager to take domestic servants, so eager that they subsidised their fares. Rye therefore recruited working-class women from the cotton towns who, although seldom trained as domestic servants, were of a comparable class. Through her intervention, several hundred women embarked for British Columbia, Queensland, New Zealand and Canada during the next few years.[26]

In November 1862 she set sail for New Zealand with a group of about one hundred women, most of them mill hands from Lancashire. Her plan was to investigate conditions in the various Australasian colonies, and to elicit support from colonial governments for female emigration. Her first port of call, Dunedin, was not encouraging. She arrived there with her emigrant women in February 1863 to discover that the immigration barracks, where they were to stay until they found employment, was being used as accommodation for a troop of mounted police, complete with their horses, brought from Melbourne to keep control in the middle of a gold rush. There was, she claimed in a letter to *The Times,* nowhere to wash, nowhere to eat, inadequate food and little privacy: 'a more demoralizing school for undecided characters could not possibly be imagined, and a more discreditable place does not exist under the sun. Two or three illegitimate children and their mothers are at present residing there ... while the upper attics are occupied by a body of women who are known only to night and evil deeds.'[27]

Her efforts to improve conditions brought complaints about interference from local colonists, reaching a climax when news arrived back in the colony of the criticisms of Dunedin she had published in *The Times.* Moving north to Christchurch, she had some success in her efforts to organise women from the local elite to raise money to establish a Servants' Home, but she met with more resistance from the colonial establishment for her interference, when she drew attention to the poor conditions aboard some emigrant ships. This led the Anglican bishop to comment that:

> It would not be altogether a bad thing if some quarantine could be established through which, unmarried ladies of a certain age with very benevolent intentions and great zeal in endeavouring to carry them out, but with no knowledge of the wants and means of our colony, might be kept for a time at least, from landing among us.
>
> Miss Rye ... has been visiting us. She has endeavoured to effect her object chiefly through the Ladies of Christchurch – by tacitly expressing that she knows more than we do, of the kind of persons wanted in the Province and dictating certain measures as necessary to be adopted – I give her full credit

for the very best intentions, but ... she knows but very little of the real condition of these Colonies, of their wants and difficulties, and the best means of supplying them, still less of the exertions that are being made among us for all religious and charitable purposes. And this ignorance is accompanied with a very high opinion of the importance of what she deems her mission, and of her own ability to direct us.[28]

The pattern was repeated throughout Rye's four-year journey through the Australasian colonies. With minimal tact, she drew attention to colonial failings in a wide range of areas, publicising her criticisms in letters to the English press, and to friends and patrons back home. The issues she raised included emigration matters, such as the condition of some emigrant ships, and the inadequate reception facilities at the colonial ports, but also ranged more widely, including complaints about hospital administration in Brisbane, and the management of the lunatic asylum outside Sydney. Colonists tended to react defensively, pointing out her ignorance of local conditions, and her lack of competence, both as a stranger and a woman, to enter the public debate in areas well beyond her legitimate sphere. Her abrasive personality, as much as her gender, lost her support amongst many of her natural allies, such as the Bishop of Christchurch, and the philanthropic Anglican women who ran the Servants' Home in Melbourne.[29]

None the less, she had some success in establishing a foothold as an emigration agent when the Governments of Victoria and of Hawkes Bay, New Zealand, both accepted her offer to recruit domestic servants for their colonies.[30] On her arrival back in England, in June 1866, she set up an office in the Adelphi, the immigration and shipping quarter of London. In 1867 the British Government recognised her services to the cause of female emigration, awarding her a Government pension of £70 per annum. During the next few years, she recruited some hundreds of women and family groups, to send to the Australasian colonies. However her experiences led her to conclude that these colonies were not an ideal destination for single women. Writing to Barbara Bodichon from Sydney, she tried to explain:

> I still think to the full as strongly as when I left home that women, educated or not, may come here with the very greatest advantage to themselves – but I see even clearer than ever that they must be women of a certain stamp – women who dislike work, or who are not very steady in their principles – are a thousand fold better off at home ... the colonies like the testing fire of the apostles tries every man's work & every man's character to the very core – It's marvellous how alone people are here, – women – men – families – it's all alike – they are here to day – gone tomorrow, & the natural result is that individuality is very prominent ... you can easily see how that would tell ...

on women who have no individuality to bring out, first they lean right – then they loll left – & then down they go.[31]

Canada, with a longer history, larger population, more mature economy and more class-based society, became her preferred destination. She made three trips to Ontario in 1868 and 1869, each time bringing about one hundred women as domestic servants. However Canadian society also proved hostile to this large-scale importation of women, especially as Canada, unlike the more recent colonies, had no imbalance of men and women, and resented the arrival of Rye's women, many of whom she had recruited from English workhouses.[32]

Still obsessed, however, by the problem of 'surplus women' in England, Rye determined that the issue must be attacked at its roots. If the colonies would not willingly accept 'surplus women' from the mother country, because of the perceived moral flaws in adult women, they might take children instead. In April 1869, in a letter to *The Times,* she outlined her plan.[33] In the United States, large numbers of slum children were taken by charitable organisations by rail from the eastern cities into the Midwest, to be apprenticed to farmers. Maria Rye had met one of the instigators of the American scheme, the Reverend Van Meter, in Chicago. She now proposed to follow in his footsteps, taking 'street arabs' from the over-crowded cities of England to find homes, and work in rural Canada. The following November, she arrived at Niagara-on-the-Lake, in southern Ontario, with sixty-nine children,[34] the first of the approximately four thousand children that she brought to Canada during the next twenty-seven years, until her final retirement in 1896.

Some of the children were paupers, recruited from the workhouses of London and the industrial towns of the North. Others were street children, brought to Rye's receiving home at Peckham, South London, by police, neighbours, and sometimes their parents, in the belief that emigration to the colonies offered them a better future than life in the slums and streets of England. Ideally, Maria Rye hoped that these children would be adopted into Canadian families; in practice, most were accepted as domestic and farm servants by impoverished families, themselves too poor to employ more efficient labour. In some cases they were indentured, but in many others, the fiction of 'adoption' allowed families to use them as unpaid labour. A long and sorry chapter of imperial child migration had begun.[35]

Unlike other philanthropists who followed in her footsteps, such as Thomas Barnardo, Rye concerned herself primarily with the relocation of girls. In this, she was largely motivated by feminist principles. Accepting unquestioningly that emigration offered improved opportunities to the immigrant, she was eager to ensure that their poorer access to migration should not disadvantage women and girls. In her preoccupation with the 'surplus woman' problem, she emphasised the need to reduce the numbers of women, relative to men, within British society. The emigration of female children could achieve the same result as the emigration of their older sisters.

At the same time, Rye's social conservatism and, perhaps, a lack of imagination, made her treat with an almost off-hand optimism the nature of 'adoption' for many of these children. Placed on farms sometimes miles from the nearest neighbour, both within the family, and outside the incest taboo, they were often in an exceptionally vulnerable position, both economically and sexually. For Maria Rye, however, it was enough that they were 'saved' from the slums of industrial England, and from the prostitution that – she implied - must be their inevitable fate if they remained there. If they remained in England, 'they would not grow up into even working, to say nothing of Christian, women, but would grow up into our habitual drunkards, our tramps, and the mothers of more tramps, and into those nameless miserable outcasts who fill the black wards of our hospitals and of our workhouses – children whose heritage here from birth to death is sin, shame, misery, and destruction.' It was far better for them to go to 'our beautiful, thrifty, kindly Canada', where they would be 'saved'.[36] Ironically, they were also being taken away from compulsory education, and the diverse work opportunities of industrial England, to be thrust into the gender-stereotyped work of domestic service.

Each generation assesses its 'good works' differently. The Victorians agonised about the problems of 'surplus women' and 'gutter children'; we worry about 'the feminisation of poverty' and the activities of 'street kids'. The poor may, indeed, be always with us, but our ways of defining them vary quite as much as our ways of dealing with them. Yet the underlying problems are often depressingly similar, and as each set of solutions fails, or turns out to have unexpected or unintended consequences, a new orthodoxy comes to prevail. Maria Rye's solution to the poverty of certain groups within her own society lay in emigration. The open borders of the British Empire at its height made the wholesale transfer of peoples less difficult than in later years, when recipient countries introduced various restrictions to control the flow. Many charitable well-wishers, with no wish to emigrate themselves, found emigration a simple solution to the problem of poverty at home, though the shipping of large numbers of peoples across the world was never a painless matter to the individual emigrants themselves. Yet it is useful, in history as in other things, to remember H. L. Menken's aphorism: 'To every problem there is a simple solution, and it is invariably wrong.' Maria Rye trod a 'primrose path', in that there was always a simple and logical progression from one step to the next, but she ended at a final point far removed in its consequences from the charitable benefits she originally set out to achieve.

Maria Rye's first imaginative leap was to see emigration as a solution to the lack of work for women in England. Her second was to see the emigration of little girls as a solution to colonial doubts about accepting large numbers of single women. Victorian sentimentality made much of the idea of childhood innocence. No question could be raised by the colonists about the morality of little girls who had yet to reach puberty, yet the demographic effect, for England and for Canada, would be the same as the emigration of adult women. In either case, the imbalance in the numbers of men and women would be alleviated.

This solution also conveniently overcame the other problem of female emigration, the unwillingness of single women to migrate. Unlike their older sisters, little girls had no choice in the decision that was made on their behalf. Childhood innocence has always been linked to childhood powerlessness, making children fair game, then as now, for the well meaning as well as the unscrupulous. Children had little concept of what was involved in a trip across the Atlantic to a new life, and those responsible for them, whether Poor Law Guardians, or relatives, or even parents, were persuaded by varying intensities of moral blackmail, that they were acting in the child's best interests.

Over a period of thirty-five years, until she finally retired in 1896, Maria Rye sent some hundreds of women, and thousands of children, as emigrants to the colonies, and through her example inspired others to follow on an even larger scale. How, then, must we judge Maria Rye's activities? When Macbeth's porter spoke of the 'primrose way to th' everlasting bonfire', he alluded to the ambiguity between cause and effect that blights many actions that begin with the best of intentions. Maria Rye trod just such a 'primrose way'.

She also trod a primrose path in another sense, foreshadowing the ideas of a later generation of conservative English woman who formed the Primrose League. From the liberal feminism that she espoused in the 1850s, Maria Rye's political beliefs became increasingly conservative. She was afraid of 'King Mob', and contemptuously characterised the Labour Party as 'the lazy party'. Like many conservative women who were successful in the public sphere, she believed in the ideology of separate spheres for men and women. She believed in the virtues of hard work, thrift, individual effort, and the idea that, whether as mistress or as servant, ideally a woman's place was in the home. It was not a principle that she felt obliged to follow herself. Instead, her life highlights the close, if vexed, relationship between traditional philanthropy and the emergence of feminism in the nineteenth century. It also illustrates the important role played by religion in motivating, and sanctioning, the activity of conservative women in the public sphere.

166

MARION DIAMOND

Notes

1 She is also included in the *Dictionary of New Zealand Biography* (Charlotte MacDonald), and will appear in the *Canadian Dictionary of Biography*, vol. 13, 1900–10. My thanks to Professor Joy Parr and the publishers for letting me see her article in manuscript.

2 Maria Rye was out of the country during the agitation for women's suffrage that preceded the passing of the second Reform Bill in 1867, but in 1884, at the British Association for the Advancement of Science meeting at Montreal, she was one of the signatories of a letter to Sir John A. Macdonald, the Prime Minister of Canada, congratulating him on his support for the cause of women's suffrage. *Montreal Herald* (5 September 1884). See also British Association for the Advancement of Science, Montreal 1884. Scrapbook (2 vols) of the meeting. Blacker-Wood library, McGill University.

3 'M.S.R.', 'The Property of Married Women', *The Englishwoman's Domestic Magazine*, 5 (November 1856), 234.

4 See Jane Rendall, '"A Moral Engine": Feminism, Liberalism and *The English Woman's Journal*', in Jane Rendall (ed.), *Equal or Different: Women's Politics 1800–1914* (Oxford, Basil Blackwell, 1987).

5 'M.S.R.', 'The Englishwoman in London: I. Dr. Elizabeth Blackwell', in *The Englishwoman's Domestic Magazine*, 8:1 (April, 1860), 13–16.

6 M. S. Rye to Tait, 8 November 1859, in Tait Papers, vol. 115, Official Letters, London, Nov. 1859–Jan. 1860, f 11, Lambeth Palace Archives.

7 'M.S.R.', 'The Englishwoman in London. VI. – Women and Workhouses', *The Englishwoman's Domestic Magazine*, 8:6 (September 1860), 177.

8 *Ibid.*

9 'M.S.R.', 'The Englishwoman in London VII: The Sanitary Movement', in *The Englishwoman's Domestic Magazine*, 8 (October 1860), 209.

10 See in particular William Rathbone Greg, 'Why are Women Redundant?' in *Literary and Social Judgements* (2nd ed., London, Trubner and Co., 1869), pp. 280–316.

11 'M.S.R.', 'An Infallible Recipe for Making Poor Relations', *The Englishwoman's Domestic Magazine*, 6:9 (December 1858), 280–3.

12 Victoria Magazine, 28 (December 1877), 90–1.

13 'Society for Promoting the Employment of Women, in connection with the National Association for the Promotion of Social Science, *English Woman's Journal*, 5:30 (1 August 1860), 388–96.

14 Arthur Mumby Papers, Wren Library, Trinity College Cambridge (by permission of the Master and Fellows of Trinity College), 30 June 1863.

15 Catherine Webber to the editor of the *English Woman's Journal*, 13:73 (1 March 1864), 64.

16 Bessie Rayner Parkes to Barbara Bodichon, 1 January 1862, Box V, no. 114, Bessie Rayner Parkes Papers, Girton College Archives, Cambridge (by permission of the Principal and Fellows of Girton College).

17 Munby Papers, 30 June, 9 July 1863.

18 'Law-Copying as an Employment for Women', *Alexandra Magazine*, September 1864, p. 305.

19 Maria S. Rye, *Emigration of Educated Women* (London, Victoria Press, 1861), p. 4

20 'M.S.R.', 'The Englishwoman in London: V. Working Hours, for Working Women', in *The Englishwoman's Domestic Magazine*, 8:5 (August 1860), 140–3.

21 Maria S. Rye, *Emigration of Educated Women, A Paper read at the Social Science Congress in Dublin, 1861* (London, Emily Faithfull and Co., Victoria Press, [1862]).

22 Details on the Female Middle Class Emigration Society are given in Patricia Clarke, *The Governesses: Letters from the Colonies 1862–1882* (Sydney, Allen and Unwin, 1985), and in the papers of the Society, at the Fawcett Library, London, and available on

microfilm through the Australian Joint Copying Project.

23 See, for instance, 'M.S.R.', 'Emigrant-ship Matrons', in *English Woman's Journal*, 5:25 (March 1860), 24–36.

24 'M.S.R.', *Emigration of Educated Women*, pp. 10–11.

25 The records of the Female Middle Class Emigration Society, comprising reports and letter-books of letters from emigrant women, are held at the Fawcett Library, London, and have been microfilmed by the Australian Joint Copying Project. A large collection of these letters has been edited in Patricia Clarke, *The Governesses: Letters from the Colonies 1862–1882* (Sydney, Allen and Unwin, 1985). A broader history of the emigration of middle-class women is A. J. Hammerton, *Emigrant Gentlewomen: Genteel Poverty and Female Emigration, 1830–1914* (London, Croom Helm, 1979). There are also older studies of the topic by Una Monk, *New Horizons: A Hundred Years of Women's Migration* (London, HMSO, 1963, and G. F. Plant, *A Survey of Voluntary Effort in Women's Empire Migration* (London, Society for the Oversea Settlement of British Women, 1950).

26 Jackie Lay, 'To Columbia on the Tynemouth: The emigration of Single Women and Girls in 1862' in Barbara Latham and Cathy Kess (eds) *In Her Own Right: Selected Essays on Women's History in B.C. [in original]* (Victoria, Camosun College, 1980) pp. 19–41; Charlotte J. Macdonald, 'Single women and immigrant settlers in New Zealand, 1853–1871' (Ph.D., Auckland, 1986), pp. 35ff.

27 Maria Rye to the editor, Dunedin, 16 March, *The Times*, 29 May 1863, p. 5.

28 H. J. C. Christchurch [Bishop Harper] to Selfe, 12 August 1863, pp. 287–8, Henry Selfe Letters, Christchurch Museum.

29 Rye approached Laura A'Beckett, the wife of a prominent Anglican layman, for help in finding work and accommodation for her emigrants in Melbourne. After giving her some initial encouragement, she resisted further efforts by Rye to send governesses to Melbourne, recommending that domestic servants should be sent instead. See also Minutes of the Governess's Home, 13 November 1865, La Trobe Library, State Library of Victoria, MS 11145.

30 On Hawkes Bay, see Charlotte Macdonald, *A Woman of Good Character*; on Victoria, Buckingham and Chandos to Sir J. E T. Manners Sutton, No. 29, 20 May 1867, Despatches of the Secretary of State to the Governor of Victoria, vol. 21, 1867, Public Record Office of Victoria.

31 Rye to Bodichon (written from Redfern, Sydney), 20 May 1865, in Fawcett Autograph Letters.

32 See, e.g., 'Miss Rye's Girls', in *Toronto Globe*, 12 June 1868.

33 Letters to the editor of *The Times* from Maria Rye on 'Our Gutter Children', 12, 20 April 1869.

34 *Niagara Mail*, 10 November 1869.

35 See Joy Parr, *Labouring Children: British Immigrant Apprentices to Canada, 1869–1924* (London, Croom Helm, 1980); Gillian Wagner, *Children of the Empire* (London, Weidenfeld and Nicolson, 1982); Kenneth Bagnell, *The Little Immigrants: The Orphans who came to Canada* (Toronto, Macmillan of Canada, 1980).

36 *Autumn Appeal: Miss Rye's Emigration Home for Destitute Little Girls* (n.d. c.1879). I am grateful to Mr Peter Rye, who kindly gave me a copy of this, and a number of other similar pamphlets from his family papers.

9

Anthropological analogies: Edith Simcox and Madeleine Pelletier

Felicia Gordon

FEMINIST history, like that of much radical politics, can be described as a history of ruptures: periods of intense activity followed by silences through which it is difficult to discern a continuous tradition. To speak of 'Wollstonecraft's daughters' is to affirm continuities of tradition, aspirations and challenges confronted. It is in this light that I wish to foreground Madeleine Pelletier (1874–1939) and Edith Simcox (1844–1901) as heirs of Enlightenment feminist radicalism. Yet how convincing is it to speak of a tradition in feminist thought? For Simcox and Pelletier, the major link between them must be seen as their effort to appropriate and utilise a traditionally masculine discourse in science and politics. They both independently recognised that women's historical exclusion from the sciences formed part of their exclusion from wider political structures within the public sphere. Separated by a generation in time and by the English Channel in space, both women operated in the contested public sphere as active socialists and feminists. Whereas Wollstonecraft, who in her *Vindication of the Rights of Woman* applied the critique of privilege to gender as well as to class in order to dramatise the case for the emancipation of women, Pelletier and Simcox appropriated the language of contemporary positivist philosophy and anthropological science for feminist ends, while simultaneously fashioning an attack on these disciplines' gendered assumptions. Though Pelletier's anthropological and primarily craniometrical research proved largely unfruitful in a professional sense, her engagement with anthropological paradigms crucially influenced her socialist and feminist development. Similarly a generation earlier, Edith Simcox employed anthropological models to deconstruct dominant Victorian theories about the foundations of culture and the position of women.[1]

Differing widely in their approaches and in many of their interests, Simcox and Pelletier followed in Wollstonecraft's footsteps in their ambition to appropriate the academic and rationalist strategies of masculine philosophic and scientific discourse. Pelletier, who called herself an 'integral feminist', was a polemical writer and political activist in both feminist and socialist circles, who thrived on debate and controversy. The most satisfying aspects of her life were in the arena of public engagement and in the masculine sphere with which she strongly identified both in her profession as a medical doctor and in her political work as a militant socialist. Like Simone de Beauvoir a generation later, she was suspicious of feminine feminists, whom she referred to disparagingly as '*demi-féministes*', an attitude which inevitably threw her into conflict with her feminist colleagues. Pelletier's combative disposition and imperviousness to lady-like behaviour reflected her loyalty to her working-class background and freed her from the bourgeois proprieties expected of her sex at the turn of the century. Her masculine identification led her to cross-dress on occasion. In her unpublished 'War Diary' she lamented revealingly: 'Oh why was I not born a man? My sex is the misfortune of my life.' Pelletier was committed to and even obsessed with achievement in the public sphere, an ambition which she partially fulfilled but not entirely to her own satisfaction. Paradoxically, her masculine identification, allied to her radical feminist and socialist views, marginalised her in those very centres of masculine power where she wished to excel.

Like Pelletier, Simcox was a political activist, but of a middle-class background. She was a member of the First Socialist International and spoke at its public meetings in Paris. She ran a women's shirt-maker's co-operative (1875–84) and was an active member of the London School Board. Far from conforming to the stereotype of retiring Victorian femininity, she operated effectively in the public sphere. Nevertheless, she seems to have been obsessively self-effacing, secretive (see her 'Diary of a Shirtmaker') and agonised over her own gender identity. Her writing, in contrast to Pelletier's directly polemical work, employed a series of codes, the personal hidden behind the academic; even the radical political message tended to be coded. My account of *Primitive Civilizations* which follows will foreground feminist and socialist arguments emerging from the text, yet these are issues which in a reading of the work are almost submerged under the weight of scholarship, designed perhaps in part to disguise the subversive nature of her argument. But, though differing markedly in temperament and class background, both Pelletier and Simcox engaged with anthropological discourse as part of their effort to draw support for feminist and socialist theories from the science of 'man'.

Anthropology was one of the nineteenth century's new sciences. From the outset it was explicitly politicised in the sense in that it was used to provide evidence for or against chosen cultural models. This overt politicisation held good not just for anthropology but for the historical and biological disciplines generally, all of which contributed to the construction of a new meta-human history.[2] Archeology, paleontology, anthropology (and its sub-discipline, craniometry) and evolutionary theory may be read as historical disciplines forming part of the the nineteenth-century European attempt to construct a theory of the past that would explain, justify or anticipate the present; an effort, in short, to reinstate the grand design, supposedly destroyed by Darwin. Anthropology, indebted both to Darwin's and Lamarck's versions of evolutionary theory, contributed powerfully, though by no means with one voice, to debates about race and gender relations, the necessity of conflict or competition and the idea of progress. In addition, much anthropological discourse (as in the work of Paul Broca, founder of the Parisian Anthropological Society in 1857) was explicitly anti-feminist and racist in arguing that women and the so-called 'lower races' were less evolved than western European males. Nevertheless such theories were also contested in anthropological circles and it is as part of this effort to reappropriate the idea of progress for radical political ends that one may situate Pelletier and Simcox.

The four key ideas which underpinned anthropological and indeed historical and other cultural theories have been outlined by Bowler, Kuper and Gould, principally in relation to racial theories though the impact of such ideas for feminist theory has been less noted by them.[3] The four linchpins of anthropological theory were: the belief in *Progress*, the concept of *The Primitive*, the *Theory of Stages of Culture* and *Recapitulation Theory*. These provided part of the theoretical foundations for Pelletier's and Simcox's writing but also the basis for their critique of scientific thinking.

Progress: Though Darwin's theories stressed random selection, it is notorious that evolutionary theory, whether Darwinian or neo-Lamarckian, was appropriated to show the working out of telos, from chaos to order, from lower to higher forms of life and culture, as, for example in the Whig interpretation of history. Archaeology, which discovered a 'primitive past' (stone, bronze age) leading to a technologically advanced present, and anthropology which looked at technologically 'primitive' races (black Africans, Aborigines), as surviving ancestral types, all contributed to this meta-fiction, the construct of progress.[4]

The Primitive: The invention of the Primitive, as Kuper shows, was founded on the idea of an inevitable movement from the simple to the complex.[5] Primitive or simple society was the cause, implying a necessary effect, namely, contemporary or complex society. Primitive society represented a mirror image of contemporary society, its customs reconstructed in an imaginary history. Thus if nineteenth-century society exhibited a territorial state, monogamous families and private property, the primitive 'horde' were constructed as promiscuous, communistic and held together by blood ties not property.[6] Surviving remnants of 'primitive' races, thought to be atavistic living records, were believed to reflect the prehistoric past. Women were also figured as primitives. Anthropology assumed an invariable progression from primitive to civilised through a series of stages. Inferior or primitive types would be left behind the evolutionary march because of being mired in the past or in nature. Curiously, however, evolution though applying universally, ceased to apply to certain categories of the 'inferior'. A basic disagreement among evolutionists centred on the question of whether evolution were selective or universal. Would the 'inferior' or 'primitive' races and genders evolve?

The Theory of Stages of Culture: The Stages of Culture through which all societies were deemed to pass were constructed as follows: (*a*) clans linked by blood ties, which were originally matriarchal, had 'progressed' to the patriarchal stage of organisation. This in turn led to (*b*) the patriarchal family tied to property through the male line. (*c*) The further universalisation of patriarchy occurred in the state.[7] A simpler version listed the stages as savagery, barbarism, civilisation.[8] Fundamentally, progression chartered a cultural move from blood ties to contract. Every culture had gone through or would go through these necessary stages.

Recapitulation Theory: This theory first propounded by the evolutionist, Ernst Haekel in 1866, held that the development of the individual mirrors in its stages the development of the species; ontogeny is the recapitulation of phylogeny. 'During its own rapid development ... an individual repeats the most important changes in form evolved by its ancestors during their long and slow paleontological development.'[9] Recapitulation theory combining Darwin, Goëthe and Lamarck argued for the inheritance of acquired characteristics. As Gould shows, the importance of recapitulation theory can be gauged from the fact that it became the conceptual foundation of such varied disciplines as criminal anthropology, racial theories, child development theories, and psychoanalysis.[10] Recapitulation too was a fictional history.

Anthropology, which rested on the theoretical premises outlined above, became both an area of contention and of inspiration for feminists because it offered a double message. On the one hand most nineteenth-century accounts of cultural evolution suggested a largely undocumented development from promiscuity (matriarchy) to patriarchal clans to monogamy and private property – the last being understood as the highest and best form of cultural development.[11] Women were clearly the losers in this progression. Their adaptive failure had caused them to be left behind by evolution and cultural history. Women's actual subordination through much of recorded history, especially in the Judeo-Christian and Graeco-Roman historical models was both explained and legitimated by this adaptive failure. In this respect, evolution theory, like myth, became a weapon of legitimation for sexual and racial subordination in an otherwise liberal economic and political climate.

On the plus side, for feminists and socialists, anthropology represented part of a historicising and relativising account of human institutions which purported to show that there was nothing inevitable or natural in any particular social arrangements. Neo-Lamarckian anthropology, which argued for the ability of individuals to pass on acquired characteristics, led socialists in particular to believe that social reform could be rendered permanent. Evolutionary theory encouraged a materialist interpretation of structures traditionally understood as natural or God-given. This was the significance of Engels's *The Origin of the Family, Private Property and the State* (1884). Though tied like most theorists of the period to the idea of progress, Engels did not see the triumph of monogamy and private property in the West as representing the apotheosis of culture, but as a material stage which would inevitably be superseded. With the abolition of private property, the oppression of women, he believed, would be ended.

The relationship between nineteenth-century anthropology, socialism and feminism emerges clearly in the early career of Madeleine Pelletier. As a medical student in Paris at the turn of the century and already committed to 'advanced' anarchist, socialist and feminist views, she attended lectures at the Ecole d'Anthropologie. Pelletier had been immediately attracted to this milieu on entering medical school. It must have seemed to her that at last science was lending empirical confirmation to her passionate belief that she as an individual woman was not inferior to men and that progress for women and the working class could be justified in the name of science as well as of more abstract Enlightenment principles of justice.

Nor did Pelletier's enthusiasm seem misplaced. The socialist, neo-Lamarckian anthropologists who dominated the Ecole d'Anthropologie, denied the fixity of species and types, thus holding out the possibility of change even in lower human forms (e.g. 'primitives' and women).[12] Charles Letourneau, for example, Professor of Sociology at the School of Anthropology and secretary to the Society of Anthropology from 1887 until his death in 1902, held that all institutions such as marriage evolved according to certain predictable laws of progress.[13] Nevertheless, the politically liberal but socially conservative Paul Broca's craniometrical system of skull measurement, believed to be an accurate index of intelligence and evolutionary development, continued to dominate anthropological practice. Craniometry catalogued human beings into higher and lower types based on racial and gender hierarchies, in which middle-class, white western males were seen perched at the top of the evolutionary tree. Pelletier had an understandably uneasy relationship with this mixed anthropological legacy, abandoning craniometrical research by 1903 after publishing an unsuccessful case-study, which was demolished by the English biometrician, Karl Pearson, as part of his ultimately successful drive to discredit craniometry itself.[14]

Pelletier's strictly craniometrical research, carried out as a young and ambitious research student, did on the whole accept the assumptions of the Broca school. Like Simcox a generation before her, she was some time in finding the intellectual confidence to challenge the dominant racial and gender paradigms of anthropology. Nevertheless she was clearly struggling in this early phase to find a way of integrating the craniometrical 'science', so much at the centre of anthropological thinking to a progressive ideology.[15] She gained support from the example and writings of such men as Mortillet, Letourneau and Léonce Manouvrier, who, though they shared Broca's republicanism, materialism and anti-clericalism, were, in addition, socialists who read Bebel, Marx and Engels. What prehistoric anthropology proved for these anthropologists was the truth of the general laws of progress which were held to shape all human history.[16] Letourneau argued that the law of progress was cumulative from animal to man and in human society through time. By tracing the evolutionary patterns of the past, anthropologists could point to the future of humankind. But like Broca, Letourneau accepted the idea of racial hierarchies which were, he believed, a continuous record of the entire history of humanity still visible on earth.

Nevertheless, Letourneau's commitment to evolution was crucial for Pelletier because he gave grounds for arguing that radical racial differences or gender differences were a product of different evolutionary pasts and were not immutable. One of her anthropological studies which engaged with some of these problems was an analysis of Japanese skeletons. This concentrated on the notorious 'elephant problem' in craniometry. If, objectors to craniometrical theory had argued, the size of the skull or brain determined the intelligence of the species, race, class or sex, why were elephants not more intelligent than human beings? Pelletier struggling against the evidence that women's smaller average skull size in relation to men was irrefutable proof of their innate inferiority, showed in her Japanese skeletons that relative to weight and height, women's skulls in these examples were actually larger than men's. Thus Pelletier made use of the elephant problem, not to undermine craniometry but to undermine some of the assumptions about evolutionary superiority between the sexes.[17]

For Pelletier, craniometry proved a cul-de-sac in terms of her own research and would probably, in spite of the radical orientation of the School of Anthropology have remained an obstacle to finding a place for feminist aspirations within its supposedly scientific assumptions. But the more generous and socially adventurous side of anthropology continued, fortunately, to dominate the French school. It had been articulated as early as the 1860s by Abel Hovelacque who had declared that anthropology's mission was:

> to reveal all that remains of the savage and barbaric in our modern civilization: the clergy, the belief in gods, militarism, the suppression of the weak and the poor, the inferior condition of women, the cult of authority, the respect for bureaucratism, the contempt for individual liberty and social inequality. These are survivals from which the development of anthropological science is called upon to liberate us.[18]

It was this belief in the capacity of science to shake off the dead hand of the past which appealed to socialists and feminists alike.

What Pelletier retained as a dominant influence for the rest of her career was not so much the belief in a system of inevitable progress (a faith which did not survive the débâcle of the First World War) but a commitment to the possibility of neo-Lamarckian 'transformation' (a dominant metaphor in her writing), both personal and political, and to evolutionary rather than revolutionary social change. The political impact of anthropology was crucial to her feminism, on the one hand suggesting that institutions like marriage could be understood relativistically, as social, not natural constructs, and, on the other, forcing her to confront and to do battle with the scientific orthodoxy of women's supposed evolutionary inferiority and with what she identified as the 'masculinism of scientific culture'.[19]

Whereas Pelletier carried out her anthropological research at the beginning of her academic and professional career at the turn of the century, Edith Simcox's work engaged with aspects of the new science towards the end of her life. Anthropological models allowed her to contest many of the dominant ideas of her age, though she remained suspicious of the conjectural side of its prehistorical vision. Her last article was on an anthropological topic, 'The Native Australian Family' *The Nineteenth Century* (July 1899), and was a comparative study of marriage customs. Simcox's scholarly and dense history of ancient Egypt, Mesopotamia and China, *Primitive Civilizations* (1893), takes as its starting-point the liberating relativism that anthropology brought to the study of human cultures while criticising many of the cultural biases and the conjectural rather than empirical historical method of anthropological theory from which

she wished to distance herself as a 'serious' historian.[20] A reviewer in
major journals, a committed trade unionist, Simcox was a lifelong political activist of the Left. Yet in her published work her ambitions seem to
have been academic rather than political. *Primitive Civilizations* (1893) is
one of three major works by Simcox, the others being *Natural Law* (1877),
a work on ethics, and a volume of short stories, *Episodes in the Lives of Men,
Women and Lovers* (1882). Perhaps unfairly to her reputation as a scholar,
thinker and political activist, she has remained best-known for her
unrequited passion for Marian Evans, the novelist, George Eliot. The
writing of *Primitive Civilizations*, probably begun in 1878, spanned a
difficult period in Simcox's life including the death of George Henry
Lewes, Eliot's companion, in November 1878 and that of George Eliot in
December 1880. The book was completed in 1890 but took almost three
years to find a publisher.[21] Unlike *Natural Law*, the critical response to it
appears to have been minimal.

   Primitive Civilizations is a study of ancient Egyptian, Mesopotamian and
Chinese civilisations from an explicitly materialist standpoint, a history of
ownership. It rejects the hypothetical histories of anthropological lore, (a
good example of which, still read today, would be Freud's *Totem and
Taboo* (1913), in favour of empirical historical evidence which can be
verified through textual and other records. Simcox demonstrates that
there have been enormously successful, prosperous and long-lived civilisations which did not follow the prescribed nineteenth-century progressive pattern from communistic clan, to 'civilised' competition, to
capitalism. In describing ancient Egypt, Mesopotamia and China she
draws implicit and explicit contrasts with nineteenth-century *laissez-faire*
economic individualism but at the same time, she shows the limitations of
the culturally progressivist assumptions of Morgan, Bebel, Engels, Bachofen
and McLennan, assumptions which excluded women from culture and
history.[22]

   Engels, accepting the theses of Bachofen and Morgan, argued for a
pre-historic period of matriarchy which had been swept away in 'the
world historical defeat of the female sex' by patriarchal reorganisation
and had led to the beginning of history and progress. Conversely,
Simcox, by describing the property and other material arrangements of
three 'archaic' civilisations (e.g. civilisations with hieroglyphic not alpha-
betic writing, but nevertheless with clear historical records), demonstrated that in a whole range of social arrangements (excluding the
directly 'political'), women enjoyed status undreamt of in Victorian
Britain. In Simcox's account, these societies were neither matriarchal nor
patriarchal but enshrined the idea of the reciprocity of wealth and
ownership between the sexes.[23]

It was indeed the case that the position of women or at least that of propertied women in ancient Egypt, in particular, was in many respects very favourable. Their legal status can be gauged by the rights over property which a woman acquired at marriage from her parents and husband, as well as from their deaths. 'In ancient Egypt, women commonly owned property; could inherit and testate it to others and hold it independently of their husbands. They enjoyed the same legal capacity to transact business as men'.[24] This historical record, Simcox suggests, renders quite unnecessary notions of a mythical pre-historic past in which the reign of women was surpassed by patriarchal progress. There was nothing 'pre-historic' about ancient Egyptian or Chinese society. The position of women and the contentment of the working class in such societies, were, in Simcox's analysis, the pre-condition for national prosperity. In *Primitive Civilizations* Simcox was in effect constructing an alternative historiography for the West. She looked not to Graeco-Roman political patriarchal culture as the foundation of western civilisation, a myth in the process of reconstruction and revalidation in the nineteenth century, but at the much older 'domestic cultures', as she termed them, of Egypt, Mesopotamia and China.

Simcox, encased in the armour of scholarship, was engaged in contesting a series of dominant ideas. The first was that of economic progress, which was held to depend on increase of wealth, which in turn depended on competition within and between nations, thus reflecting 'the struggle for existence' of evolutionary law. Simcox suggested, on the contrary, that economic and social tranquillity , depended partly on a static social hierarchy and on providing reasonable subsistence for the populace, sufficient to maintain that social stability. The ruler's prosperity was measured by the prosperity of his people.[25] Competition, the key idea of evolution as interpreted by Herbert Spencer, progress and *laissez-faire* capitalism, were irrelevant in this account:

> The condition of the conservatism of ancient States was the content of all, and especially of the most numerous class, with their social status and the degree of material well being habitual to it. The condition of this content, as we shall see, lay in the abundance of the food supply, and its distribution so as to meet the wants of all, and especially of the largest labouring class.[26]

The second major theme of the book is that these cultures emphasised what Simcox termed the domestic or feminine virtues, that is to say, they emphasised the importance of domestic life over the political. Simcox argued that in the Graeco-Roman model of cultural transmission, domestic relations were seen merely as a reflection of the authoritarian, patriarchal, political model. Here, inversely, the domestic model was reflected in the political sphere:

In the domestic States, the unselfish kindness shown by the normal father and mother to their children furnishes the model which the Government, in the comparatively narrow sphere assigned to it, is expected to initiate and reproduce. In political States ... the natural relations of parents and children, husbands and wives, masters and servants are apt to be obscured or perverted by the intrusion of analogies of political authority and subordination.[27]

Simcox almost certainly had been influenced by Alexander Kropotkin, the Russian anarchist exiled to England, and by his book, *Mutual Aid,* which first appeared in *The Nineteenth Century* between 1890 and 1896. Kropotkin, a convinced evolutionist who first read *The Origin of Species* in 1862, tried to interpret the notion of the struggle for survival in a more ecological sense. He stressed less the competition and more the interdependence of living forms. Specifically, between the members of the same species, Kropotkin argued that survival depended not on internecine struggle but on the principle of 'mutual aid'. Even in human society this principle could be observed to operate in the clan, the family, the village, within trades unions and in 'the alliance of mothers among the poor'.[28] Kropotkin's general observation about the biases of most historical writing also bears upon Simcox's project:

Historians ... hand down to posterity the minute descriptions of every war ... but [their histories] hardly bear any trace of the countless acts of mutual support and devotion which everyone one of us knows from his own experience; they hardly take notice of what makes the very essence of our daily life – our social instincts and manners ... Nearly all historical documents ... deal with breaches of peace, not with peace itself.[29]

Simcox, like Kropotkin, wrote a history of peace, seeking to establish the historical continuity of maternal and domestic cultures, to re-interpret the idea of progress. The book's dedication to her mother but implicitly also to an imagined George Eliot whom she also called 'Mother', offers insights into the personal source of her historical vision:

To J.H.S.
In correcting these volumes for the press, you will have observed, Sweet Heart, that a great part of the wisdom of the Egyptians and the wisdom of the Chaldeans, not to speak of the Chinese or other ancient nations lay in this: that they thought much of mothers. To whom then, but you can I dedicate these echoes of world-old humanity, gathered to show by what habits and forbearances the sons of women may live long and gladly, in all regions where heaven gives, earth brings forth, and the waters bear along the fruits of industry.

One is struck by the unfamiliar 'sons of women' (an assertion of a female line of descent) and the stress on habits and forbearances, rather than competition, rights, progress.

Another feature of Simcox's work in terms of her debts to and dissension from anthropological and socialist orthodoxy is her description of the family which, like Engels, she historicises. Undermining contemporary assumptions about the cultural superiority of monogamy Simcox observes:

There is no one of the leading traits of modern family life which can be put forward as so pre-eminently and absolutely natural as to be universal. Polygamy flourishes along with rarer experiments in monogamy and has been practised by women as well as men ... Marriage is sometimes a light relation during pleasure on both sides, sometimes an indestructible bond, trebly woven of duty, inclination and convenience, and sometimes it rests on a one-sided utility, involving the virtual slavery of wives.[30]

Particularly revealing, in the context of relativising marriage, was Simcox's discussion of brother–sister marriage customs in ancient Egypt. A. H. Huth in *The Marriage of Near Kin* (1875), noting the wide variations in marriage customs within and beyond the family, had observed that in Egypt, Greece, in Jewish culture and among the Persians, but not among the Romans, varieties of incest, either brother–sister or parent–child were permitted.[31] Conversely anti-incest taboos extending even to intercourse with sixth cousins became a feature of Christian Europe.[32]

In spite of the known wide variations on intra-family marriage, nineteenth-century anthropologists had early fastened on to the incest taboo as a universal basis of culture, which, they asserted, was the root of the moral order and fundamental to social life itself. This remained a staple assumption of anthropological theory, and was adopted as a foundation stone of psychoanalysis. In *Totem and Taboo* (1938) Freud like anthropologists Tylor (1887), Parsons (1954) and Lévi-Strauss (1949) concurred in identifying the incest taboo as the fundamental prohibition without which culture could not be said to develop.[33] However, the empirical evidence had long been shown to be otherwise. In Egypt, it was not only kings and queens who broke the alleged incest prohibition, which Freud had asserted was a violation permitted only to the privileged, in fact there does not seem to have been a taboo at all. The nobility and commoners found nothing untoward in brother–sister marriage, a custom rendered respectable, as Proust said in another context, by its universality. Hamer has noted that as late as the Roman period in Egypt, brother–sister marriage continued to be common among all levels of society and that Cleopatra's two marriages to younger brothers would have been among the Roman cultural prohibitions which in imperial eyes rendered her especially dangerous.[34] It is likely that women's enjoyment of property rights in ancient Egypt may have been linked to the sister–brother dyad, as property would remain within the family.

Simcox's discussion of incest is entirely uncensorious and de-dramatised.

Indeed she does not use the term 'incest' at all. It is also true that she deals only with brother–sister marriage and not sexual relations between parents and children. It is possible that her own sexual marginalisation, her lack of an appropriate language in which to articulate her desires with regard to sexuality and to affection, left her freer to perceive the relativity of arrangements governing human relations, such as marriage. Furthermore, if the supposedly unspeakable crime of incest could be a perfectly acceptable custom in an advanced culture such as Egypt, she must have wondered whether same–sex relationships between women, tacitly prohibited in her own lifetime because unacknowledged, might not in another age be viewed as beneficent.

Through her research Simcox adduced evidence from Egypt, Babylon and China about the respect in which women were held in marriage, their often considerable rights of inheritance and their ability to control their husbands' and their own property in their lifetimes. As with Engels, marriage and the family are seen by Simcox to be founded on economic ties. Because the bonds of affection, she argued, were linked to concepts of property, the strong family feelings shown in the written records of her three cultures offered convincing evidence of a harmonious process of social bonding, rather than of competition between individuals. The importance of domestic relations in medieval China, for example, did not suggest that women were emancipated, but that some women (mothers-in-law) were extremely powerful and that domestic relations were not a retreat from the struggle for existence, as Ruskin had argued in *Of Queens' Gardens*, but the very essence of social existence, the terrain where real power was exercised.[35]

In another significant dissension from current anthropological orthodoxy, Simcox nearly rejected the racial hierarchies dear to conservatively-minded theorists like Broca, Mclennan and Morgan and threw into doubt any sense of the necessary superiority of western civilisation over all others: 'There is no portion of the human race naturally incapable of assimilating any sound doctrine or useful custom preached or practised by yellow, red, or white philosophers since wheat first grew in Mesopotamia'.[36] If the real point of *Primitive Civilizations* was to furnish alternative models of social organisation to nineteenth-century liberal individualism, then prevailing ideas about the meaning of racial difference needed to be addressed. Racial hierarchies from 'primitive' to 'civilised' were based on the assumption that 'lesser breeds' represented a less evolved or alternatively an atavistic return to older forms of the evolutionary chain. Individuals within those races were restricted to the developmental limitations of the race – because ontogeny was held to replicate phylogeny, both biologically and culturally. Such arguments were as much the

application of imperial ideology as of biological research but the one reinforced the other.[37] It is noticeable that when Pelletier became involved
in the militant Hervéiste faction of the Socialist Party from 1906 to 1911,
she too was exposed to its critique of imperialism and thus of racial typo-
logy. Simcox, in any case, dismissed the cultural recapitulationist
argument with a brisk pragmatism. 'There is no portion of the human race
naturally incapable of assimilating any sound doctrine or useful custom.'[38]
The ontogeny/phylogeny model was shown to be irrelevant if one
looked at the empirical rather than the conjectural development of human
cultures. Simcox devoted her scholarship to demonstrating that human
beings could adapt to whatever system best suited them.

However a striking limitation to Simcox's synthesising vision of
humankind occurs in her short chapter on Egyptian slavery. Slavery must
have constituted a problem for her in accounting for the prosperity of the
Egyptian economy based on a contented society. Was not an alternative
explanation possible, namely that Egypt was prosperous precisely because it was a slave culture? Simcox's admiration for ancient Egypt led her
virtually to endorse slavery on the grounds that those enslaved in Egypt,
namely black Africans, were naturally inferior. She also implied that the
lack of rebellion among the slave population suggested contentment with
their lot:

> Even if every other ingredient of stability had still been present, it is self-
> evident that the duration of Egyptian or Chinese society would have become
> impossible in the face of a growing population of malcontent slaves. But there
> was no fear of such a class in Egypt where, in the first place, only members of
> an inferior race ran any risk of being reduced to slavery at all, and where,
> moreover, the lot of the domestic slave was in no respect worse than that of
> the labourer or artisan accustomed to do his daily work 'under the stick' of an
> overlooker.[39]

Such a passage seems particularly surprising given the presumption
that Simcox must have been familiar with the argument frequently
advanced against women's emancipation, namely that women's natural
inferiority was demonstrated by the fact that so few overtly rebelled or
when asked, wished to cast off their oppression, attitudes in common
with the black African slaves of ancient Egypt. The link between the
emancipation of slaves and the emancipation of women was a staple of
nineteenth-century liberal thought. Simcox, it seems clear, still clung in
this instance to the concept of the hierarchy of races. The fairly cursory
treatment of slavery in a work in which almost every topic is treated
exhaustively, suggests that Simcox felt some unease, though cultural
relativism could allow, to some extent, for a positive reading of this form
of oppression. But because *Primitive Civilizations* clearly has a political

application to nineteenth-century industrial Britain, the issue of racial hierarchy, or the necessary oppression of 'inferior groups', remains a stumbling-block to Simcox's socialist and feminist vision. The problem would not have arisen were she merely describing Egyptian customs; it arose in the clear contrasts she implied between ancient Egypt and nine-teenth-century Britain, where the latter, through most of the book suffers from the comparison.

Primitive Civilisations constructs an account of three societies based, in Simcox's version, on the sympathetic identification of each with all. This was arguably the social ideal also offered in George Eliot's novels. In its validation of domestic cultures *Primitive Civilizations* represents a tribute to George Eliot's idea of a maternal ethos as well as to Edith Simcox's own much loved mother, of whom she wrote: 'I rank her above my other love in perfection for all human relations.'[40] But the book also forms part of an ongoing debate which Simcox may have been too diffident to articulate in Eliot's lifetime; it seeks to suggest that socialism might be the nine-teenth-century expression of a maternal or domestic culture. *Primitive Civilizations*, one may argue, is her attempt to reconcile the conservative and the socialist, the feminine and the feminist, as both a tribute to, and intellectual engagement with, her Madonna.

The title of Simcox's book becomes freighted with ironic overtones by the end of her scholarly demonstration of complex cultures. In reading her exhaustively detailed study, one sees that the notion of 'the primitive' applied to the sophisticated cultures under discussion, is indeed a cultural fiction. Simcox almost certainly saw through the myopic western view of the primitive, and saw it for what it was, an invention of the western imagination.[41] Simcox, marginalised as a woman, and unhappy in her sexual identity, seems to have largely escaped the contagion of the orient-alist or imperialist imagination.

Simcox's re-interpretation of historical tradition created scarcely a ripple in its own time, if one takes as evidence the absence of reviews in *The Academy*, *The Nineteenth Century*, *The Fortnightly Review*, *The Cornhill Magazine*, *The Pall Mall Gazette*, journals to which she regularly con-tributed. It is heartening to see her *Primitive Civilizations* listed in Jack Goody's bibliography *The Oriental, the Ancient and the Primitive* (1989). While we know that the history of the Egyptians, to go no further afield, was well documented in the nineteenth century, for example, Huth (1875); Hobhouse, *Morals in Evolution* (1906); Westermarck, *The History of Human Marriage* (1891), yet its customs with regard to women and marriage, property rights and incest practices seem to have been ignored by those constructing the supposedly universal laws of cultural history. The importance of the Graeco-Roman model of cultural descent for the late nineteenth and early twentieth centuries lay in the perceived need to justify the law of the father in an increasingly egalitarian political and social climate. Ancient Greece and Rome and their myths provided a story of origins which legitimated gender and racial inequality in an invented history of progress. Across the political spectrum there came to be wide agreement that culture had always been patriarchal; before that was pre-history, matriarchy, sexual promiscuity and non-culture. In this account, civilisation and patriarchy became synonymous. The irony is that this version is still accepted in some feminist discussions on the construction of patriarchy, and its universalist implications.[42] Simcox allows us to see the fictional quality of this history. She demonstrates that what are asserted to be cultural universals, are empirically speaking, relative customs.

Of course *Primitive Civilizations* is not only about these issues; it is an exhaustive study of climate, topography, agricultural practices, patterns of ownership, legal codes and so on. But at every stage, women, their property and power appear in Simcox's account. If nothing else, *Primitive. Civilizations* confounds Bachofen and Engels's defeated female principle. And like every good Victorian tale, this history has a moral: prosperity and stability are shown to occur in those societies which care for all their members and in which women exercise material, not just symbolic, power and responsibility. Like Wollstonecraft in her attack on the limitations of Rousseau's concept of equality and individual development, and like Madeleine Pelletier, recognising that the strategies of anthropology constituted an opportunity for feminism and socialism, Simcox exposes not only the limitations of liberal economic orthodoxy, but also those of socialist thought, immune to the revolutionary potential of a gendered analysis.

Mary Evans in her review of Virginia Shapiro's *A Vindication of Political Virtue* (Chicago, 1992) has written of Wollstonecraft as 'the last great woman writer of the Enlightenment to believe passionately in the masculine project of reason.'[43] Simcox and Pelletier, to continue the metaphors of genealogy, were children of the Enlightenment and daughters of Wollstonecraft who while implicitly and explicitly attacking 'masculinism', resisted throwing out the rationalist baby with the masculine bathwater. They wished to include women within the discourse of reason, within meaningful human activity and within history. For both, the tools of anthropology contributed towards this project. Simcox's idea of a society based on 'reciprocity' between the sexes, a version of Kropotkin's 'mutual aid', represented her attempt to overcome the dualism of gendered power relations. Pelletier's application of evolutionary paradigms to socialist and feminist projects similarly enlisted the language of science for political ends. Though Pelletier's faith in the inevitability of progress was fatally undermined by the Great War, her commitment to Enlightenment ideals – that the 'Rights of Man' should apply to all humankind – never faltered. Simcox's appeal to another historical tradition is a reminder that like Kropotkin's, hers was a voice seeking to build an alternative, a less competitive ethos for western societies. Pelletier and Simcox's reinterpretations of cultural history form a significant if neglected chapter in the construction of a female tradition, offering continuity and identity, though not necessarily progress. For both writers, evolutionary paradigms which simultaneously reflected continuity and change mirrored women's historical reality and their best hope for the future.

Notes

1 This chapter is partly the fruit of a long-held and continuing interest in the complex interfaces between feminism and materialist theories of history. Among the most persuasive discussions of convergences and discontinuities one may cite Barbara Taylor's *Eve and the New Jerusalem* (London, Virago, 1983), see p. ix on the issue of ruptures. The key study on Edith Simcox is still K. A. Mckensie's *Edith Simcox and George Eliot* (Oxford, Oxford University Press, 1961). Professor Gillian Beer has given a number of papers on Simcox, notably 'Edith Simcox, Ethics and Activism' (The Society for the History of Philosophy, summer, 1991). Her generosity in sharing her scholarship and enthusiasm about the variety of Simcox's work and experience has stimulated many students. I wish to express my debt to her for alerting me to *Primitive Civilizations* when I was first researching Madeleine Pelletier's anthropological career. Madeleine Pelletier's socialism has been chronicled in Charles Sowerwine's *Sisters, or Citizens: Women and Socialism in France* (Cambridge, Cambridge University Press, 1982). There are now two biographies available: Felicia Gordon, *The Integral Feminist: Madeleine Pelletier, 1874–1939* (Cambridge, Polity Press, 1990) and Claude Maignien and Charles Sowerwine, *Madeleine Pelletier, une féministe dans l'arène politique* (Paris, Editions Ouvrières, 1992). A collection of essays edited by Christine Bard, *Madeleine Pelletier: logique et infortunes d'un combat pour l'égalité* (Paris, Côté Femmes, 1992) has also been published. In the following discussion I have deliberately not placed Pelletier and Simcox in chronological order to avoid linking the idea of a feminist tradition with the idea of progress (see Bowler and Kuper, below).
2 Peter J. Bowler, *The Invention of Progress: The Victorians and the Past* (Oxford, Basil Blackwell, 1989), 'Introduction' and Michael Hammond, 'Anthropology as a Weapon of Social Combat in Late Nineteenth-Century France', *Journal of the History of Behavioural Sciences*, 16 (1980), 118–32.
3 Bowler, *The Invention of Progress*, p. 12. Adam Kuper, *The Invention of Primitive Society* (London, Routledge, 1988), pp. 1–5. Stephen Jay Gould, *Ontogeny and Phylogeny* (London, Harvard University Press, 1977), ch. 4. Nancy Stephan, *The Idea of Race: Great Britain 1800–1960* (London, Macmillan, 1982). I am grateful to Dr Peter James for background on Recapitulation Theory.
4 Bowler, *Invention of Progress*, pp. 101–10.
5 Kuper, *Invention of Primitive Society*, p. 2.
6 Bowler, *Invention of Progress*, pp. 33–5. Kuper, *Invention of Primitive Society*, p. 5.
7 Henry Maine, *Ancient Law* (London, 1861).
8 Lewis Henry Morgan, *Ancient Society* (London, 1877).

9   Ernst Haekel, *Generelle Morphologies der Organismus* (Georg Reimer, Berlin, 1866), p. 300, quoted in Gould, *Ontogeny and Phylogeny*, p. 77.

10 Gould, *Ontogeny and Phylogeny*, 150–5.

11 Bowler, *Invention of Progress*, p. 33. Johann Bachofen, *Myth, Religion and Mother Right*, ed. R. Marx (London, Princeton University Press, 1967). Froma I. Zeitlin, 'The Dynamics of Misogyny: Myth and Mythmaking in the Oresteia', *Women in the Ancient World* (Albany, SUNY Press, 1984), 159–91.

12 Hammond, 'Anthropology as a Weapon of Social Combat', 123–85.

13 Charles Letourneau, *The Evolution of Marriage* (London, 1891). Gordon, *The Integral Feminist*, p. 34.

14 Gordon, *The Integral Feminist*, 38–9.

15 Madeleine Pelletier, 'Les signes physiques de l'intelligence', with N. Vaschide, *Revue de Philosophie*, 1 October, 1903, 1 February, 1904.

16 For a discussion of Cuvier and anti-evolutionary theory see Hammond, 'Anthropology as a Weapon of Social Combat', 119–22.

17 Madeleine Pelletier, 'Recherches sur les indices pondéraux du crâne et des principaux os longs d'une série de squelettes japonais', *Bulletins de la Société d'anthropologie de Paris*, 15 November 1900, pp. 514–29, also Maignien and Sowerwine, *Madeleine Pelletier*, 31–7.

18 Adrian de Mortillet, *Les Débuts de l'humanité* (Paris, Droin, 1881), quoted in Hammond, p. 126.

19 Gordon, *The Integral Feminist*, 71–4. Maignien and Sowerwine, *Madeleine Pelletier*, p. 33.

20 Gillian Beer, 'Edith Simcox: Ethics and Activism'.

21 Mckensie, *Edith Simcox*, p. 75.

22 Edith Simcox, *Primitive Civilizations* (London, Sonnenschein, 1894), p. 19.

23 Simcox, *Primitive Civilizations*, p. 125.

24 Jack Goody, *The Oriental, the Ancient and the Primitive* (Cambridge, Cambridge University Press, 1989), p. 326.

25 Simcox, *Primitive Civilizations*, 2, p. 30.

26 Simcox, *Primitive Civilizations*, 1, p. 11.

27 Simcox, *Primitive Civilizations*, 1, p. 8.

28 Peter Kropotkin, *Mutual Aid, A Factor of Evolution* (1902) (London, Allen Lane, 1972), p. 241.

29 Kropotkin, *Mutual Aid*, p. 114.

30 Simcox, *Primitive Civilizations*, 1, p. 9.

31 A. H. Huth, *The Marriage of Near Kin* (London, 1875).

32 See Jean Louis Flandrin, *Families in Former Times* (Cambridge, Cambridge University Press, 1979), and Roderick Phillips, *Putting Asunder* (Cambridge, Cambridge University Press, 1988).

33 Goody, *The Oriental, the Ancient and the Primitive*, 320–1.

34 Mary Hamer, *Signs of Cleopatra* (London, Routledge, 1993), p. 19.

35 Simcox, *Primitive Civilizations*, 2, pp. 65–72.

36 Simcox, *Primitive Civilizations*, 1, p. 12.

37 Bowler, *Invention of Progress*, relates that after the Indian Mutiny, the supposed innate inferiority of Indians was thought by the British to be manifested by their rejection of the self-evident benefits of British rule, p. 32.

38 Simcox, *Primitive Civilizations*, 1, p. 12.

39 Simcox, *Primitive Civilizations*, 1, p. 91.

40 Mckensie, *Edith Simcox*, p. 137.

41 See Joanna Groot, ' "Sex" and "Race": the Construction of Language and Image in the Nineteenth Century', in *Sexuality and Subordination*, eds Susan Mendus and Jane Rendall (London, Routledge, 1989), 89–130, and Edward Said, *Orientalism* (Harmondsworth, Penguin, 1978).

42 See Zeitlin, 'The Dynamics of Misogyny', and for the feminist reading of the all-
    embracing power of patriarchy see Gerda Lerner, *The Creation of Patriarchy* (Oxford,
    Oxford University Press, 1986), whose wide-ranging analysis of women historic and
    pre-historic oppression omits, however, the history of Egypt.
43 *The Times Higher Education Supplement*, 9 Oct. 1992.

10

Wollstonecraft's daughters, Marianne's daughters and the daughters of Joan of Arc: Marie Maugeret and Christian feminism in the French Belle Epoque

James F. McMillan

BY the 1890's a women's movement had established itself as a small, fragmented but permanent feature of the French political scene. The triumph of republicanism and the establishment of a viable democratic regime encouraged the feminists of the Third Republic to believe that they might succeed where earlier generations of women's rights campaigners in the 1790s and the 1830s and 1840s had failed. The movement essentially replicated the ideological and political divisions of French national politics. There was a bourgeois–republican majority, which, like the male republican politicians themselves, was split between moderates and radicals. Only the latter – women like Hubertine Auclert, Eliska Vincent and Caroline Kauffmann – could be accounted militant suffragists. The moderates, the heirs of the founders of modern French feminism, Léon Richer and Maria Deraismes, considered the pursuit of the vote less of a priority than legal reform, the abolition of the double standard of morality and the opening up of economic opportunities for women. Their ranks were reinforced by an even more moderate set of feminist leaders who had come to feminism by way of philanthropy (often Protestant philanthropy) such as Sarah Monod, first president of the Conseil National des Femmes Françaises at its foundation in 1901. On the left wing of the movement was a tiny group of socialist feminists, headed by Elizabeth Renaud and Louise Saumoneau. Finally, on the Catholic Right stood the least known and, for most historians, the least significant of the feminist *groupuscules*: the group founded by Marie Maugeret in 1897 which campaigned under the banner of *Le Féminisme chrétien*, or Christian feminism. It is their story which is the subject of this chapter.[1]

The appearance of Maugeret's organisation needs to be be appreciated against the background not just of the emergence of organised feminism but also of another important phenomenon of the 1890s, namely the development of social Catholicism. Stimulated by Pope Leo XIII's encyclical *Rerum novarum* of 1891, which examined the problems associated with the coming of an industrial society and the development of a liberal capitalist state in the light of Catholic doctrine, it manifested itself in the guise of Catholic trade unions, study groups, propaganda organisations, and a renewed interest in 'Christian Democracy', notably among a new generation of priests who came to be known as the *abbés démocrates*.[2] Women. too, were among the most active social Catholics of the turn of the century, founding female trade unions, workers' settlements, holiday camps for children and the like.[3] Particularly dynamic was *Action sociale de la femme*, a study circle founded by Jeanne Chenu in 1900. Viewing itself not as a confessional organisation but as one inspired by Christian social thought, *Action sociale* described its aims as being 'to inform women about their role in society, to make them understand better how their action can be influential in the family, in education, in the professions, in the city, and to assist them to defend the principles on which our French way of life has always rested'.[4] Though neither *Action sociale de la femme* nor any of the other female social Catholic organisations subscribed explicitly to feminism, they all shared Marie Maugeret's preoccupation with the larger question of women's place in society and were at least potential recruits to 'Christian feminism'.

It should perhaps be stressed that social Catholicism requires to be carefully distinguished from liberal Catholicism. Whereas liberal Catholics believed in representative government and were alarmed by doctrinal developments such as the *Syllabus of Errors* of 1864 and the proclamation of papal infallibility as a dogma of the Church in 1870, social Catholics were enthusiasts for the intransigent, ultramontane Catholicism which became established as orthodoxy during the papacy of Pius IX (1846–78). French social Catholics were overwhelmingly right-wing in their political sympathies, reluctant to heed Pope Leo XIII's appeal in the 1890s to abandon their attachment to monarchism and to rally to the republic. They invariably held traditional views on the family and on women's place in society.[5] Leo XIII himself, it should also be said, despite his policy of *ralliement* was no liberal. Doctrinally as conservative as his predecessor, he was undoubtedly genuinely concerned at the plight of workers victimised by the worst excesses of the capitalist system, but his interest in the social question was prompted in large part by fear of socialism. French social Catholics shared these fears and saw themselves as the defenders of an avowedly Christian civilisation. Fundamental to their outlook was the belief that religion was not a private and personal affair, as the anti-clerical politicians of the Third Republic made out, but a social pheno-menon which should pervade the life of the community as a whole. As the academician and well-known Catholic polemicist, Ferdinand Brunetière, told a gathering of Catholic youth in 1903, not only had Catholics never accepted that religion was a matter solely for the individual conscience, the Church had always taught that 'Christian society extended beyond this life: witness the devotion to the Virgin, the intercession of the saints and prayers for the dead'.[6] Social Catholics were working for nothing less than the rechristianisation of society.

In this work of rechristianisation, women were deemed to have a crucial role to play. Catholic commentators constantly reiterated that Catholicism more than any other religion or creed gave women the opportunity to fulfil themselves. The prominent Dominican preacher and professor of moral philosophy at the Institut Catholique in Paris, Père Antonin Sertillanges, was only one of many who claimed that it was Christianity which had rescued women from slavery and made them hu-man persons.[7] Charles Turgeon, a professor of political economy at the University of Rennes and the author of a two-volume study of French feminism, admitted that there was certainly a misogynous strain within the Christian tradition, evident particularly in the writings of the Early Fathers of the Church, but he argued that this was more than compen-sated for by the cult of the Virgin Mary, which proved that 'the Catholic religion has veritably ennobled and magnified woman'. Indubitably, he maintained, woman was the equal of man before God.[8] According to Etienne Lamy, who published a widely read book on women which ran through over twenty editions, 'to serve Catholicism is for women to serve their own cause'.[9] Women, these writers suggested, should be the spearhead of a spiritual revolution which would regenerate society and raise it to a higher level of morality. As Lamy saw it, they would spread what he described as the 'feminine' values of sweetness, mercy, pity, goodness and love.[10]

To a significant number of Catholics around 1900, the 'woman question' was recognisably on the political agenda and could not be ignored. As the Countess Marie de Villermont put it: 'Feminism is an important part of the social question, and the mistake of Catholics was not to have understood this immediately'. In the present state of society what was necessary was that women become 'something other than dolls who amuse themselves and amuse others'.[11] A prominent *abbé démocrate*, the abbé Naudet, warned that it would be disastrous for Catholics to remain indifferent to the issues raised by feminists, because this would leave the field to the enemies of religion, as had happened in other areas of life.[12] Indeed, to many Catholic commentators it appeared that the time had come to extend women's influence into the political arena. Convinced that they would bring a new moral dimension to politics, abbé Henry Bolo wrote that 'the political exclusion of women appears as an astonishing injustice for a century and a regime which make such a fuss about proclaiming the rights of man'.[13] The crucial point was to distinguish 'good' from 'bad' feminism. Naudet had no time for 'the noisy action of a few citizenesses who, the better to emancipate their sex, begin by emancipating themselves from all moral laws'.[14] Bolo mocked the 'few state-school primary teachers who aren't very happy, the few female politicians who aren't altogether healthy in mind' who allegedly made up the greater part of the feminist army. This kind of feminism, he affirmed, was not even French, having originated in the United States, 'a country known for its eccentricity where women, less protected by traditions, had more need to defend themselves'. Feminism had then entered Europe by way of England 'where pauperism and drunkenness keep women of the popular classes locked up in the most abject misery, where two and a half million spinsters have declared war on men guilty of not having married them, and where even in the upper classes women were beaten like beasts'. Finally feminism had taken off in the Protestant countries of Europe 'where the liberty given to fantasies of dogma undoubtedly diminishes the influence of evangelical legislation'.[15] Turgeon likewise denounced the 'professionals' of feminism, by which he meant 'the advanced portion who ... aim straight for free love by suppressing marriage and overthrowing the family'.[16] Paul Acker castigated those feminists who were 'resolute revolutionary and sectarian materialists', and unfortunately the ones who received most publicity.[17]

On the other hand, all of these commentators were strongly in favour of the development of a distinctively Christian feminism which would be an antidote to the anti-clerical, republican and socialist varieties. Turgeon, usually identified as one of the most outspoken opponents of 'the new woman' of the 1880s and 1890s,[18] was a strong supporter of women's suffrage (though not of women deputies). Christian feminism, in his eyes, was 'a reasonable feminism which deserves the approval and the encouragement of the laity and even of the clergy' on the grounds that it was 'above all a conservative force which aimed at defending marriage and society against the audacity of the revolutionaries'. If women voted, he argued, it was hardly likely that they would vote in favour of freemasons and freethinkers. Christian feminism could unleash a force of devastating power which would shake Catholicism out of its torpor and serve to rejuvenate the faith.[19] Naudet argued that feminism need not lead to a war of the sexes, since, on the contrary, it wanted to unite the efforts of both men and women in a common enterprise, 'for country, family and humanity'.[20] With approval he quoted an extended passage from an article written by Madame Pierre Froment in Marie Maugeret's journal *Le Féminisme chrétien*, which both summed up the objectives of Christian feminism and suggested why Catholics had everything to gain by its expansion. She wrote:

> Women must be taught that the domestic and practical virtues are no longer enough, if they neglect, ignore or misunderstand the social virtues, those Christian virtues par excellence.
>
> We will teach the social virtues – that is to say consecrated not to oneself and one's relations but to others – the duties, I say, of the modern Christian French woman.
>
> It is necessary that women learn to take an interest in general things: that they understand that religion does not consist solely in going to Mass, making one's Easter Duties, baptising the children, or marrying in church, but much more in the penetration of religion into the whole social body ...
>
> The essential thing is not only to make one's way in the world and achieve social position, but to make society more moral, more pure, more exalted, more nobly human'[21]

In the late nineteenth century, therefore, it was evident that at least some sections of Catholic opinion were eager to engage with feminism from a Catholic, and particularly a social Catholic, point of view. If the movement attained a degree of celebrity, however, this was undoubtedly thanks to the efforts of its leading exponent, Marie Maugeret.[22] Born the daughter of a doctor in the Sarthe in 1844, she grew up in a comfortable bourgeois milieu and received a conventional convent education from the Ursuline sisters. Having been left a substantial fortune, she used it to indulge her literary and journalistic inclinations, founding *L'Echo littéraire de l'Ouest* in 1883 while living at Le Mans. She also published several novels and a small book *Pensées*, not a few of which seem to suggest a certain sadness in her character deriving from disappointment in love ('To love someone is to give him the power to martyr you': 'Are you very, very sure that life is worth living?').[23] One of her earliest publications was a robust attack on Protestantism, symbolised by Luther, who personified heresy and revolt, coupled with a vigorous defence of orthodoxy, as championed by the founder of the Jesuit Order, Ignatius Loyola, the epitome of 'straight and rigorous submission'.[24] An extreme ultramontane, she extolled 'the immortal canons of the holy Council of Trent', and rejoiced at the outcome of the Vatican Council of 1870 which, by proclaiming the Pope to be infallible, added 'a dogma dear to the piety of the faithful'.[25] A liberal Catholic Maugeret was not.

An intransigent Catholic, Maugeret was also a die-hard political reactionary ideologically aligned with the French integral nationalist Right. The Dreyfus affair revealed her to be a rabid anti-Semite. Revision, she claimed, was obtained 'by intrigues and by gold', the latter furnished by 'the brothers of Iscariot'.²⁶ Loubet was only the nominal president of the Republic. Its real king was Rothschild.²⁷ 1898, the year of Zola's, *J'accuse*, she described as 'the year of the Jew' and in a veritable diatribe she denounced Jews as 'the people whom God has vomited from his mouth' and as 'this eternally foreign and incurably evil-doing race, naturalised in law but never in their hearts, obstinately resistant to all assimilation', which, according to her, was draining the nation both of its gold and its vitality. Anti-Semitism, she ranted, was 'a work of national defence', 'a struggle between races' and 'more simply still, the struggle of the robbed against the robber'.²⁸

Freemasonry was another target of her invective, especially at the time of the separation of Church and State in 1905. The law was 'the work of the Lodges'.²⁹ Citing her friend and Christian feminist collaborator, Mme Françoise Dorive, as an authority on the 'masonic question', she railed against 'the efforts of the diabolical sect to deform the national character in taking away from it its very essence: the faith and patriotism'.³⁰ For Maugeret, as for the French Right as a whole, there were two Frances, 'the France of God and the France of Satan, the Church of Christ and the Church of the Grand Orient'.³¹ Masonry, however, she saw only 'as an intermediary, a servile instrument in the hands of a still more secret power, whose orders it transmits without even knowing its leaders' – the Jews, 'those beings without altars and without a homeland, those cosmopolitans forever and everywhere condemned to be foreigners'. The real goal of 'the jackals of judaeo-masonry' was clear: the dechristianisation of France:

> Now, to dechristianise France is to assassinate her, historically speaking. France is not a nation like any other: her special role, her providential *raison d'être* is to be God's soldier in the world, to carry everywhere the Cross of Christ, which is both the sign of eternal salvation and the flag of civilisation.³²

If Maugeret urged women to become politically active it was primarily to allow them to lend their strength to the fight to keep France Catholic. What was required was the unity of all Catholics, male and female. For too long men had overlooked the contribution which women could make and it was her mission to try to persuade them that the time had come to cast off atavistic prejudices.³³

Maugeret, then, was an unlikely feminist. Yet feminist she called herself. Where other Catholic women hesitated to accept the label, Maugeret openly flaunted it, and constantly chided her reluctant sisters. As she told them in 1905:

> I can't prevent myself from telling you that you are very ungrateful to feminism,

for it is at the origin of everything which Christian women are doing at present, and which they would never have had the idea of doing if the women free thinkers, coming out of their habits of women of their interiors to do what we call evil, hadn't taught us also to come out to do what we call good ... don't sport the word if it still shocks you: for myself, I have taken it and I shall keep it, all the more so that the clergy is currently adopting it and using it.[34]

Maugeret may not have been a 'liberal' or 'individual' feminist or a disciple of John Stuart Mill, but she certainly espoused a brand of that 'relational' feminism which has rightly been identified by Karen Offen as the characteristic form of European feminism in general and French feminism in particular throughout the nineteenth century.[35]

Her conversion to the cause can be dated from 1896, when she attended a feminist congress held in Paris on the condition and rights of women. Convinced by the debates that feminism had justice on its side, she was alarmed that so many of its champions seemed to come from the worlds of free thought and socialism. What was required was a Christian feminism, one entirely in keeping with the tenets of the Catholic religion. She therefore changed the title of her journal to Le Féminisme chrétien and began her crusade to convince Catholic opinion that feminism and Catholicism were not incompatible. Without denying that women's primary role remained that of wife and mother (though she herself was never to marry), she argued that society was undergoing a process of change and that women aspired to a better future. They wanted 'the right to be what we are: human beings gifted with intelligence as well as heart, not identical with, but equal to men, as capable as they are, and sometimes more capable, of taking on, always more conscientiously and with a greater sense of duty, not only the lowly positions they scorn, but the majority of those over which they have until now maintained a monopoly'.[36] Women should have the right to prepare themselves for all careers compatible with their physical and moral faculties. They should have economic rights, whether they were working women forbidden by the law to dispose freely of their own earnings or whether they were propertied women who ought to have more control over the fortunes they brought to a marriage:

At a time when marriages are often only financial arrangements, we energetically demand the abolition of the intolerable iniquity whereby a man, under the pretext that he is the head of the family, can, the day after the wedding, dispose of his wife's dowry without any controls, not just to compromise it in the most risky speculations, but even to pay off debts he had incurred as a bachelor, and to continue, if it is his fancy, the pleasures and associations of his previous life.[37]

Since the law on this point consecrated an injustice, insisted Maugeret, it had to be changed. As far as its provisions on marriage were concerned, the Code was a 'Code of slavery'. This state of affairs was not of divine origin but the work of men. They had cause to be satisfied with the existing order of relations between the sexes, but women wanted emancipation.

How were they to achieve it? Maugeret proposed, essentially, 'the education of women in view of the new role of which they dreamed without fully understanding its implications'. They needed to be taught their 'right to rights', which her journal would expound to them 'from the point of view of our sentiments as Frenchwomen and Christians'.[38] The right to work was also fundamental. Like other republican feminists, (and unlike most social Catholics) Maugeret was vehemently opposed to 'protective' legislation which denied women the right to work:

> We say and we maintain that liberty (in the work place) must be as absolute for women as it is for men, because work is par excellence the right to life, and that no human power has a right against this right, sacred and intangible among all. On this point we do not admit any regulation, any limitation, any fetter of any sort, and under any pretext whatsoever, either economic or sentimental.[39]

But perhaps the most distinctive feature of Maugeret's feminism was its insistence, from the outset, on the need for women to involve themselves in politics and to campaign for women's suffrage. At a time when many of the mainstream republican feminists hesitated to support votes for women, Maugeret and other Christian feminists sought to lead the way. Countess de Villermont argued that the logic of 'universal' suffrage was that the vote be given to all women as well as to all men and, with aristocratic hauteur, expressed her indignation that depriving half of the human race of the right to vote 'placed the most intelligent woman below the lowest manual labourer, the most imbecile coal-man and the most sottish drunk'.[40] Maugeret insinuated the suffrage issue onto the agenda of a congress of Catholic women convened by a group of upper-class and aristocratic ladies in 1900 under the patronage of Cardinal Richard, the Archbishop of Paris and presided over by Mgr de Cabrières, Bishop of Montpellier. Few were prepared to follow her at this time, but Maugeret persisted in her attempts to convert them.

Her strategy was to unite all Catholic women under the banner of Joan of Arc – a shrewd move since Joan was increasingly venerated in Catholic circles as the symbol of Catholic nationalism and the *pays réel* ('real', 'eternal' France) as opposed to Marianne, the peasant girl who symbolised the Republic, whom the Right referred to contemptuously as *la gueuse*, the slut. French Catholic women's groups such as the *Ligue des Femmes Françaises* (LFF), an organisation of royalist women founded at Lyon in 1901, and the *Ligue Patriotique des Françaises* (LPF), founded in 1902, were among the most enthusiastic supporters of the case for Joan's canonisation which was being strongly pressed by the French Church at precisely this time.[41] Maugeret therefore founded the *Fédération Jeanne d'Arc* with the intention of holding an annual congress – to be known as the *Congrès Jeanne d'Arc* – which would bring together women from the entire spectrum of female Catholic initiatives. The first took place in 1904, and in addition to discussing purely religious, charitable and social issues, addressed the questions of women's political rights and women's suffrage which Maugeret had placed on the agenda. No resolutions were passed, but for Maugeret it was an important exercise in consciousness-raising.[42]

In 1906 she returned to the theme at the third *Congrès Jeanne d'Arc*. Once again the proceedings were dominated by religious and social issues, but on the last day Maugeret devoted the session to 'women and politics' and lined up a succession of speakers all of whom favoured women's suffrage. They included Mme Vincent, the President of the militant suffrage group *Egalité*, not only a non-Catholic but a former supporter of the Paris Commune of 1871. Vincent, who specialised in the historical dimensions of the woman question, nevertheless impressed her audience with her thesis that women had been entitled to vote under the Ancien Régime and that it was the French Revolution which had taken away their rights. Maugeret, conscious of the distaste which many Catholics felt for any kind of collaboration with the Republic, argued that 'In order to clean up a house, it is first necessary to enter it. Let us enter this house'. After the speeches, two motions were passed. A vague call for the representation of women in the political arena was endorsed by the four hundred or so women present. A second, more specific, motion calling for the introduction of women's suffrage was passed by only 83 votes to 67, with most delegates abstaining.

Maugeret's triumph was short-lived, however. Indeed, her manoeuvre had succeeded only because many delegates who were either opposed to women's suffrage or uninterested in the question did not attend the final session of the congress. Both the LPF and the LFF rejected suffragism and their stance was reinforced in 1909 when it became known that the Pope himself, Pius X, had made known his disapproval at an audience granted to leaders of the two leagues. Even Maugeret's collaborator, Françoise Dorive, the editor of *Le Devoir des femmes françaises* (which specialised largely in diatribes against Freemasonry) came to have second thoughts, and concluded in 1907 that Catholic suffragism was more likely to offend than to rally Catholic women. When Maugeret dared to air the subject once more at the seventh *Congrès Jeanne d'Arc* in 1910, the pro-suffrage speakers failed to carry their audience with them. After this defeat, without renouncing her own suffragist views, Maugeret effectively retired from the campaign.

Yet her fight had not been in vain. Certain sections of Catholic opinion, including a number of clerics, had already been won over to the idea
of a Christian feminism. Abbé Bolo stated that Maugeret and other Christian feminists deserved to be supported from every point of view.[43] Abbé
Naudet rejected the case against women's suffrage as mere camouflage for
the continuation of male supremacy, though, he was pessimistic about the
prospects for change in France in the short term.[44] Père Sertillanges was
more ambiguous. While admitting that there could be no objections in
principle to women's suffrage he thought that there might be objections
of a practical order – such as the anger it might provoke among French
anti-clericals – but even he favoured giving women the right to vote in
local elections.[45] Similarly, lay Catholic intellectuals like Charles Turgeon
had nothing but admiration for Maugeret's movement and lent their voices to
the cause. Thanks to Maugeret, wrote Turgeon, free thought had been
taught that it had no monopoly on the advancement on women's rights.
As we have already seen, he was entirely convinced that women should be
entitled to vote on the same basis as men, declaring that it was difficult to
imagine 'an institution worse named' than 'universal suffrage':

> Can one call it universal without derision or deception, when it excludes half
> the members of society. In reality, our universal suffrage of today is only a
> restricted suffrage, a male privilege, a masculine monopoly.

All the arguments invoked against votes for women were entirely
spurious – including that which cited their non-performance of military
service. According to Turgeon, 'the blood tax' (*l'impôt de sang*) was more
than compensated for by 'the heavy burdens of maternity'. Moreover, if
women had the vote, Turgeon was sure that they would vote against
extremism, since their Christian education would incline them to support
moderation in politics (i.e. conservatism).[46]

Maugeret's defeat in 1910 was in any case only a temporary setback for
Catholic suffragism and she herself lived to see her position vindicated.
By the time she died in 1928 the Catholic women's suffrage movement
had become the largest in France.[47] Even before 1914, groups such as
Action sociale de la femme and the LPF began to show greater sympathy for
Maugeret's position. The experience of the First World War and the
Russian Revolution served to convince much of conservative opinion that
women needed to be mobilised as bastions of the social order and when
the successor of Pius X, Benedict XV, made it plain in 1919 that the
Church positively welcomed the prospect of female electors the way was
clear for the emergence of Catholic suffragism as a mass movement.
Jeanne Chenu's *Action sociale* took the lead in bringing together the LPF,
the LFF and other Catholic organisations as the *Commission d'éducation*

sociale civique de la femme (CESC), a federation with over a million members. At its congress of 1920, it passed a resolution committing Catholic women to the struggle for votes for women. In 1925 the head of its suffrage section, Madame Levert-Chotard founded the *Union nationale pour le vote des femmes* as the first Catholic association devoted entirely to the cause of female suffrage. By 1939 it had 100,000 members. In 1925 also, Andrée Butillard founded the *Union féminine civique et sociale*, one of whose aims was to prepare women for the exercise of the vote. The real expansion of Catholic suffragism thus came after the First World War, but it is clear that the foundations had been laid earlier by Maugeret and the other pioneers of Christian feminism. At the age of eighty-two Maugeret was still well enough to address the twenty-second *Congrès Jeanne d'Arc* held in Paris in June 1926 and in her journal (now called *Questions féminines et questions féministes*) looked back with pride on the progress made since the first congress of 1904.[48]

Marie Maugeret and Christian feminism, therefore, are by no means peripheral to the story of women's rights in France. On the contrary, any account of 'Wollstonecraft's daughters' in a French context needs to find room for the daughters of Joan of Arc as much as for the daughters of Marianne. Indeed, if anything, their very success in building up a Catholic suffrage movement was perhaps the most significant factor in the refusal of the political masters of the Third Republic to accord the vote to women. In May 1919 the Chamber of Deputies passed a women's suffrage bill by a majority of 344 to 97. Over three years later it was thrown out by the Senate by 156 votes to 134, largely on the grounds that it would imperil republican institutions and invite clerical rule.[49] Republicans had no intention of enfranchising those who might choose to vote the wrong way. Only when the Third Republic was no more, in 1944, did French women finally receive the right to vote not as a result of pressure from any feminist lobby but on the decision of a great, machiavellian statesman – Charles de Gaulle.

Notes

1   The classification of French feminist groups given here is that suggested by S. C. Hause with A. R. Kenney in *Women's Suffrage and Social Politics in the French Third Republic* (Princeton, Princeton University Press, 1984). The standard history of the women's movement in French is L. Klejman and F. Rochefort, *L'Egalité en marche: le féminisme sous la Troisième Républic* (Paris, Presses de la Fondation Nationale des Sciences Politiques, 1989). The only study of Christian feminism to date is S. C. Hause and A. R. Kenney, 'The Development of the Catholic Women's Suffrage Movement in France, 1986–1922', *Catholic Historical Review* 67 (1981) 11–30. The present chapter is indebted to this pioneering article but seeks to clarify the ideological basis of Christian feminism by correcting the error of interpretation whereby the authors

confuse and conflate 'liberal' Catholicism and 'social' Catholicism.

2   On French Social Catholicism and Christian democracy in this period, see H. Rollet, *L'Action sociale des catholiques en France*, 2 vols (Paris, P.U.F., 1951–58) and J-M Mayeur, *Catholicisme social et démocratie chrétienne: Principes romains et expériences françaises* (Paris, Les Editions du Cerf, 1986).

3   Cf. J. F. McMillan, 'Women in Social Catholicism in Late Nineteenth and Early Twentieth-Century France', in *Women in the Church. Studies in Church History*, 27 (Oxford, Blackwell, 1990), ed. W. J. Sheils and D. Wood, pp. 467–80: S. Fayet-Scribe, *Associations féminines et catholicisme: de la charité à l'action sociale xix–xxe siècle* (Paris, Les Editions Ouvrières, 1990).

4   *L'Action sociale de la femme*, 1 (10 April 1902), 18.

5   Cf. E. Poulat, *Eglise contre bourgeoisie: Introduction au devenir du catholicisme actuel* (Paris, Casterman, 1977): Y. Tranvouez, *Catholiques d'abord: Approches du mouvement catholique en France xixe–xxe siècle* (Paris, Les Editions Ouvrières, 1988): and the important essay of J-M Mayeur, 'Catholicisme intransigeant, catholicisme social, démocratie chrétienne', in *Catholicisme social et démocratie chrétienne*, pp. 17–38.

6   F. Brunetière, *L'Action sociale du christianisme* (Besançon, ACJF, 1904), p. 96.

7   A. D. Sertillanges, *Féminisme et christianisme* (Paris, J. Gaball et Cie, 1908).

8   C. Turgeon, *Le Féminisme français*, 2 vols (Paris, L. Larose, 1902), vol. 1, esp. p. 58ff and pp. 64–5.

9   E. Lamy, *La Femme de demain* (Paris, Perrin et Cie, 1901), p. 193.

10 *Ibid.*, pp. 47–8.

11 Comtesse Marie de Villermont, *Le Mouvement féministe: ses causes, son avenir, solution chrétienne*, 2 vols (Paris, Bloud, 1900–04), vol. 1, p. 30.

12 L'Abbé Naudet, *Pour la femme: études féministes* (Paris, Albert Fontemoine, 1903), *avant-propos*.

13 H. Bolo, *La Femme et le clergé* (Paris, René Haton, no date: 1902?), pp. 309–10.

14 Naudet, p. 14.

15 Bolo, p. 16, pp. 141–2.

16 Turgeon, I, pp. 33–8 (the translation here is that of Karen Offen in S. G. Bell and K. M. Offen (eds), *Women, the Family and Freedom*, vol. 2 1880–1950 (Stanford, Stanford University Press, 1983), p. 50).

17 P. Acker, *Oeuvres sociales de femmes* (Paris, Plon, 1908), p. 5.

18 Cf. Bell and Offen, II, p. 46.

19 Turgeon, I, chapter 2, esp. p. 71 and p. 73.

20 Naudet, p. 9.

21 *Le Féminisme chrétien*, 15 July 1897, quoted by Naudet, pp. 37–8.

22 On Maugeret, see BHVP, Fonds Bouglé, Dossier 523, Marie Maugeret, and issues of *Le Féminisme chrétien*.

23 M. Maugeret, *Grains de sable*, (2nd edition, Paris, 1892), p. 51, p. 26.

24 M. Maugeret, *L'Attaque et la défense: Luther et Loyola* (Le Mans, Leguicheux-Gallienne, 1881), p. 89.

25 *Ibid.*, pp. 83–4.

26 *Le Féminisme chrétien*, 13 (20 July 1899), 553.

27 *Le Féminisme chrétien*, 19–20 (5–20 November 1899), 739.

28 M. Maugeret, 'A bâtons rompus', *Le Féminisme chrétien* (5 January 1899).

29 *Le Féminisme chrétien* (February–March, 1905), 2–3, 36.

30 *Le Féminisme chrétien* (June 1905), 69.

31 *Le Féminisme chrétien* (December 1905), p. 19.

32 *Ibid.*, pp. 1–9.

33 *Ibid.*, p. 27.

JAMES F. McMILLAN

34 *Ibid.*, pp. 30–1.
35 K. Offen, 'Liberty, Equality and Justice for Women: The Theory and Practice of Feminism in Nineteenth-Century Europe', in *Becoming Visible: Women in European History* (2nd edition, Houghton Mifflin, Boston, 1987), ed. R. Bridenthal, C. Koonz and S. Stuard, pp. 335–73.
36 *Le Féminisme chrétien*, I (1896), 'Notre programme'.
37 *Ibid.*, 3.
38 *Ibid.*, 5.
39 *Le Féminisme chrétien*, 8 (25 June, 1896), 'Le Travail', 116.
40 Villermont, II, p. 34.
41 J. F. McMillan, 'Reclaiming a Martyr: French Catholics and the Cult of Joan of Arc, 1890–1920', in *Martyrs and Martyrologies, Studies in Church History*, vol. 30 (Oxford, Blackwell, 1993), ed. D. Wood, pp. 359–70. On the LPF, J. F. McMillan, 'Women, Religion and Politics: The Case of the Ligue Patriotique des Françaises', in *Proceedings of the Annual Meeting of the Western Society for French History*, vol. 15 (Flagstaff, Arizona, 1988), ed. W. Roosen, pp. 355–64.
42 This and the following two paragraphs draw on the account of Hause and Kenney in the *Catholic Historical Review*, esp. pp. 20–5.
43 Bolo, p. 247.
44 Naudet, p. 199.
45 Sertillanges, p. 170.
46 Turgeon, I, pp. 33–43.
47 Hause and Kenney, *Catholic Historical Review*, esp. p. 25ff.
48 *Questions féminines et questions féministes*, 7 (15 July 1926), 203–4.
49 Cf. J. F. McMillan, *Housewife or Harlot: the Place of Women in French Society 1870–1940* (Brighton and New York, Harvester, 1981), p. 179; Hause with Kenney, *Women's Suffrage and Social Politics*, p. 221ff.

INDEX